BLACK ROOTS, WHITE FLOWERS
A history of jazz in Australia

Andrew Bisset's interest in music began in primary school when his family lived for four years in the USA. He played trumpet in the school orchestra. While studying history at the Australian National University as an undergraduate, he was able to combine both interests in his honours thesis on early jazz in Australia. This work formed the basis of further research throughout Australia with the assistance of a grant from the Australia Council which led to publication of this book. Andrew works for the Australian Public Service in Canberra and pursues an interest in vocal and choral music in his spare time. He recently wrote and presented the ABC Radio Adult Education series, 'Jazz Transplant'.

Bruce Johnson's interest in jazz developed in his home town, Adelaide. He is currently a Senior Lecturer in the School of English at the University of New South Wales. He has written extensively for most Australian jazz journals and recently completed work on *The Oxford Companion to Australian Jazz*. His main performance activity has been as a trumpeter in Australia, England and the USA. In Sydney he is a long-time member of bands led by Dick Hughes and Paul Furniss, and he also heads his own quartet. He is currently Jazz Co-ordinator and Secretary of the Music Broadcasting Society of New South Wales.

BLACK ROOTS, WHITE FLOWERS

A history of jazz in Australia

ANDREW BISSET

Afterword by Bruce Johnson

To my dearest Frankieboy,
For you to remember
Oz land by the Jazzy side
with lots of love
and laughter
Big LOVE xxx
quizzy rider 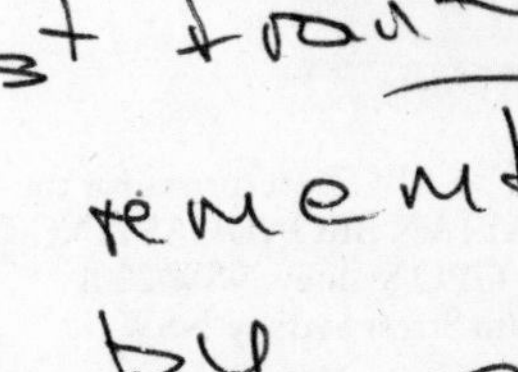
06/07/15

SMOKO - LA PAUSE CAFÉ
Radio Skid row 88.9f
Marrickville, NSW
2204

Published by ABC Enterprises for the
AUSTRALIAN BROADCASTING CORPORATION
Box 9994 GPO Sydney NSW 2001
150 William Street Sydney NSW

National Library of Australia
Cataloguing-in-Publication entry
Bisset, Andrew.
   Black roots, white flowers: a history of jazz in
Australia.

New ed.
Includes index.
ISBN 0 642 53067 X.

1. Jazz music – Australia – History and criticism.
I. Australian Broadcasting Corporation. I. Title.

785.42'0994

Set in Stempel Garamond
Printed and bound in Australia by The Globe Press, Melbourne.

FOREWORD

by Don Burrows

I am glad somebody has finally produced such a book as this. I think it is important.

I've been around jazz all my life. I was born in 1928, and grew up in Bondi, during those marvellous thirties, when the likes of Frank Coughlan and so many others were establishing this 'new music' on these shores.

The book reveals that numerous pioneers had begun to spread the word quite a while before, but it was during the thirties that the foothold was achieved in Australia. As a kid I was very much aware of this and my earliest recollections are spiced with treasured moments of discovery of this music called jazz.

It was heady stuff. The sounds were brash and toe-tapping, everything about it seemed to be in something of a hurry and even today, thinking back, the sound impression is to my ear not unlike the visual effect of old news reels of the time to my eye.

Jazz has always had a capacity for spawning 'characters', like no other music. I've known many of them. They alone could form the basis of a very funny book. The sense of humor possessed by jazz musicians, particularly Australians, is something special.

Because I have been in music full-time since the age of fourteen, I have been witness to many of the events recounted in these pages. Australia has indeed produced some notable jazz talent but we have yet to produce a 'great'. We will though.

A remarkable aspect of Australia's jazz history is the enormous role played by the musicians from New Zealand. When you consider the tiny population and isolation of that country, it is quite astonishing that they could produce so many outstanding jazz musicians. Their contribution and influence here has been immeasurable.

Jazz has flourished in Australia, that's for sure. But I think it is pathetic that so little time is given it on radio and television.

Frankly, I think our airwaves put forth an imbalance of content which is nothing short of a disgrace. It's a sad fact that jazz-eum-popular music was far more readily available to the public during the 30s and 40s than it is today. More often than not it was free. Groups of two or three guitars, ukelele, harmonica, maybe clarinet and a snare drum and brushes were familiar sights on the sands of Bondi Beach any weekend. Tightly packed around the players twenty or thirty deep would be eager listeners, shivering and wet just out of the surf, mesmerised by the beat of the music and catchy tunes like 'Twelfth Street Rag', 'Sweet Georgia Brown', 'Some of These Days', 'Brother, Can You Spare A Dime' and so on.

Radio shows boasting good bands offered the public free seats to make up an audience. There were many of these.

City theatres offered big bands and variety shows as an additional attraction to the movies.

Even the Manly ferries had bands—more in the role of buskers, I guess—but live music, just the same.

Anyway, what matters is that we do indeed have a strong, well-established jazz movement in Australia and at long last our players are judged on their own merits and not by how closely they resemble somebody from overseas. Importantly, our groups are producing more and more original music, too.

I think it's fair to say that Australian jazz has come a long way and the future looks awfully good.

CONTENTS

ACKNOWLEDGEMENTS

THIS BOOK would not have been completed without the assistance of a grant from the Music Board of the Australia Council. I am grateful for the time which so many jazzmen and women gave to me. I would like to thank the staffs of the State Libraries of Western Australia, South Australia, Tasmania, Victoria, Queensland, the National Library of Australia, the Commonwealth Archives in Canberra and Melbourne, the Australian War Memorial, and in particular the Mitchell Library and the Australian Music Centre in Sydney.

For permission to use their photos I thank the Mitchell Library, the National Library of Australia, the Australian War Memorial, the State Libraries of Victoria and Queensland, Neville Sherburn of Swaggie Records, The Shepparton *News* and Horst Liepolt Jazz Productions and '44' Records. Roger Beilby, custodian of the Jazz Archives in Melbourne gave helpful guidance.

My months of research around Australia were made easier by the many friends who offered me accommodation while I was in their town, especially, in Melbourne, Nancy McIntyre, and in Sydney, Ian Bisset. Jack Mitchell's *Australian Discography*, the only guide to recorded jazz in Australia, was invaluable. Three people who aided me throughout and read my work in its draft stages were Mike Sutcliffe, Peter Burgis, and Humphrey McQueen, who suggested the idea to me in the first place. I owe a great debt to my mother, Hazel Bancroft, for her help and support while I finished the book.

The views, and, in spite of all this help, the mistakes, are my own.

Andrew Bisset

JAZZ TEAS AT THE TIVOLI

HALFWAY around the world from the land in which it originated, jazz has taken root in Australia. The speed with which it travelled and the dedication and enthusiasm it has inspired from Australians, whose lives are very different from the uptown Negroes of turn-of-the-century New Orleans, makes the story of the development of jazz in Australia as interesting in its way as the beginnings of jazz itself.

Sydney may have heard jazz before Chicago. The first important jazz band to play in Chicago in February 1915 was the Original Creole Band from New Orleans, billed as coming 'direct from the Hippodrome Theatre in Sydney, Australia'. Extensive efforts to confirm the band's visit to Australia have failed but the possibility cannot be dismissed; advertising has always had to be at least remotely plausible, and who in Chicago in 1915 would have bothered to promote a band in that way unless the journey to Australia was made regularly by American vaudeville performers?

The journey to Australia became common in the 1850s when clippers joined the Pacific trade and it became easier in the 1870s when steam ships challenged sail, but Negroes had come to Australia long before in crews of earlier Yankee whalers. Joseph Banks had a Negro valet on the *Endeavour* when Captain Cook claimed Australia for Britain and there were a few Negroes in the First Fleet, probably West Indians. Australia has had small numbers of non-Aboriginal black residents ever since.

It was the gold discoveries of the 1850s which brought over a rush of Americans, some black. These black Americans contributed their share to life on the diggings. Of the thirteen men tried for treason after the Eureka Stockade Rebellion at Ballarat in 1854 two were black, one from USA and the other from Kingston, Jamaica.

Where miners went, entertainers followed. American circuses and nigger minstrel shows toured the goldfields and cities. The Melbourne *Argus* of 26 January 1853 advertised that Rainer's Original Ethiopian Serenaders would be appearing at the Mechanics' Institute before going on to Hobart. The show was comprised of Negro melodies and original burlesques. The program began with an overture followed by songs such as 'Commence Ye Darkies All'; 'As I View Now' from *La Sonambula*; 'The Sweep's Refrain' with Tyrolean imitations; 'Stop that Knocking'; and 'Phantom Chorus'. Part two included a banjo solo 'with oddities, absurdities, comicalities, profundities, contradictories, incongruities, improbabilities, hoping that all will show their infirmaties by granting indemnities to patronise his disquisition on. sheep's meat, pig's meat, and every other kind of meat that you should feel meet to listen to withal'. This to be performed by Mr Moran, alias Brudder Bones. The whole evening's entertainment would conclude with 'A PLANTATION JIG!'

The same issue of the *Argus* also carried a notice that Mr J. Hore, formerly of the circus, was now available for functions with his sax-horn band. This is remarkable because the sax-horn was invented by the Belgian, Adolph Sax, only eight years earlier.

Miss Josephine Gassman and her Piccaninnies were a big attraction on the Australian vaudeville circuit in 1914. Second from left is Eva Taylor who later married Clarence Williams.

From the original *Australian Variety and Show World* (Sydney), Vol. II, No. 12, 25 March 1914, front cover.

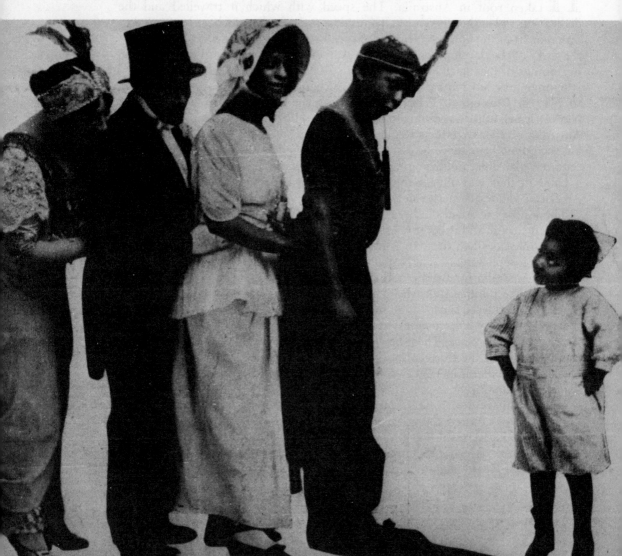

Nigger minstrelsy and spirituals introduced the public to an entertainment based on Negro elements of story, dance and song. Australian vaudeville audiences so enjoyed the shows from the cottonfields that by 1880 a classical music enthusiast, writing about trends in popular taste in the *Victorian Review*, thought it shameful that instead of liking his type of music the great mass of the labouring classes of the city had a 'mania for nigger minstrelsy'.

The Fisk Jubilee Singers were the most famous performers of spirituals to travel to Australia. Between 1887 and 1919 they made five tours across the Pacific and their performances created sufficient interest for Allans the music publishers to print a collection of their jubilee and plantation songs in 1905.

'Coon' songs were popular favourites and annual song books included such tunes as 'Ol' Folks at Home', 'I'se Goin' Back to Dixie', 'Old Kentucky Home', 'Home Sweet Home', 'Mississippi Cakewalk', 'Creole Belles' and 'Rastus on Parade'.

A soprano from the Jubilee Singers, Bertha Haynes Miller, married a Mr Willis and stayed behind in Melbourne when the choir returned to USA. They had a son they named Harry who grew up to be a bass player and after World War II was for many years secretary of the Professional Musicians' Union.

A variation of minstrelsy was the piccaninny show, performed by Negro children usually led by one adult. Salicia Bryan and her Pics toured Australia in 1898. One of the Pics was Princess White who made her first studio recording at age ninety-four in 1975 with Clyde Bernhardt's Harlem Blues and Jazz Band. Miss Josephine Gassman and Her Piccaninnies was the most popular of this type of act. They left San Francisco on their first trip in 1900 and returned for a year long tour of Australia and New Zealand in 1914–15. On both occasions a young singer named Eva Taylor was part of the show. She later married Clarence Williams, an important figure in American jazz. In every city where the Picaninnies appeared they had to give encore after encore before the audience would let them go.

Some notable Negro dancers strutted the Australian circuit. In 1911, two years before their European tour, Charles J. Johnson and his wife Dora Dean held a great reputation in Sydney as cakewalkers. Johnson claimed to have begun the Soft Shoe in America in 1891 and introduced the Cakewalk to Broadway in 1895. He usually wore full evening dress, monocle, gloves and cane. Dora Dean was the first Negro woman to wear thousand dollar costumes on stage. Without intentional malice a Sydney theatrical magazine, *Footlights*, esteemed Johnson to be 'one of the swellest coons in vaudeville'. Johnson's younger brother and his partner also toured Australia at the same time with a similar act called Johnson and Wells.

There were many minstrel troupes and individual Negro acts in Australian vaudeville and in USA at least, jazzmen could be found in almost any troupe by the turn of the century. Bunk Johnson is rumoured to have reached Australia while working on ships.

Vaudeville made people aware of musical trends in America in much the same way as records, radio and cinema would later. Vaudeville theatres were to be found in the big coastal cities and a visiting artist would be likely to visit Sydney, Newcastle, Brisbane, then Melbourne and Adelaide, and less often Hobart and Perth. Acts rarely travelled to country districts unless they were with a tent show or circus. Australia was one stop in a large Pacific vaudeville circuit. After doing Australia, artists would troop off to New Zealand, Singapore, Shanghai, Hong Kong and Manila before returning to San Francisco, or they might continue westwards to Calcutta, Colombo and South Africa or Egypt, playing mainly to expatriate European communities.

The leading vaudeville managers were Ben J. Fuller, J. & N. Tait, Harry Rickards, Jack Musgrove, J. C. Williamson and Hugh Macintosh, whose secretary, Tom Holt, was the father of Harold Holt, a Prime Minister in the 1960s. They did not leave the choice of their performers to chance but had

A young Buddy Rich during his eighteen month tour of the Australian vaudeville circuit, 1924–25.
From the original *Sun News-Pictorial* (Melbourne) 12 June 1925, p. 11, in the State Library of Victoria.
By courtesy of *The Herald and Weekly Times Limited.*

FRIDAY, JUNE 12, 1925 *PAGE ELEVE*

THE TAPS OF TRAPS.—Traps, the six-year-old jazz musician at the Tivoli Theatre, is beating his way into the hearts of patrons. Next to Jackie Coogan, he is, it is stated, the highest paid juvenile in the world.

representatives in England and America who actively sought out acts they thought would please Australian audiences.

Some of the visiting artists were famous. Houdini the Handcuff King escaped from his bonds at the Tivoli in 1910; Little Tich, one of the greats of British music hall, made a tour; W.C. Fields took Sydney by storm with a silent comedy juggling act before World War I. Traps, a child jazz drummer, beat his way into the hearts of patrons of the Tivoli during his eighteen month stay in Australia in 1924–25. As an adult, Traps became one of the world's best jazz drummers under his real name, Buddy Rich.

Australians also performed on the circuit in their homeland and in Asia, though they often complained that the English and Americans were taking their work. Popular artists had as much trouble as their literary contemporaries with audiences which fawned on foreign artists and underrated local efforts. Two of the many Australians who owed their start to vaudeville were Mo (Roy Rene) and Arthur Tauchert, the Bloke in the 1919 film 'The Sentimental Bloke'.

Patrons of vaudeville were mainly from the lower class but after the King went to a music hall several Australian State Governors followed suit. Vaudeville managements tried to extract as much snob value as they could by advertising that their leading artists received salaries equal to that of the Prime Minister but their pay packets usually told an entirely different story.

Ragtime or ragged-time, as Eric Pearse knew it, was all the rage before the Great War. Pearse (b. 1890) was a 'black note king' on piano, playing at private parties in homes around Sydney. This meant he played mainly in the black keys such as D flat, G flat, B natural and E flat minor. Pearse's father was a sea captain from Plymouth working on ships serving the north coast of New South Wales. Eric got his interest in music while growing up in Paddington, Sydney, from a friendship with an intensely musical family of Jamaican blacks, Madame Hendrix and her two daughters. When he started in dance work he had to play the waltz, schottische, lancers, mazurka, quadrille, alberts, polka, valeta, larika and the two-step. Then came the foxtrot which was most important when jazz came in. Novelties like the Turkey Trot, Bunny Hug and Apache Dance were as fashionable as the Cakewalk and one-step. The visit of the American Fleet in 1908 boosted a craze for such tunes as 'Mosquito's Parade', 'Teddy Bears' Picnic' and 'Frog Puddles'. On the eve of the war the Tango introduced a Latin-American flavour to dancing and if one booked early one could take a Tango Tea at the Tivoli. Sydney was right up with the dances then popular in New York.

John Philip Sousa's tour in 1911 did much to popularise ragtime. Sousa and his military band of sixty played to overflowing houses in Sydney, and then in Brisbane, Adelaide, Ballarat, Tasmania and New Zealand. In Melbourne Sousa was welcomed at Spencer Street Station by forty brass bands who escorted him and his band down Collins Street to an official welcome at the Town Hall.

Ragtime had immediate appeal. While Sousa was making his world tour, Irving Berlin composed 'Alexander's Ragtime Band' and within a year George Sorlie was making a big hit with it at the North Sydney Coliseum. For six weeks his audiences compelled him to bring forth their favourite number. Sorlie was a West Indian who had a travelling tent show for years and made many records for Parlophone and Regal Zonophone in the twenties and thirties, though they were not jazz but popular tunes.

SATURDAY, 12th APRIL

In the School of Arts

CARLSON'S MUSICAL FOLLIES

Direction—FRED CARLSON and NORMAN T. LEON

Present their

1924 SHOW — THIRD ANNUAL TOUR

HEADED BY HUGE JAZZ BAND

SPECIAL ADDED ATTRACTION

Bailey's Statuary and Posing Dogs

LATE WIRTH'S CIRCUS.

Bring the Children to see the Wonderful TRAINED ANIMALS

WING FAN SUN
Chinese Illusionist
(Late Sir Ben Fuller's Theatres)

MISS MAVISINA
The Poetry of Motion
(Late Cristie Film Studios Bathing Chorus, Hollywood, Los Angelos)

The Royal Musical Carlsons

World's Greatest Musical Act

A Scream A Roar A Feast of Music

Prices: 4/4 3/3 2/2. Children Half Price

Poster of a touring show, Murwillumbah, 1924.

Meanwhile in Melbourne, a violinist called Rinaldo had so much success with his 'Rinaldo Rag' that a tobacco merchant manufactured the 'Rinaldo Fag'.

The 'blue note' was noticed then but the best *Footlights* could explain was that it was 'an old American expression amongst musicians' and equated it with discord.

For six months from September 1913 Gene Green, 'The Emperor of Ragtime', played the Australian circuit. Charlie Straight accompanied him on piano. Ten years later back in USA Straight led his own jazz band and made records. While here Straight composed 'Australian Rag' and Green's records sold well on the Pathé label.

Many touring artists gave lessons to interested local musicians and ragtime spread quickly from vaudeville to the dance halls. In 1913 ragtime could be heard at the Crystal Palace Dance Hall in George Street, Sydney, or for 2/– one could dance to ragtime on the garden roof of the Grand Pacific Hotel at Coogee.

All this traffic primed popular taste to embrace jazz when it came. Jazz was an alien thing but a lot of people were comfortable with the idea of a Negro-derived rhythm music and eagerly danced the latest American craze.

Jazz is a music of the city and has thrived where there have been enough interested musicians to devote their time to it; competition amongst them driving them to peaks of excellence, which, in turn, has attracted new talent to their company. Australia's small population should be borne in mind when making comparisons with the United States. At the turn of the century the population totalled three and three quarter million, of which the two largest cities, Sydney and Melbourne, had half a million each. Even today, Australia's total population is less than that of Greater New York city. There are just not the same number of people available to play jazz.

As Sydney and Melbourne grew, so did the demand for professionally organised mass entertainment. Competitive football, vaudeville and public dance halls catered to this need. Organised dancing as a commercial business proposition got under way a little later than football and vaudeville, just prior to the First World War. Much of the credit for Australia's dancing vogue goes to an American, Billy Romaine, and a Canadian, J. C. Bendrodt.

Romaine arrived in Sydney from San Francisco on 28 October 1912 as Roaming Romaine, the Wandering Violinist. *Footlights* promptly criticised him for being too much like Rinaldo, of Rinaldo Fag fame. Romaine's (1891–1972) real name was William Harold Pittack and he came from a theatrical family. His sister, Wanda Hawley, co-starred with Rudolph Valentino in several silent films. Romaine opened the Crystal Palace Dance Hall opposite the Regent Theatre which went well until larrikin behaviour forced it to close. But he had seen the possibilities of public dancing and in 1914 he, Jim Bendrodt and George Irving opened the Salon de Luxe at the lower end of William Street. Billy's American Ragtime Music played for dancers; three violins, flute, clarinet, trumpet, trombone, drums, piano and bass.

The Salon de Luxe was formerly the Imperial Skating Rink which Bendrodt had opened in 1912 for roller skating. Bendrodt was an actor, boxer, lumberjack and all-round athlete. Between the wars he became the most important private entrepreneur in the Australian dance and jazz world.

Evening and afternoon dancing gradually caught on and another promoter opened the Centennial Palais de Danse at Bondi Junction.

The Salon de Luxe closed when the war started and Bendrodt enlisted, but though dancing declined during the war it did not vanish. The ballroom of the White City amusement partk at Rushcutters Bay was finished in December 1914 and the manager, T. H. Eslick, contracted with Romaine to supply the music. From 1915 to 1917 Romaine played the summer season at White City and winter at the Salon de Luxe which was renamed the Palladium.

The White City ballroom was huge; it catered for two thousand dancers and fifteen hundred spectators. The band played from the centre of the floor on a stand fashioned to resemble an immense chalice supported by four beautiful female figures and decorated with lead lights illuminated from inside. But the walls were for the most part lattice-work ventilators and it was destroyed by a storm in 1917.

During 1917 came reports of a new jass or jazz music sweeping America. Jazz ceased to be an underground music of the Negro community when five white men from New Orleans playing hot and by ear made their debut as the Original

The advertisement which appeared in Sydney newspapers in June 1918 for the first Australian jazz band. From the original *Music Maker*, 1 Dec. 1933 p. 40 in the Mitchell Library

Dixieland Jazz Band at Reisenweber's Cabaret in New York on 26 January 1917. As described by Australian magazines and newspapers, jazz seemed to be a synonym for anything loud, discordant or noisy.

Vaudeville acts gave a better idea. Nieman and Kennedy, the American Hoboes, was one act which claimed to present jazz. They arrived in Sydney in October 1917 and soon had Tivoli audiences calling for three encores of their song 'Mr Jazz'.

At this stage records were not important. There was little jazz available on disc and there was no hurry to import them as there was no market. The Original Dixieland Jazz Band first recorded on 26 February 1917 but their records did not appear in Australian catalogues until 1920. In the twenties this time lag was reduced to six months, or a year.

Ben Fuller wanted to be 'first again in introducing the most curious of musical ideas' so he asked Billy Romaine to form a jazz band. The other four members of this first band were all Australians: Wally Smith—piano, Harry Mehden—trombone, Jock Thompson—sax, Don Royal—drums. It was thought that a jazz band had to have a saxophone but they were rare in Australia. Finally Romaine discovered that Jim Tougher, the conductor of the State Military Band, had imported a set of saxophones from France.

Sydney audiences crammed into Fuller's National Theatre in June 1918 to catch twenty-five minutes of the Big American Musical Craze. Belle Sylvia, an Amazonian lady baritone, sang with them. They were an immediate hit. For six weeks they did their act in Sydney on the same bill as a yodelling comedian, dancing conversationalists, some jugglers, a revue called 'Candy Ship', the singing Falvey Sisters and a boxing kangaroo.

Similar success followed at the Bijou Theatre in Melbourne. Belle Sylvia was replaced by another massive Australian, Miss Mabelle Morgan. Miss Morgan had spent five years in USA from 1911 doing musical comedy, vaudeville and drama, and had appeared in Great Britain in a revue called 'Hullo Ragtime', so it is possible she had genuine feeling for jazz.

Quiet Adelaide was taken by the 'violent' music at the Majestic Theatre and the band was fêted at a society picnic in the National Park. The audience was sent delirious by the drummer's routine at the Empire Theatre in Brisbane. There the tour ended and the band broke up.

There were probably other musicians playing jazz tunes or calling themselves jazz bands but in mid-1918 none had made more than purely local impact. Romaine's band made jazz known nationally and it is from his tour that the history of Australian jazz begins.

The big influx of American bands did not begin until 1923. They were the biggest influence on Australian musicians but there was a five year period from 1918 to 1923 in which jazz was played mainly by Australians or by Americans who were already resident here. Musicians struggled with the new style as best they could and made some advances; dancing boomed and more hot dance and a few jazz records were imported so that by the end of the five years Australia had its own flourishing young entertainment industry.

Romaine left for a few months in New Zealand with his violin act. Returning by ship he was reunited with Bendrodt who had finished his service with the Flying Corps and come back through the United States. Bendrodt was

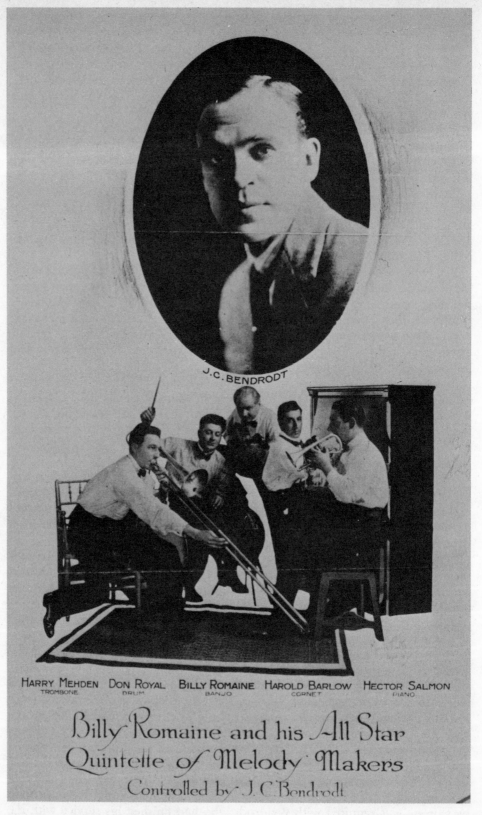

Romaine's second jazz band, 1919.

enthusiastic about the bands and dances he had seen and together they planned to open another dance hall. On board ship was Mr Sargent of Sargent's Pies whom they convinced to back the venture and in June 1919 a series of jazz dances was inaugurated through Sargent's chain of stores with the headquarters at Market Street, Sydney. Romaine got some of the originals together again in a new band — Billy Romaine and his All Star Quintette of Melody Makers.

Simultaneously Bendrodt directed Jazz Teas at the Tivoli for Hugh MacIntosh. Adami and Flo, London society dancers, were engaged to demonstrate the latest steps to those who wanted to 'get the jazz habit'. Harry Mehden was often praised by variety magazines for his trombone work at these places.

Harry was the son of Baron von der Mehden of a German family which settled in San Francisco. The Baron became Champion Cornetist of the World. He married into a performing family which came to Australia in 1884 with Signor Chiarini's Royal Italian Circus. Harry and his brother Carl (b. 1889) were born in Sydney and learned to play with the Newtown Brass Band. When they were old enough the family toured with a circus through southern Asia to India. In 1905 the brothers went to San Francisco, survived the Great Earthquake and Fire, and played jobs at the Barbary Coast, San Francisco's red light district. Unlike other Australians, the Mehdens could get work because their father was an American citizen. They took this opportunity to learn American rhythm music.

Jazz developed in black communities all over USA; though New Orleans was the unrivalled leader of jazz, other cities had their own rudimentary forms of it. The route of jazzmen to Chicago was not always up the Mississippi on a steamboat in 1917. Perhaps Freddie Keppard's Original Creole Band did not make it to Australia but they had certainly come as far as San Francisco by 1915 and they were not the only Negroes in town. Romaine chose Harry Mehden for the first jazz band because he could play in the right style.

Miss Nellie McEwen's Jazz Quartette, Melbourne, 1919, Jack Lazarus (trombone), Paul Jeacle (flute, drums), Nellie McEwen (piano), Steve Jeacle (violin).
From the original, *Footlight Star*, November–December 1919, p. 22

Harry and Carl returned to Australia in 1914. Union trouble prevented them from working with Bendrodt so they played ragtime in the pit at the National. Their cornetist was Carl Oberdorf (b. 1885, Melbourne) who thirty years later became music copyist for 2GB. In the library with him was a young clarinetist named Don Burrows who thought that reading Oberdorf's sheet music was like trying to play from the Dead Sea Scrolls.

The success of dancing at Sargents induced Bendrodt to lease the Hall of Industries at Moore Park from the Royal Agricultural Society. He called it the Palais Royal and from 6 October 1920 to 1936 it was Sydney's premier dance hall. Larger than the White City ballroom, the Palais covered half an acre of polished maple. Billy Romaine fronted the Six Super Kings of Syncopation, giving dancers 'all the newest Jazz music in the most refined and classical manner'. Already musicians had to dilute and 'refine' their jazz if the public were to accept it.

Soon other bands were playing what they called jazz. Bert Howell imported American sheet music during the war for his band at the Djin-Djin Secundas Cafe in Collins Street, Melbourne. Some pieces proved so popular that he formed the First Society Jazz Band which played at private parties and dances in the rich Toorak area. These parties were posh affairs; it was the custom of the time for musicians to eat at table with the guests and if they were late the party would wait for them.

A handful of women had their own bands. Miss Nellie McEwen conducted the Olympia Jazz Band from the piano for the ball in honour of H.R.H. the Prince of Wales at Government House in Melbourne. She had been in vaudeville as a child and had her own orchestra before the war. She formed a jazz quartet after her flute player, Paul Jeacle (b. 1897, Melbourne), returned safely and advised him to take up drums and reeds because the flute was hardly of any use then. Jeacle's specialities included xylophone and ocarina solos.

War service brought a lot of musicians into contact with jazz overseas. Keith Connolly, leader of the Syncopating Jesters from 1924, got the idea for his vaudeville act after hearing some of the bands which accompanied American troops in France. Troops waiting to be repatriated may have grown to like jazz. Australia had 167,000 men abroad at the end of World War I and the last transport did not leave England until 23 December 1919. Jazz was very popular by then and the Original Dixieland Jazz Band was playing in London. Like Bendrodt, many Australians took the opportunity to return via USA.

Ragtime at least made an impression on the army. A wartime song which was sung at Anzac Balls for years afterwards was 'The Ragtime Army':

> *We are a ragtime army,*
> *The A.N.Z.A.C.*
> *We cannot shoot, we won't salute,*
> *What earthly use are we?*
> *And when we get to Berlin,*
> *The Kaiser he will say,*
> *Hoch! Hoch! mein Gott!*
> *What a bally rotten lot*
> *Are the A.N.Z.A.C.*

The British army had a similar version of this song.

Advertisement for Leslie and Dare's Syncopas Jazz Band in The Sun *(Sydney), 15 October 1920. From the original in the National Library.*

When the Original Dixieland Jazz Band was at the Hammersmith Palais two Australians paid sixpence a time to learn how to jazz dance while keeping a close ear on the drummer and saxophonist. Leslie and Dare were pilots with the Australian Flying Corps who formed a band in the officers' mess when they weren't up in their Sopwith Camels and Snipes dropping bricks on the enemy. On piano was Leslie whose real name was Harold Fraser (b. 4 July 1893, Sydney). On drums was Captain A. H. Cobby, Australia's air ace, and on banjo was Major Wackett, later Sir Lawrence Wackett, head of the Commonwealth Aircraft Corporation. E. H. Battershill (Eric Dare) took over from Cobby. They played at large country houses near the airfield. Leslie and Dare soaked up as much jazz as they could before they were sent home in December 1919 and when they got back to Sydney they thought the jazz scene was pretty weak.

They told Mrs Maclurcan of the Wentworth Hotel that the jazz was the thing now and formed the Syncopas Jazz Band to audition for her. Their instrumentation—cornet, trombone, sax, piano, banjo, drums—differed from New Orleans bands by using sax instead of clarinet. The clarinet took second place to the saxophone in Australian bands right up to the mid-1930s. These combinations were primarily dance bands with jazz influences, not jazz bands playing for dancers.

Mrs Maclurcan liked the sound and built the Wentworth Cafe Ballroom onto the hotel for Leslie and Dare to open on April Fool's Day 1920. When their six months contract was up, Will James's band took over and they opened their own dance hall at Clifton Gardens on 15 October 1920. They called it Dixieland. Illuminated ferries were hired to bring patrons from the city. Leslie and Dare also taught jazz dancing but only the one-step, foxtrot and jazz-waltz; the shimmy-shake was taboo. 'Margie', 'Rose' and 'O By Jingo' were popular tunes.

During the season one of the Carlyons came up from Melbourne to ask them to play at the new ballroom of Carlyon's Esplanade Hotel at St Kilda. This is one of the few places remaining from those days where jazz is still played. Leslie and Dare accepted and Ernie Derriman replaced them at Dixieland.

They discovered a booming dance scene in Melbourne. One block along the beach from Carlyon's was the Palais de Danse. It was built in 1913 but the war, and the restrictions enforced to combat the 1919 influenza epidemic, checked the rise of entertainment at St Kilda. The Palais de Danse made great strides ahead when two Americans, Herman and Leon Phillips, took up the lease and hired a peculiar fourteen piece band led by George Arnold. Peculiar because it had three banjos, four saxes, one violin, one trumpet, one trombone and three piece rhythm section. Alongside the Palais were the Palais Theatre and Luna Park; opposite from 1923 was a competing dance hall, the Wattle Path.

Leslie got out of professional music in 1923. He flew in the aerial display at the opening of the Sydney Harbour Bridge and became manager of Mascot Airport. Carl Mehden led the new eight piece Carlyon's Famous Players. He had just returned from a further three years in California where he had played traps for a promising vaudeville act by the Marx Brothers and was on contract to D. W. Griffiths to play for his silent movies.

Adelaide and Brisbane did not lag behind. Two thousand people with the rhythmic assistance of Val Royal's Jazz Band helped the Lady Mayoress celebrate the opening of the 1920 Adelaide Palais Royal season and a Maison de Danse was

An advertisement from Table Talk, *3 Dec. 1923.*

soon built at Glenelg. Dancing was conducted in various city halls in Brisbane until the Trocadero was opened in 1923.

It is a mistake to think that only musicians with overseas experience were playing jazz or that Australians were only nudged forward twelve times a year by the monthly releases of new records. There were highly skilled locals who had been too young to serve who were making their own independent improvements to their music. Trombonists especially were getting fed-up with blirting oom-pah to a scraping violin lead. They took a new rôle for themselves.

Dave Meredith (b. 1901) was the trombonist in Linn Smith's Royal Jazz Band in vaudeville. In those days there were no orchestrations of dance tunes, only the piano part, and in a small five piece band—violin, sax, trombone, piano, drums—like Linn Smith's, Meredith was expected to play the bass part or raucous effects like a turkey gobbler which he would do with a glass mute. The trombone was not a respected instrument but Meredith was not content with this. He listened to cellos and tried to develop a vibrato, which was uncommon then. The new music gave the trombone more to do on the chord and Meredith thought a trombonist should provide a counter melody. His style may sound corny by today's traditional jazz standards but it was an innovation in its time.

Linn Smith's Royal Jazz Band

Linn Smith's Royal Jazz Band, a high voltage crew of musicians, who tumble into gay and glad-some jazz with an artistic finish. At times they are dreamy, but never draggy, and they make a chop suey of the fox trot, whilst retaining time and melody. Their grotesque trombone warblings and waltz oddities are the real thing in stimulating, seductive jazz. Linn Smith, the pianist, develops tremendous motive power, and the trombonist (Dave Meredith) presents a slithery-footed inebriated trombone, which joins in the happy hysteria led by the reckless saxophonist (Paul Jeacle), shrieking with delight and giving an impersonation of an educated turkey gobbler. The Drummer (Sammy Cope) smites out right and left amidst his noisy appliances: the Violinist (Arthur Curnick) fiddles with zest and the whole effective combination is spectacular jazz.

A popular band on the vaudeville circuit in the 1920s.

From the original Fuller News, No. 4, 14 March 1925, p. 2, in the Mitchell Library.

Advances were made in technique. Americans leapt ahead in their brass and sax methods. Though the sound was heard on records it was difficult to tell exactly how it was done, but a few Australians picked up some clues in a variety of ways. Harry Larsen, sick of playing the gallops at Wirth's Circus, improved his slide technique by studying photos of overseas players. Somehow Meredith developed a semi-non-pressure system of blowing.

Meredith graduated to jazz from brass bands. He was the son of a Welsh carpenter at Cobar, N.S.W., and began in the Cobar Brass Band at the age of seven, and at the prestigious brass band competitions conducted by the South Street Society at Ballarat he was awarded several medals. While busking in the streets of Sydney with one of the many bands of disabled and out-of-work diggers he was approached by two Woolloomooloo cowboys, Jack and Eden Landeryou, who were pretending to be Americans. Through working with them he met Linn Smith at a Royal Easter Show.

Leslie and Dare, Harry Larsen and Linn Smith's Royal Jazz Band were the musicians in Sydney which a talented seventeen year old trombonist went to hear when he came down from the Northern Rivers District of N.S.W. determined to make his name in jazz. And make it he did. Frank Coughlan (b. 1904, Glen Innes, N.S.W.) became the single most important and able jazzman in Australia between the wars. His colleagues dubbed him 'The Maestro' and if anyone is to be called the Father of Australian Jazz it must be Frank Coughlan. He is one of the outstanding musicians in Australia's jazz.

Coughlan was one of five sons of William Coughlan, shire clerk of Glen Innes and conductor of the municipal band. Frank, Jerry, Charles, Jack and Tom all became adept at brass instruments under their father's tutelage. William Coughlan was a friend of Baron von der Mehden and admonished his sons by saying if they didn't practise they would never be like the Mehdens.

Although at least three quarters of dance musicians had their start in brass bands and although Frank Coughlan was a gold medallist, he found he had a lot to learn before he made it on the dance scene. Brass bands had given him a good grounding but the standard repertoire was no preparation for the new style. At the end of two weeks in Sydney, Coughlan was sacked from his first dance job and after he put £10 down on a new trombone he realised he was in trouble. He approached Harry Larsen playing in the pit at the Haymarket Theatre but Larsen was too busy to teach him, but he advised Coughlan to virtually start again and work through a book of exercises. Meanwhile Coughlan had to get a day job. He demonstrated piano rolls for The Confidential Pianola Company in George Street and tried again with Milburn's Orchestra in the northern suburbs. It was only a small obscure band without a bass and he got sick of the deadly trombone part. Before long he shifted to Rose Bay.

There he was stopped one night by an aspiring jazz pianist who had learned to play from piano rolls, Ernest Barbier. He invited Coughlan to audition for his jazz band and asked him if he'd heard Linn Smith's band at the Tivoli because Smith's brother had been to the United States and told Linn exactly how to do it, and if Coughlan were to join his band he'd have to learn how to laugh on the trombone like Dave Meredith. Coughlan was better at the audition than expected but not as good as was hoped, so Barbier told him to come round to listen to some records. Barbier's father was a successful butcher and could afford a Brunswick Panotrope to which Ernest applied all sorts of gadgets to bring out the best sound and plasticine to stop the rattle.

The first one Barbier played was a Brunswick pressing of 'Hot Lips' by the Cotton Pickers with Miff Mole. Coughlan was by turns shocked and delighted and thereafter worshipped Mole as the greatest white pioneer of jazz trombone. Up to the Depression the records of Mole and Red Nichols were the most influential among the jazz fraternity, but only slightly more than records by the Original Memphis Five, Mound City Blue Blowers, California Ramblers, Bailey's Lucky Seven, Pollack, Goldkette, Ted Lewis, Coon-Sanders and Bix Beiderbecke's imaginative solos with Paul Whiteman's band. Louis Armstrong was not a force until later; Coughlan heard him first in 1928. Even though Australians knew jazz came from Negroes they were generally influenced by white bands. This was simply because records by black artists were unavailable. Until 1942 the record industry of the United States made a separate catalogue of 'race records' by Negro artists which were sold mainly in black districts. Until Negroes were also recorded for the general catalogues of companies which had outlets in Australia it was nearly impossible for musicians to hear them.

Different methods of record manufacture complicated the problem. Not many musicians seem to have been aware of the bands on Edison cylinders or Edison discs because they did not own the machinery necessary to play them. Edison discs were a 'hill and dale' cut as opposed to the more general and currently used 'lateral' cut. Record collectors today rarely mention the Edison bands for the same reason. As well as needing a different machine to play the different cuts, a musician was faced with the choice of buying a phonograph to play cylinders or a gramophone to play discs.

Coughlan immediately set about saving enough to buy a table model Rexonòla, borrowed Barbier's records and listened to them until they played both sides at once. He played along with them and his brother took off Phil Napoleon's trumpet passages. Then he saved again to buy new records for Barbier and some for himself. Barbier's band was getting occasional jobs around town and Coughlan decided to try the big time again.

By this time Will James had finished at the Wentworth and begun at the Bondi Casino. Too late Coughlan heard that they had just taken on a new trombonist but he went along anyway to badger James into auditioning him. Finally James relented and was impressed; Coughlan took over the seat. He could not believe his salary, £10 a week was ridiculous for an unknown, but the first American band had arrived at the Palais Royal and driven up wages for proficient dance musicians.

The advent of the Americans ended the first five year period of Australian jazz. Australians had muddled through with often hazy notions of what jazz was, gleaning what they could from records and the few musicians who had been overseas. Serious jazz bands had made good progress in combining the right instruments and lead violins were at last done away with. But this was no Golden Age if that term implies a blossoming of talent; recording began in Australia in 1925 and shows that jazz here was still in the bud. Australia's Golden Age came in the mid-1930s. Before then a lot more had to be absorbed from the Americans.

TONGUES LIKE LIZARDS

THE second period of Australian jazz, 1923–28, was dominated in palais and on stage by American and British bands which gave Australians their best chance yet of quickening their ideas about jazz. Frank Ellis and his Californians were the first and most influential of the American bands to visit and were a revelation to dancers and musicians alike. Even the huge Palais Royal in Sydney could not accommodate the crowds which clamoured for admission on opening night, 4 May 1923; it was packed by 8.15.

This commotion was orchestrated yet again by Bendrodt who talked a flour merchant, Mr Gillespie, into importing the band. The Californians were the nucleus of Art Hickman's band from San Francisco which had America-wide popularity when Bendrodt saw them on his way back from the war. Hickman's band is regarded as one of the first real dance bands; with ten players it was unusually large and it used string bass instead of brass bass, an innovation not often followed until the late twenties. Bendrodt wanted to bring the whole band out but they could not all come, so the band's pianist, Ellis, brought seven of them.

The huge Palais Royal, Sydney's leading dance hall from 1920 to 1936.
From the original *Music Maker* 1 April 1934, p. 44, in the Mitchell Library.

Famous Palais Royal—gigantic—yes—but will it be big enough on those opening dates ! !

The first American dance band to come to Australia, Frank Ellis and his Californians, at the Palais Royal, 1923.
L to R: Bob Waddington (an Australian bassist), Monte Barton (trombone), Danny Hogan (drums), Frank 'Shorty' Rago (trumpet), W. Loris Lyons (tenor sax), Frank Ellis (piano), Walter Beban (soprano/alto sax), Bob Kruze (banjo).

Their bass player refused to accompany them to Australia because he was fed up with their constant practical joking, so when they arrived in April 1923 Ellis searched the theatre orchestras of Sydney until he found a man better at staccato bowing than any he had seen in USA: Bob Waddington (b. 1889) who became the first Australian member of a touring American dance band. Waddington was a reader, not an improvisor, so while the band played for a week in the Haymarket Theatre he learned the tunes for their opening at the Palais. He was dedicated to the double bass because he was sure its sound moulded a band together more than the brass bass; if he sat on Lady Macquarie's Chair listening to bands on ferries going to Clifton Gardens or Manly he could always pick which ones had a double bass as the sound travelled better across the water. In the days of the large palais, before electric amplification, how well the sound carried was vitally important. Ellis would not sign the contract unless a sound shell was built for the band. A sound shell projected the music into the hall and was better to play in than many modern stages because the band could all hear each other.

The Californians were a lesson for Australians. Until then, if an Australian band had eight players they would have eight different instrumentalists, but Ellis had his men doubling on instruments to achieve a greater depth of tone colours. Coughlan recalled their impressive style (*Music Maker*, Dec. 1936): 'Beban, as alto saxophone, did not improvise far from the melody . . . while the trumpet and trombone alternated Dixieland style with a fine pulsating rhythm from the rhythm section . . . Their influence on dance music was tremendous, introducing correct vibrato for saxophones and trombones, drumming for rhythm instead of noise, swinging bass on piano, pizzicato bass, and featuring of artists . . . vocalists were yet unknown with the exception of Danny Hogan singing 'Beale Street Blues' through a cardboard megaphone.' The Californians introduced vibrato for saxophones to locals who had no idea of what vibrato meant. Australians played the saxophone the way they played clarinet in the pit orchestras, with a classical still tone which sounded strident when applied to the sax. The Americans showed them the nice sobbing tone a vibrato gives. Walter Beban played alto and B flat soprano sax, he did not play clarinet and had no idea of New Orleans style, but he did play in a way which weaved around the melody.

Already the public had succumbed to the myth that jazzmen could not read music so everyone was surprised to see them playing from printed parts, though these were not orchestrations, just verses and choruses, two saxophone and two brass parts on which they improvised. Improvisation was probably the main thing Australians could learn from the Americans who were generous with their time and skill. They demonstrated that you were not necessarily better if you played fast with a lot of notes; superiority lay in choice and timing, in a word, taste. It has always been a valuable experience to see overseas performers in the flesh and the Californians gave much needed pointers to local efforts and confirmed for many that they were on the right track.

Up to two thousand dancers continued to pack the Palais every night, paying 2/6 (women 2/-) admission, and more for the Friday night dress night, and threepence for each dance. Many just came to sit in the loges and listen to the infectious beat, which really set the band apart. Ellis discovered that the tempos were much slower in Australia than in America and, unknown to the dancers, he slowly speeded up from 36 to 56 bars per minute over a period of weeks. Every dance hall followed.

The Californians stayed in Australia for four years, playing in Sydney and Melbourne, winter at the Palais Royal in Sydney and a short summer season at the Palais de Danse, St Kilda.

Bert Ralton's Original Havana Band was the second band to come to Australia, in November 1923, from the Savoy Hotel, London. Its origins were not British but Californian, yet another link in the long established interchange between San Francisco and Australia. Like Ellis, Ralton started in Art Hickman's band, left for New York then formed his own band in Cuba in 1919, took it to London and called it the Savoy Havana Band. One of Ralton's trumpeters was George Eskdale who became a fine classical soloist. His other trumpeter was Eddie Frizelle, formerly the Californian Boy Wonder who played with Al Jolson, and with Paul Whiteman at a skating rink before he became famous. When Ralton left Cuba, Frizelle temporarily returned to the St Francis Hotel, San Francisco.

A web of coincidences surround this venue. When the Mehdens returned in 1914 they brought with them Al Tatro, pianist at the hotel; Art Hickman's band played there; when Ellis got back he recorded on Columbia in 1927 as 'Frank Ellis's St. Francis Hotel Orchestra'; Carol Laughner's Palm Grove Orchestra performed there after their tour of Australia and made six records in 1931 labelled 'Lofner-Harris St. Francis Hotel Orchestra'. Phil Harris the film star was the band's drummer but also in the 1931 band was the American-born son of an Australian, Lu Watters, who was later a key figure in a world-wide revival of traditional jazz. Another son of Australian parents later to gain fame in California, though not at the St Francis, was Gil Evans, an outstanding arranger of modern jazz.

Ralton's trombonist dropped dead just before he left England, so Ralton cabled Harry Mehden, whom he knew from Harry's days in San Francisco, asking him to join the band. After several short theatre appearances the Original Havana Band featured at Sydney's lavish new £250,000 Ambassadors night club in December, opened by Stuart Dawson, a wealthy jeweller, who had even imported the chef and waiters from London. The story circulating among musicians was that Dawson built Ambassadors to drive the Wentworth out of business after his son got drunk one night and was asked to leave. Well-heeled bookmakers and their diamond-studded dames often patronised the club. Inside, it was an elaborately decorated, alabaster and marble palace with period furniture adorning a Palm Court.

The Havana Band played at Ambassadors for twelve months and then at Carlyon's new venture in Melbourne, the Ambassador Plantation Restaurant, but its influence was not as marked as the Californians' at the Palais. Ralton's band had showmanship and their arrangements were more developed than the Californians' but they lacked the dance swing of Ellis's combination. The Havana Band recorded in Melbourne in 1925 before they left but their style was schmaltzy. This was due partly to their venue; already it was considered that real jazz was an inappropriate entertainment for an exclusive club and the clientèle would accept only an even more diluted style than was being offered to the general public at the Palais. Dawson disliked trumpets and trombones and the succeeding band at Ambassadors boasted no brass section.

Bert Ralton and the Californians' tenor man, W. Loris Lyons, both met violent deaths. Lyons returned to America in proud possession of a large diamond ring. A bandit drew a gun on him in Oakland and Lyons fought with him but was accidentally shot dead by a policeman trying to shoot the bandit. Ralton died of a gunshot wound sustained while hunting game on the African Veld. According to reports in the *Australasian Band and Orchestra News* (26 March 1927) 'he faced the end with a brave demonstration of his characteristic cheeriness, playing the ukulele and singing to his attendants while waiting to be borne to hospital'.

A better band than Ralton's was Ray Tellier's San Francisco Orchestra, the first band to make a jazz record in Australia. They played only in Melbourne at the Palais de Danse from May 1925, and were so successful that their contract was extended to November 1926 and they returned for another six months in May 1928.

In the period 1923–28 the following bands came to Australia, all from USA except Ralton's and Roy's which were from England: 1923—Frank Ellis and His

Californians, Bert Ralton's Original Havana Band; 1924—Yerke's Flotilla Dance Band, Jimmy Bachelder and His Californian University Collegians; 1925—Tom Brown and His Original Six Brown Brothers, Ray Tellier's San Francisco Orchestra (and 1928); 1926—Henry Santrey and His Symphony Orchestra, Carol Laughner's Palm Grove Orchestra; 1927—Harvey Ball and His Virginians, Ruth Varin and Her Maryland Maids; 1928—Sonny Clay's Colored Idea, Five Red Peppers (a college band), The Ingenues, and Sid Roy's Lyricals. J. C. Williamson's tried to secure Jack Hylton's band from England in 1928 and in April 1929 it was rumoured that Paul Whiteman's band would visit, but both tours failed to eventuate.

Ellis's and Tellier's bands were the most important for Australian musicians because they played the best and they stayed long enough for Australians to learn a great deal from them. Some of the bands were palais bands and some were stage bands, and though not all were wholly jazz oriented, in a 'jazz age' virtually anything from America which was not strictly classical contributed to the jazz climate, the same way as today when ballad singers are lumped under the same heading as raving rock and rollers. The Six Brown Brothers were a clown saxophone band and a pioneer ragtime recording group; their first disc was made in 1911. The Colored Idea was not the only Negro group to travel to Australia in the period but the others were minstrel troupes. The Maryland Maids and the Ingenues were all-girl bands and excited a lot of interest.

Not all overseas bands were successful; Carlyon's persevered with Australian bands until the publicity surrounding the Americans proved too much, so Tom Carlyon decided to import the Californian University Collegians. They were terrible. Carlyon had to do a quick deal with the Tivoli to get the Original Havana Band in.

Dedicated ambitious young Australian musicians seized the opportunity to play with the visiting bands and turned this experience to good account later when some of them led their own bands. The high cost of travelling, pressure from the musicians' union, disagreements with management and sheer misadventure created vacancies for Australians to fill. The Original Havana Band took Harry Mehden back with them to England where he stayed for a couple of years. Bendrodt and Ellis fell out when it came time to renew the contract in 1924 and Ellis and Lyons went home. Beban took over and enlarged the band to ten pieces with Frizelle and Australians Ern Pettifer, Dave Grouse, Keith Collins and Frank Coughlan, and renamed it the Palais Royal Californians. It continued the success of the original band and they recorded in 1926. Frank and Jerry Coughlan and Pettifer were three of the five Australians who built up Carol Laughner's band to strength. Ray Tellier led a combined American-Australian band on his second trip and left Pettifer his book of arrangements to use in Pettifer's new Rhythm Boys orchestra at the Palais de Danse in November 1928.

Pettifer's (1903–1974) interest in reed instruments was sparked as a child when he heard a bassoon player in Sousa's band, which his father took him to see at the Melbourne Exhibition buildings. Pettifer was given a flageolet when he was seven and a 'C' clarinet at nine, on which he made such good progress that he attended the Melbourne Conservatorium of Music. A few others who had conservatorium training were Carl Oberdorf, Al Hammett and Sam Babicci who won the first clarinet scholarship to the Sydney Conservatorium and toured New

Zealand with Ralton's band. Pettifer could earn an extra pound a week in the pit at Her Majesty's Theatre if he learned to play the sax, and when the Mehdens heard him they invited him to join the dance profession at Carlyon's.

Continuing influences came from musicians left behind. Tellier's trumpeter, Joe Watson, stayed to show Pettifer how to play the book and they achieved a similar sound to the original. Watson led the Green Mill orchestra in 1929 and the band at the Wentworth Cafe. Tellier's banjo player, Eugene Pingitore, took up residence in Australia and worked with dance and theatre orchestras into the 1950s. Pingitore's brother Michael played banjo and guitar in Paul Whiteman's orchestra. Danny Hogan and his double action drum pedal could not go home

Joe Aronson, the Rajah of Jazz and his band at the Green Mill, Melbourne, 1928.
Back Row L–R: Wally Walters (trumpet), Bill Meredith (bass), Jack Smith (banjo), Charlie Rainsford (piano), Ken Cotton (trombone), Neville Stoneham (violin).
Front Row L–R: Les Whitty (alto), Clarrie Aronson (Joe's son, drums), Joe Aronson, Gus Schultz (tenor), Jock Robertson (sousaphone).

with the Californians because he was a gambler and unable to pay his income tax. He led his 'Frisco Six at the Bondi Casino until he was smuggled on to a ship. The Havana Band left Saatman and Wallace behind and they formed a combined British-American-Australian band at Ambassadors.

Some came back later to settle; Charles Navarro, on banjo-mandolin in Yerke's Flotilla married an Australian and returned in 1935; from the same band came Leon Van Straten; 'Shorty' Rago from the Californians returned in 1937. Yet their influence was slight because their style had been overtaken by then and there were better Australian players.

Other Americans came without the stork-like assistance of a touring band. Tom Swift from Nebraska was invited to Australia by Carlyon to take over after Ralton left. He formed the Black Diamond Band. In America, Swift had played piano on recordings with Eddie Elkins, and the Knickerbockers. Coughlan (*Music Maker*, Jan. 1937) considered Swift to be the first real arranger and some of this must have rubbed off on to his drummer, Harry Bennett, who became an arranger for the ABC. At the Wattle Path, Walter Rudolph featured a repertoire of light classical works but this was less successful than the popular policy followed at the Palais de Danse.

More popular than Swift and Rudolph was Joe Aronson, 'The Rajah of Jazz'. He arrived via the Far East about 1922 and with his son Clarrie on drums led bands in Sydney, Melbourne, Adelaide and Perth for over a decade. His peak of popularity came when he broadcast in Melbourne over 3LO for a year in 1927 playing new pieces sent to him from overseas. The only drawback he encountered in training Australian musicians was teaching them syncopation, but by 1928 he was saying in *Everyone's* (12 Dec.) that now the general public had a sense of it. To musicians he told a different story. In the union's journal (*The Professional Musician*, Dec. 1928) he said that the better class Australian bands were not jazz bands but syncopating rhythm bands like Whiteman's or Lopez's. He was broadly correct.

The jazz traffic was not all one way. Bands continued to work the Asian circuit as they had in vaudeville and there are isolated instances of Australians playing with important bands in USA. Clarrie Collins left Australia in 1927 and deputised on trombone for Boyce Cullen of Paul Whiteman's band while they made the 'King of Jazz' film in Hollywood in 1930. Collins played with other 'sweet' bands including those of Fred Waring (1937), Xavier Cugat (1941) and even once in Walt Disney's Mouseketeers (1952). Three enterprising young Australians, Ross, Barker and McLennan toured the Keith circuit in USA and the world 1925–34 with a jazz act, the 'Three Australian Boys'. They recorded in England in the late twenties. Hec McLennan was taught banjo by Bob Kruze of the Californians. McLennan's son Rod enjoyed success as a pop singer in the 1960s. More Australian jazzmen would have gone to the United States had not the immigration laws made it difficult.

Though the Americans dominated the Australian dance scene 1923–28, they did not have the running all to themselves as there were successful Australian bands competing with them.

Linn Smith's Royal Jazz Band was among the first to 'throw out a challenge to America in the provision of real dance music', partly by appealing to their audiences' patriotic feeling for the new national symbol, the Anzac; all the band

Jimmy Elkins' Orchestra.

A leading Sydney band, 1924–28, which was mentioned in American Variety *magazine.*

were 'Dinkum Diggers' except Meredith who was too young. Vaudeville audiences roared themselves hoarse for more 'Bow Wow Blues' and 'Yes We Have No Bananas' in 1923 and for the next two years the band toured Australia and New Zealand as the Hells Bells Jazz Band in J. C. Williamson's stage shows 'Good Morning, Dearie' and 'Kid Boots'. The trend begun by the Americans was always to make the band larger but Linn Smith could not read music and was holding them back. After an argument Smith was eased out. Meredith played with Tom Swift at the Green Mill for a season then they reformed a seven piece band under the pseudonym of Fred Haywood's Palm Grove Orchestra and went back across the Tasman. At the Adelphi Cabaret in Wellington in 1928 they fostered a craze for 'The Yale Blues' and 'Breeze' even though these two songs had been out for years. Dave Meredith afterwards led his Melody Five at the Adelphi and at Kings Cross, Sydney, until 1934 when the Depression caught up with him and he got out of professional music.

Sydney Simpson led a seven piece band at the Wentworth Cafe 1926–28 and his was the first all-Australian dance band to record, in July 1926.

One local band played so well that it was mentioned in the American *Variety* (6 April 1927) which considered Jimmy Elkins's to be 'the best jazz band in Australia at present'. Elkins (real name—Jimmy Tucker) began playing piano for silent films in Sydney and formed his band in 1924. It mostly worked as the musical attraction at cinemas in Sydney and Melbourne. Like other successful band leaders influenced by the Americans, Elkins enlarged his band when he could, to nine pieces. They made the first electric recordings in Australia, for Columbia at Homebush, Sydney, in October 1926. As famous as it was in the 1920s, Elkins's band should be remembered for the potential it held for the next decade because the two best swing bands of the 1930s grew out of it. Elkins's drummer was Jim Davidson who became leader of the Sydney ABC Dance Orchestra. In 1927 Jim Gussey came across from New Zealand to play trumpet with the band; he was Davidson's successor at the ABC. Gussey brought a saxophonist with him, Maurie Gilman, whose band at the Ginger Jar in 1935 was the nucleus of Frank Coughlan's Trocadero Orchestra of 1936.

Towards the end of the 1920s more Australian bands came to the fore. On 13 February 1928 Harry Jacobs's band at the Palais Theatre, St Kilda, combined with Harvey Ball and His Virginians for the Australian premiere of Gershwin's 'Rhapsody in Blue', four years after Whiteman recorded it. Art Chapman played at Melbourne's Rex Cabaret 1928–33, and Billy Romaine popped up again in 1928 leading the first all-Australian band at Sydney's Palais Royal, the Palais Royal Orpheans, who 'threaten to finally squash the suggestion that you must go to America for a good dance band'.

Jazz was able to spread world-wide as quickly as it did because of the invention of radio and records. Commercial radio broadcasting began in Australia in 1923, the same year as the first American band arrived. Sydney listeners to 2FC regularly heard Eric Pearse, the Black Note King now leading his five piece Astoria Band, and over on 2BL Cec Morrison and His Gloomchasers. Pearse had Bert Heath on trumpet for a while. Heath was the brother of Ted Heath, the famous English band leader. Bert also played with Al Hammett's Ambassadors Orchestra when it recorded. Radio soon spread to the other cities and many more dance bands were rapidly included in the weekly program. Every top-ranking band broadcast regularly over the air.

The main difference between programming then, and any period since the Depression, was that most of the broadcasts were live from the studio or cabaret where the band was working. Record companies were against radio stations playing their product and this antipathy still surfaces today. The public preferred live bands because early reproduction of records was not good and programs

One of the early dance bands on Sydney radio, Eric Pearse and his Astoria Band, 1923. Frank Smythe (banjo), Arthur Bennett (sax), Eric Pearse (piano), Jack Irvine (trumpet), Lisle Pearse (drums).

comprised solely of records became common only when technical improvements were made and when air time became too expensive for live bands to be employed.

Music houses influenced what went to air. If Allans got the contract to supply 3LO with a listeners' program then the musicians had to play sheet music sold by Allans 60% of the time, but if Alberts got the contract then they had to play 60% Alberts. Reward for this was neither very great nor binding because the same bands performed for every publishing house. Before radio, artists had plugged songs at dance halls and from the stage, but now 'hits' could be made quickly in city and country. As usual, the least enduring songs by less than the best artists were often bestsellers. Publishing houses nominated The Ingenues as the best plugging combination for 1928, followed by a vocal group The Big Four, Henry Santrey's band and the Tom Katz Saxophone Band. Only the top band leaders bothered to work out their own arrangements; the others were content to subscribe monthly to the orchestral club of a music house and receive their stock numbers.

This is not to say the development of Australia's own Tin Pan Alley was a bad thing. There has been and always will be a vast amount of ephemeral rubbish heaped on the hit parades but it is no use condemning the lot or trying to uphold some exclusive ideal of 'good taste' because you will inevitably be confounded by something good from that genre if you have the ears for it. Jazz was initially thought to be garbage and unmusical by the canons of the time but few condemn it now. The same applies to rock and roll. Admittedly, the pieces that survive are often more subtle and developed than what was on the hit parade but the one could not arise without the other. An occasional wallow in musical junk can be amusing and sinless, but it is unfortunate that as more money is invested in the music industry, what should be its basic purpose, the sharing of human experience, becomes subverted to the drive to show a return on invested capital and a policy develops of getting as large an audience as quickly as possible by making the music 'safe'. Unfortunate, yes, and widespread but not unavoidable; musicians, aficionados and sometimes even the general public keep the good coming—jazz is not 'safe'.

Australians began importing records and machines in the 1890s and have continued to be good customers. *Everyone's* (2 May 1928) reported that for the period January–October 1927, £62,407 of American talking machines and £600,000 of pianos had been sold here. Manufacture of record cylinders began in 1910 in Glebe, Sydney, and record discs were first made in Darlinghurst in July 1924. These were Brunswicks pressed from imported masters.

The first Australian dance records being recorded acoustically by Ray Tellier's San Francisco Orchestra in the studios of the World Record Co., Brighton, Victoria, 1925.

The first company in Australia to record a master, press and retail it, was the World Record Company (WoCord), Brighton, Victoria, in 1925. This firm acoustically recorded Ray Tellier's San Francisco Orchestra. It was started by a British ex-parliamentarian, Mr Noel Pemberton-Billings. He designed his own records, multi-layered cardboard pressed to one quarter of an inch thickness surfaced on both sides with shellac. These were issued on the Austral label. WoCord manufactured gramophone and wireless sets and had its own radio station, 3PB, which played its own records. WoCord immediately ran into stiff opposition from other companies which refused to supply stores which stocked WoCord's records. WoCord closed in 1926.

Henceforth the major record companies were foreign subsidiaries. The principal five companies manufacturing and importing records were: The Gramophone Co. (known as HMV), Columbia, Parlophone, D. Davis and Co., and in Melbourne, the Vocalion Co. Only Davis was an American firm, the rest were English owned. Domination by English companies had one good effect of mitigating some repressive American policies. In 1929 the interlocking directorates of powerful music publishers embarked on a campaign to suppress jazz in the United States because they were influenced by the Hays Office and wanted to protect American morals. This organisation, the Radio Music Company, was able to do this by dictating through its control of copyright a good proportion of the music sold in shops and heard over the air. English companies were less affected and in the Depression many American jazzmen escaped their intolerable domestic situation by seeking exile in England and Europe.

All the companies had a popular and classical label. Parlophone sold their popular ten inch discs with a red label for 4/– and their classical twelve inch discs with a purple label for 6/–; HMV priced some classical records at 18/–! The companies got federal tariff protection against cheap imports in 1927 but in the Depression all the smaller ones collapsed and Columbia took over Parlophone and merged with HMV to create the forerunner of EMI, which is still the biggest record manufacturer in Australia. Their cheap labels were combined and called Regal Zonophone.

Department stores like Coles, Selfridges and Woolworths sold records but musicians favoured the specialist music stores like Suttons, which, during the middle and late twenties, fortuitously imported Gennett, a label on which many early jazz artists appeared.

Although overseas recordings vastly outnumbered the local product in the catalogues, companies did make the effort to record Australians. About fifty sides of what is almost jazz were recorded by 1930. Some of the early recordings like those by Eric Pearse and His Astoria Band in 1926 show faint traces of a distinctive Australian style of dance music that had not yet succumbed to the impact of the Americans. It was not as professional, but it was a combination of jazz, English dance band and Australian music hall pit orchestra. The Australian band which first properly assimilated the American style was Jim Davidson's Palais Royal Orchestra on its recording of 'Forty Second Street', made 6 June 1933. Recordings of the 1920s show that even though the jazz content may be low, as dance bands, Australians were the equal of most overseas dance bands.

An intriguing artist who recorded in 1929–31 was a lady baritone, Des Tooley, 'The Rhythm Girl'. Her voice lacked that vital timbre and drive which made

A 1926 newspaper advertisement for a large Melbourne dance hall.

Tom Swift's Green Mill Orchestra, Melbourne, 1926.
Back Row L–R: Charlie McPhee (clarinet, alto), Bill Meredith (bass, tuba), Jack Smith (violin, banjo), Harry Bennett (drums), xylophone, bells), Harold Moschetti (saxes, violin).
Lower L–R: Tommy Torrens (tenor, clarinet), Dave Meredith (trombone), Alex King (trumpet, mellophone), Keith Way (trumpet, mellophone).
Centre: Tom Swift (piano).

some Negresses so great but the way she sang 'He's So Unusual' and 'I Wonder What Is Really On His Mind' gave an odd slant to the ambiguous lyrics and makes one believe they were getting away with a lot more in the twenties than is commonly thought. She was usually accompanied by a trio or quartet, often Abe Romain on sax and clarinet, or Frank Coughlan on trombone. These recordings show how white dance music developed with a minimum of black contact; Romain's sax is bouncy, supportive and confident, and Coughlan displays beautiful lifting improvisations and rhythm but there is something missing: the music is peppy but not hot.

After making nearly fifty recordings for Parlophone, Tooley was heard of only a few times again, on ABC radio in 1933–34 and in the mid-1940s. She died in obscurity, probably in the mid-1950s.

The vogue for dancing went from strength to strength 1923–28. Dancing had long been enjoyed by all classes but never before had it been embraced by so many. More dance halls and cabarets opened. In Melbourne the classy Embassy commenced in 1925 and the Rex Cabaret in 1928. The building which formerly housed Wirth's Circus and Menagerie was miraculously transformed into the Green Mill—'the decorations are Dutch landscapes . . . the ceiling is a sky after the Turner school . . . a rainbow illuminates a small waterfall, and during waltzes the ceiling is lit by futuristic stars' (*Argus*, 8 Sept. 1926). The Green Mill was so huge that when the main hall burned down in 1941, what had merely been the foyer was converted into the Melbourne Trocadero. An extra squad of police was called to control more than three thousand people wanting to attend opening night.

Martin Kett's band played from a stand in the centre of the hall for the first six months but he could not overcome the echo. As dancers went into the corners they faltered because they heard six beats instead of four. Hessian was slung from the ceiling but that failed to damp it. Meanwhile, Tom Swift told the management he could solve it, but they would have to sign up his band before he did. They took him on, so while Kett worked out his contract, Swift went to the Adelaide Palais Royal with the nucleus of his band to rehearse them into shape, brought them back and set up stage at the end of the hall, not the centre. That was all it needed.

Different crowds of dancers gravitated to different parts of the Mill and the management employed about twenty redcoats (bouncers) to keep proceedings at a civilised level, but brawls still got out of hand. Fights, if not over women, were sometimes the result of the intense interest accorded dancing competitions. Good dancers could win silverware or two Baby Austin motor cars at the 1928 Amateur Dancing Championship of Victoria at Leggett's Ballroom. A system of popular voting occasionally caused tempers to flare because carloads of people would go from hall to hall to stack the voting, and if their favourite did not win then the band played 'Dinah' until the furniture returned to the floor.

The *Footlight Star* (June 1919) reassured readers that it was unnecessary to wear a dress cut above the knee as a properly cut ankle-length dress could accommodate a jazz dancer and that the jazz as taught in Australia was considerably more refined than that in America. The best known dance was the Charleston. Reports came to Australia in April 1926 about the new craze; in June, J. C. Williamson's released a series of film lessons on the dance, 'The Charleston Kid' was shown at a city cinema and in August Henry Santrey's band arrived playing the right music. A lot of people complained about being kicked by Charleston experts. All the media was tapped to bring the dance to the public.

More cabarets opened in Sydney. The Cavalier run by Lebbeus Hordern was a rendezvous for the cream of society. Stuart Dawson's London chef left Ambassadors in 1929 to open his own high class restaurant, Romanos. Smith's Oriental, a less ambitious place, opened below Her Majesty's Arcade, Pitt Street. All the big department stores had ballrooms which they hired out for social functions, and small orchestras would play light classical and popular tunes for 'tea dansant' in the afternoons while customers ate, listened and sometimes danced. There was much more live music to be heard in the cities in the 1920s.

The atmosphere at a large dance was exciting, heightened by the antics of the musicians who abandoned themselves in the required ways. *Australian Variety and Show World* (5 July 1918) described one: 'While the music is moaning and the dancers are swaying, they get into action until the air is full of flaying feet, grabbing hands and delighted exclamations, such as "Oh Boy", "Hold me tight",

"Swing me dizzy", "Alexander's got a 'Jazz' Band now", or similar exclamations of joy.'

This excitement led to some bizarre excesses. In August 1927 thousands flocked to the Green Mill to watch the unedifying spectacle of an exhausted man dragging himself mile after mile trying to break one hundred hours' continuous dancing. He had a team of girls with slings over their shoulders taking three hourly shifts who ended up almost carrying him. Police intervened. A similar attempt was made in December by a man who had Hubert Opperman, the champion cyclist, to advise him. The silly season got into full swing in 1928 as the following headings from the *Argus* show:

6 Feb.	*B. Nichols Dances 100 Hours on Floor*
16 Apl.	*B. Preston Dances 120 Hours in Katoomba*
30 Apl.	*B. Angus Dances 135 Hours at Adelaide*
1 May	*S. Watts Dances 136 Hours at Mt. Gambier*
17 May	*T. Milton Arrested for Imposing on Public: Continues Dancing in Cell*
26 May	*E. Sunderland To Attempt Dance from Geelong to Melbourne*
12 June	*Road Dancing Contest at Perth*
16 June	*D. Young Dances from Hurstville to Martin Place*
26 June	*B. Angus: 142 Hours 'Non-stop' at Broken Hill*

Complaints were frequently made in letters to newspapers. Well before electric amplification was invented jazzers were accused of making weird, loud and discordant midnight noises. Why should honest workers have to tolerate the carousals of layabouts, they demanded. Why not, retorted others less impressed with 'the utter worthiness and ingrained respectability of the Melbourne mind' and who favoured brighter leisure hours 'to dispel Melbourne's drab commercial gloom' (*Argus*, 8 May 1924).

Australia's liquor laws hindered the evolution of her jazz and entertainment. Liquor is the principal catalyst for social functions, or perhaps social functions are the principal excuse for consuming liquor, but because it was illegal to sell alcohol after six in the evening it was nearly impossible to open a good restaurant where one could have dinner, see a good cabaret and dance in an atmosphere of flowing wine well into the night, for without profit on drinks a proprietor could not afford to pay a band. The need for a profit on drinks is still a sore point with traditional jazz musicians today long after adult licencing laws have been effected because they are liable to be sacked if the customers put down their glasses and get up and dance.

Less reputable clubs exploited a loophole in the law which provided that liquor could be consumed on premises if it was paid for by six o'clock. For the benefit of the law the club would tie name tags to the bottles to indicate they were reserved, but going by the tags, half the clientèle were called Smith and the rest Jones. These small dives were frequented by dwellers on the fringe of society, pithily described by Merv Acheson, Sydney saxophonist, as 'the racetrack mob, the bookies, the urgers and the organisers, and the gambling fraternity', but they had little effect on the course of jazz. Unlike those American jazzmen who found Al Capone to be one of their best bosses, Australian musicians were not in the pay of the underworld.

The law was engaged to uphold traditional social mores and it obstructed new forms of entertainment. Proprietors of several Melbourne dance halls were warned in 1926 that exhibitions of dancing were deemed to be cabaret entertainment and thereby rendered themselves liable to prosecution for breaches of the Theatres Act of 1890, under which every person in such a place could be arrested as a rogue and a vagabond. Court proceedings sometimes took an unexpected turn though. One judge was so intrigued by a plaintiff's complaints of a loud jazz band with accompanying animal imitations and merrymaking that he held the application over for a week so he could see for himself. The law also tried to ensure that clubs and halls were safe for the public by forcing them to provide adequate exits and fire protection.

The second period of Australian jazz, 1923–28, was an exciting time for musicians and the public. Musicians made the most of their chances to hear and play with visiting Americans and the public were captivated by the infectious rhythms of the overseas bands and by some of their own. Jazz was the spearhead of the dancing boom and radio and records brought it to everyone's attention.

WHAT COULD A POOR GIRL DO

As soon as jazz appeared some people wished it would go away. All over the world jazz had its opponents. It was criticised for everything from its supposed lack of musical qualities to its effect on morals, and was accused of causing nearly all changes which alarmed older generations.

Under the heading 'Garbage Destructor for Jazz', Australian *Variety* (18 Dec. 1919) denounced jazz as 'merely a combination of noise, discord and horseplay' and reported from America a female vaudeville pianist decrying jazz as 'but the illegitimate outpourings of a brain either diseased by the use of drugs or accelerated by a desire to create pandemonium'. 'Jazz is to Pass Out' predicted *Everyone's* (8 March 1922) in the year Louis Armstrong left New Orleans to join King Oliver in Chicago; 'Australia . . . should rejoice that the craze for absurd syncopation, like the futurist and cubist periods is to be but short lived,' it continued hopefully, and revealed that a prominent instrumentalist had told them that seven-tenths of the jazz bands of Sydney were comprised of men who had little or no knowledge of music or tempo.

The members of the Sydney Conservatorium of Music were curious to listen to ragtime but one of them who was touring the USA despised jazz as 'the most abominable distortion of musical sounds known to humanity', and feared for the effects of jazz on morals, warning that it was responsible for 'perverting the taste, weakening the moral fibre and injuring mind and body' (*Conservatorium Magazine*, June 1919).

Many attacks stemmed from a sense of insecurity caused by the Great War. Sixty thousand dead Australian soldiers helped to shatter the idea that western civilisation was on the road of inevitable progress. Where formerly society had seemed to march forward with God's blessing and every new invention added to the greater glory of mankind, now that seemed to be threatened and sometimes modernism appeared to be a threat in itself. Jazz, which symbolised the period like nothing else did, became a focus for doubts about modern developments. In the arts, to which some élitists confidently clung as evidence of their own supposed superiority, there were unsettling developments like cubism and futurism, or strange dissonances in classical music, and poems which were stark and dry. People who thought about such things generally found evidence of a general malaise afflicting the world. Fritz Hart of the Melbourne Conservatorium attacked the modern world in these terms: 'The vicious influence of the jazz spirit is to be discerned today not only in music, but also in painting, poetry, and, to a certain extent, in sculpture. To me it appears to be an almost entirely evil thing . . .' (*Argus* 6 July 1926). Jazz was linked with communism and with attempts to undermine religion.

Not everyone shared this extreme view nor considered that everything should be condemmed just because it was different and happening in the twentieth century. The *Age* (31 May 1919) carried a short story remarking on the era's shallowness and the constant desire for superficial stimulation, but it concluded with a jibe at the fearful ones: 'While they are dealing with Jazz, why don't they mention Jazz painting, and Jazz poetry, and Jazz dressing, and Jazz music, as well as Jazz thinking and reading, and revolution making and all the rest? What's the good of condemning just one Jazz thing, when they've got the chance of denouncing a Jazz era?' New developments seemed to trouble entertainment personalities least of all. Bendrodt's business partner in the Sydney Salon de Luxe, George Irving, demonstrated the Walking Waltz, the Jazz and the Tickle Toe with Miss Ethel Bennetts to inaugurate a special jazz week at the Globe Theatre for the premiere in August 1919 of the Australian made film, 'Does the Jazz Lead to Destruction?', a comedy filmed at Rushcutters Bay, which was originally titled, 'Why Mabel Learned to Jazz'.

Jazz was accused of being materialistic and less sentimental than earlier popular music. It was supposed to embody the noises of modern machinery and large cities, though the only sound which jazz has used is that of the steam locomotive, usually as a symbol of escape to freedom and not as a recital of the joys of industrialised life.

Established social patterns changed considerably during and after the First World War. Many younger women would not accept the social constraints of their elders and because the new codes of behaviour could be seen most readily at a social function like a dance, jazz again came under attack as the cause of the changes. The *Argus* (30 April 1920) reported that girls from eighteen years of age were ordering cocktails in the city with complete assurance on any day of the week, which the *Argus* thought was a direct result of the 'freedom and independence permitted during the war, and of association with men . . .'.

Alcohol at dances provoked adverse reactions from many quarters. Between the wars, there were many women who chose not to exercise their new freedoms but instead took it upon themselves to be the moral protectors of society, and they wanted the law amended to protect young women from moral, physical and spiritual degradation. In 1935, the Premier of New South Wales, Mr Stevens, received a deputation asking that people who took intoxicating drink to dance halls should be punished. The deputation was comprised of representatives from the Council of Churches, the Catholic Women's Association, the Hibernian Society, the Catholic Guild, the Irish National Foresters, Country Women's Association, National Council of Women and the Country Press Association. They stressed that they were not a temperance delegation, they objected to drink only at dance halls, for only 'designing people' wanted liquor at dances.

An amazing thing about the palais then was that technically they were all dry. The big crowds which came to dance were supposed to drink tea or lemonade all night, and of course that just would not do. Overcoats were the fashion, so men sewed pillow cases inside and filled them with bottles and, in the loges around the floor, couples would be constantly reaching under the table to top up their drinks. Musicians were among the best offenders and an instrument case served ideally for smuggling in drinks.

Many parents were convinced that jazz was essentially vulgar and commonplace and feared that jazz fostered a release of sensuality. A shocked father wrote to the *Argus* (19 September 1925) asserting that 'a dance is but an excuse for kissing and cuddling, and even worse'. How much jazz was responsible for any release is hard to tell, but in the twentieth century women have become less and less content with the double standard. Social codes discouraged women from learning to be jazz performers or musicians but did not extinguish the desire for self-expression. In the inter-war period a lot of the best Australian books were written by women, but often they were women with an unusually good education and 'a room of one's own' to work in. But what could a poor girl do?—Dance!

The most publicised opposition to dancing came from the religious leaders of the community, especially the Nonconformist churches. In 1925, the South Australian Methodist Conference, after a spirited discussion on 'The Lure of the Dance', passed a motion earnestly recommending to the trustees of their properties that their connexional halls should not be used for 'mixed dancing' which was 'an inexpedient pastime'. One speaker testified that the white slave traffic (prostitution) was under the wing of the dance hall and that 90% of the women of the streets of the city sustained their first fall there. A year later the General Conference of the Methodist Church of Australia passed a similar motion. The Presbyterian Assembly in Brisbane in 1926 was in a dilemma over dancing. They agreed that while it was not in itself wrong, it unfortunately had 'deplorably evil associations'. Their discussion hinged on whether dancing could be done 'to the Glory of God and to the advancement of His Kingdom'. With unusually progressive reasoning, the *Argus* (2 June 1926) did not support the churches but argued strongly in favour of dancing, believing it should be encouraged in association with the church to build young persons' characters.

Attacks on jazz were bound up with opinions as to what was in good taste. Taste is response notoriously affected by age and aspirations. The upper classes pretended to their idea of the best of British culture, a calm, sophisticated assurance based on centuries of successful achievement in art and business, a tradition in which exuberant, unfamiliar and new music from the outcasts of a different country could take no part. Rarely was any real jazz played at the exclusive night clubs. Guests at Romano's never had a topnotch combination even though many of the best dance musicians played there at various times. 'Ambassadors' advertised that they catered for 'Merrymakers who seek Charm and Refinement, and who are satisfied only with superb music and a cuisine unequalled in Australia . . . minimum charge 10/6'. Charm, Refinement and half a guinea were incompatible with jazz.

This attitude was clearly observable in cinemas. *Everyone's* (11 April 1928) snootily stated: 'There is every evidence that many motion picture houses throughout Australia are fostering a taste for classical music amongst their audiences. These theatres are attended by a different class of people than attend cinemas in which the musical part of the programme is sadly neglected, or is composed entirely of red hot jazz'. In every discussion of jazz in the popular press the implicit assumption was made that jazz was not a valid musical form; there was good music and there was jazz.

Conductors for cinema orchestras were chosen for the type of audience they would attract. Albert Cazabon, conductor at the Prince Edward Theatre, judged his listeners to be the best people, attending 'because they know they will get the best music. I think that other than straight jazz should be confined to vaudeville. Jazz is played at the Prince Edward, but it is played straight'. Jazz was acceptable to the 'best people' only if it was played straight, in other words, only if it was diluted of its unique characteristics until it ceased to be jazz. By contrast, Will Quintrell at the Sydney Tivoli estimated that '95 per cent of Tivoli patrons are more or less tickled pink with jazz'. (*Everyone's* 7 March 1928).

Patterns of social prestige were changing and the establishment was no longer the sole arbiters of what people should be like. Instead, figures from the entertainment world increasingly captured public attention. There was one view of society which fondly believed that everything was guided by the best ideas trickling down through the population from the élite to the common people, but jazz upset all this. Jazz bubbled up irresistibly from what were considered the lowest sections of society: not by any virtue of the lower classes though, because popular uneducated taste is fairly conservative with a penchant for gimmicks and novelties.

Jazz bubbled up from the lower classes because they were more exposed to it; it came through their channels, the palais and vaudeville houses, whereas the upper classes favoured to import Italian opera companies for their concerts. No class has a monopoly on intelligence, and there were independent thinkers from all classes who became musicians who decided that jazz would be a rewarding style of music to play and study. But in the days when jazz was regarded as vulgar, a musician from a lower class would be more likely to embrace jazz than one from a wealthier background because he had less social prestige to lose by doing so. Quite often he could gain if he rose high in the music trade. Jazz was all the more disturbing to élitists because it was an art form which contained many 'barbaric' elements and unlike brass band music, owed almost nothing to the high tradition of Europe.

A fear grew that the high culture would be overwhelmed by popular culture. Academics despaired for the future if the young were allowed to continue in their way. P. F. Rowland in an article entitled 'Five Thoughts on Education' (*Australian Quarterly* 14 September 1932) wrote: '. . . speaking generally, in music do we ask anything more than "jazz", in art the jazz equivalents, in literature the latest naughtiness in novel form? Is not this due to the fact that in our age . . . the cultural subjects are being crowded out of our curriculum?'. Jazz and all that it symbolised was not considered worthy enough to be 'cultural'.

The equivalent today of a jazz band in the 1920s is a hard rock group; jazz then was the latest bizarre emanation from America. Jazz was criticised in part simply because jazz came from America; it would have been much harder to mount an attack on it if jazz had developed in Britain. Australia's infant national pride was piqued that unlike the Norman invasion of England, this non-personal cultural invasion absorbed nothing of the country it conquered and it was perceived as a threat to the national identity. Another academic anxiously wrote an article called 'Pacific Penetrations' (*Australian Quarterly* No. 8, December 1930) which concluded: 'We dance to their tune and the pied piper is leading our young race to the sounds of syncopated music into the hillside where our characteristics may be lost forever'.

Australia has survived sixty years of jazz and still remains 'Australian'. Although it is a young country still searching for traditions to guide it, the extent to which it has become less 'Australian' in the twentieth century and more like another country is no more than the extent to which any other western country has changed under the impact of modern technology, especially in the English-speaking world. If jazz could be regarded more as a discipline like nuclear physics instead of a sinister American miasma, then there would be less confusion. The people who applaud Australian scientists yet regard brilliant Australian jazz musicians as a mixed blessing fail to realise that jazz has not somehow captured their brains, but instead, Australian musicians have taken jazz and made it their own. Quite unconsciously, an Australian style of jazz has developed. It is still immediately recognisable as jazz to anyone in the world, but while it is the same meal, all the herbs and spices are subtly different. Whatever it is that makes people 'Australian' has been able to withstand the advent of jazz, and inject jazz, as played here, with its essence.

That Australians should so slavishly bow to the fashions of another country rankled with some but others took a more lighthearted view. The *Argus* (23 July 1921) satirised the dance craze in a short story about a hopeless dancer who returned from New Guinea with a native dance and the word went round that the 'Bulea' was the latest thing from America. True to form, 'Whether it's the latest Yank comedy or the latest Yank song or the latest Yank fad, dear, jolly old Sydney will swallow it hook, line and sinker everytime'. Melbourne was not spared either, because 'if you didn't "Bulea" you were branded a "dud"'.

The guardians of good taste found one major stumbling block in their drive to dismiss jazz—a few independent-minded classical musicians defended it. Percy Grainger, Australia's internationally renowned pianist and composer, and Bernard Heinze, Professor at the Melbourne Conservatorium, both publicly argued that jazz was a most excellent and beautiful music. Their opinions threw into relief the reasons why people liked the established styles of music or found it hard to accept new ones. The real reasons were not all musical, but classical musicians, unlike many of their patrons, could be enthusiasts of jazz because they appreciated its intrinsic merits more than they bothered with its social context.

Heinze thought that jazz excellently took the place of the minuet and waltz and other old dances which people talked about so lovingly. This was a provocative comment because it was well known that classical music derived much from European folk traditions and here was an expert saying that this despised music could take a place in it. Grainger reminded concertgoers that Bach had introduced the clarinet into classical music when it was similarly scorned. He advocated that Australia and the USA were now presented with the opportunity to form a new type of orchestra which would be an 'extremely expressive and soulful medium' if they utilised such modern instruments as the saxophone. Such combinations would not be a substitute for a symphony orchestra but would have to evolve their own systems of expression and balance, different from but on a par with classical music. This was an essential step that only a few were prepared to take, to recognise that jazz was a legitimate and worthwhile form of expression. The move to accept jazz was helped along when, in 1926 and 1927, the influential South Street Society of Ballarat included in its competition a section for jazz bands.

These few favourable opinions were vastly outnumbered by the views of 'musical purists' who detested jazz, who said that jazz had no melody, it would never be taken seriously by musicians, a jazz opera would never come off and it would never become a music in its own right. Among classical musicians Heinze and Grainger were in the minority.

A curious aspect to Heinze's and Grainger's remarks was that no-one from the dance scene in the 1920s championed what they had to say. Overseas, every chance comment Grainger made that was favourable to jazz was seized on to bolster up jazz.

In Australia, while musicians were not about to give up syncopation for one minute, they were slow to come to its defence. They almost agreed with their detractors by default, dodging around the issue saying, so what, but we like it; or that jazz had a right to exist because while it was worthless, it was harmless. The *Australian Band and Orchestra News* (26 July 1926) feebly suggested that since jazz consisted of Joy, Animation, Zip and Zest, 'then why should Professor Bernard Heinze and others bother to try and hear anything in it?' This weak attitude changed in the next decade when dance men came to know more about jazz.

Jazz caused a big split in the Sydney Musicians' Union. Dance musicians were looked upon almost as a new breed of men, and 'legit' musicians were jealous and would not speak to them. At one stage relations were so bad that the dance musicians were forced to make their headquarters in the pub across the street from the union. Eventually this split was healed but not before it created resentment against the idea that art was only for élites. The *Footlight Star* (February 1919) sullenly concluded: 'We have been taught that . . . if the multitudes admire it, it ceases to be art'.

While the uncertainties created by the First World War caused some people to clutch the European high tradition ever closer to their breasts as one sure bastion in a cranky, drifting world, there was another factor that was equally responsible for the outbursts against jazz. This was the Australian's fluctuating concept of himself in terms of his race. Australia began as one of Britain's far flung outposts of the empire and up till the Second World War many Australians were content to see themselves as Austral-Britons. Near the end of the nineteenth century some Australians developed ideas that our origins, the land and the climate had combined to produce a new social order and a racially distinct type, different especially from the English. This new concept weakened and vanished about the turn of the century when Australians perceived a threat from the yellow hordes to the north in Asia. The dominant concept took over again, that we were all transplanted Britons, but this was undermined by the Great War. How could they claim there was a unity of blood in the Anglo-Saxon world when the United States delayed so long before entering the conflict, and refused to join the League of Nations? Thousands of Australian troops saw for themselves that they were different from the English, and the Anzac became the expression of the national identity. On one hand there were people who emphasised how British the Australians were in an effort to ensure that Britain would defend her small dominion; on the other hand there were people who felt they were not really British. There was some slight competition for allegiance to either concept.

Underlying this small division of loyalties was a disquiet fuelled by events in Russia and Ireland after 1917, that the internal stability of Australia was at risk. Jazz, because it had vigour and definite non-European characteristics, did not allay these fears. The dominant classes wanted everyone to listen to British music in the hope that they would act in a British, or conventional, way. If they listened to jazz, it was feared they might not. An editorial in the *Argus* (11 July 1925) said that British music expressed 'essentially British qualities and British ideals. It is for the most part, sane and wholesome . . . and it evinces a determination to go ahead and develop its own special characteristics'. The *Argus* hoped that if more people came to like English folk songs, that might 'yet redeem a popular taste perverted by an imported vogue of sheer barbarism, with inspiration no loftier than the savagery of the African negro'. This attitude was a fawning on what was thought to be the font of culture, Britain, and it discouraged the development of an Australian expression of life, but the opinion leaders were prepared to sacrifice that for social stability. Jazz was disliked because it was alien to the high tradition and the upper classes feared that it would provide an identity for the lower classes which was separate and oriented away from the approved way of thinking.

Whether one saw oneself as Australian or British was less important than whether one was white, or not; not nearly white or almost white or a very light brown, but pure white. The major political parties all upheld the White Australia Policy, the aim of which was to exclude coloured races. Jazz, with its Negro origins, could not have been better designed to aggravate the misconceptions Australians held about non-whites. Jazz was seen not as just a music but as a threat to the fabric of society. The *Argus* (6 July 1926), not a gutter rag but a respectable Melbourne newspaper, ranted in an editorial that jazz represented:

> an imported vogue of sheer barbarism. Jazz is a direct expression of the negroid spirit . . . it affronts the ear at every turn . . . It has degraded the modern fashion of dancing to represent more and more the dreary posturing and ugly contortions of the primitive African people from whom it emanates . . . It is a matter for anything but pride that British people should have turned from their own delightful heritage of song and dance to a noisily concealed perversion of the musical instinct . . .'

Notice that this paper took the attitude that we were 'British people', not Australians. It was also suggested that jazz was some kind of divine retribution visited on the generations of the white race for the horrors of the slave trade. The following is from an article in the *Sydney Morning Herald* (19 May 1934) which purported to defend jazz:

> '[The American Negro] has impregnated the whole American people, and through them the civilized world, with the barbaric culture of the jungle through the medium of jazz. American commercial genius has facilitated this spreading of jazz mania. Thus it has come to pass that these African exiles in America have wrought a far-reaching and terrible revenge for the unspeakable enormities of the slave trade . . . And, quite justly, this revenge has not been confined to the United

Real Syncopation!
Sonny Clay's Colored Idea.

The colored jazz band combination, which is one of the big features of Sonny Clay's Colored Idea, soon to play a season over the Tivoli circuit.

The first Negro jazz band to tour Australia, 1928.
Ernest Coycoult (trumpet), Archie Lancaster (trumpet), Luther Graven (trombone), Leonard Davidson (alto), Louis Dodd (alto), William Griffin (tenor), Sonny Clay (piano), Rupert Jordan (banjo), Herman Hoy (bass), David Lewis (drums).

From the original *Everyone's*, 11 Jan. 1928, p. 46, in the Mitchell Library.

States, but, like a deadly infection, has spread to every nation which profited by that lucrative, loathsome traffic in human flesh and blood.'

With friends like that jazz did not need enemies.

Australia was full of these racial fears when an all-Negro jazz band arrived in Sydney in 1928. Sonny Clay's Colored Idea was probably the best band to tour Australia to that date. Twenty-eight year old Clay had played in California with Jelly Roll Morton and Kid Ory, and the instrumentation of Clay's ten piece Colored Idea resembled Morton's Red Hot Peppers. The band was part of a troupe of thirty-five coloured performers. Singing with the band, but on a separate contract, was Ivy Anderson who later recorded with Duke Ellington. There were the four Harmony Emperors who sang southern melodies, Dick

Saunders who danced and was master of ceremonies, and The Four Covans who were one of the outstanding Negro dancing teams of the 1920s. Before they came, the Covans—two brothers Willie and Dewey and their wives—worked with Lionel Hampton at the Sebastian Club in Los Angeles in 1927. Willie Covan was the pick of the four and later Eleanor Powell recommended him to MGM in Hollywood to give the film stars dancing lesson. Among others, he coached Mickey Rooney, Kirk Douglas, Gregory Peck, Shirley Temple, Mary Tyler Moore and Dick Van Dyke.

Sonny Clay turned the SS *Sierra* into a jazz-ship as it berthed at Circular Quay on 21 January, perhaps playing their composition, 'Australian Stomp', which they had recorded for Vocalion in Los Angeles just before they left. It was immediately obvious that their style was far in advance of anything Australians had heard previously. Their 'potent, overproof brand of syncopation' proved a little too hot for local taste and their tour was cut short after nine weeks when the band was deported.

The deportation resulted from a combination of many factors set in train five years before when the first American band came out. Initially Australians had welcomed the Americans if only for the effect they had on wages—Frank Ellis was paid the fabulous salary of £65 per week and the rest of the Californians got about £40 per week, roughly ten times the basic wage—but when more Americans came out Australians started to lose jobs. The General Secretary of the Musicians' Union soon foresaw that action to gain the same sort of protection that the American union gave its members would be necessary if the importation of complete bands continued. Australian musicians were in a double bind because though they felt they were the equal of the Americans as instrumentalists, they conceded that, as jazz musicians, the Americans led the way. But jobs were more important and the union directed complaints to the International Confederation of Musicians at The Hague, the South African and British musicians' unions and the Melbourne Trades Hall Industrial Disputes Committee, and protested to the Minister for Home and Territories, Senator Pearce, urging the prohibition of tours by American jazz bands. Indeed, it is surprising that the Colored Idea was allowed in at all: Senator Pearce had refused at least two applications to import Negro bands in 1924 and had publicly asserted that 'coloured men will never be allowed to come in'. The Musicians' Union in November 1923 had passed a motion which appeared in the rule book as one of the union's objectives: 'To uphold and maintain the White Australia policy, and prohibit the admission of coloured races as members'. This seemed to have no effect on the government which, by January 1928, had done nothing to give musicians greater protection.

A more immediate reason for the deportation of Sonny Clay's band stems from the actions of the American Federation of Musicians which banned a concert tour of the USA by the Australian Commonwealth Band, an inoffensive, conventional military band. This measure incensed Australians and galled all the more because of the cordial reception given to American bands here. The Lord Mayor of Sydney, Alderman Mostyn, on welcoming the Commonwealth Band back to Australia in October 1927, disparaged the United States by declaring that he had previously believed Americans to be broadminded but, in view of the treatment given to the band, he now thought them very narrow-minded. In Federal

Parliament a member, Mr Jackson, was scandalised and urged Prime Minister Bruce to institute reprisals against Americans who came to Australia with orchestras, but Bruce would not contemplate that and could not do anything at a government level anyway because the action had nothing to do with the U.S. government.

Sonny Clay's Colored Idea arrived three months later and encountered a heated resentment towards America. They were the first American band to come out since the return of the Commonwealth Band and a few days after they arrived the press reported that Miss Eunice Hurst of Australia had been prevented from accepting an appointment as professor of violin at Wells College, New York, by the American immigration authorities. So there would have been trouble anyway, but, because the band was black, it was so much easier to organise.

Their show opened at the Sydney Tivoli on the day they arrived and was warmly received by the critics though the band was not the expected 'wow' for the audience. Clay's idea of jazz did not conform to the Australian idea which demanded a hot finish to each number with everyone blowing hard, instead of the fade-out affected by the Colored Idea. The hard-hitting finish is still favoured by Australian traditional jazz bands today. 'St Louis Blues' and 'Blue Heaven' were two outstanding numbers by the band. Despite the talented cast, the show did not go as well as it should have, and after four weeks it shifted to the Melbourne Tivoli where it opened on 20 February. Tempers among the cast frayed and they were evicted from several hotels for noisy behaviour until they took flats in Evelyn Street, East Melbourne. There, on the weekend of 24–25 March, police raided their rooms and discovered six of the band with six white women in various stages of undress and sobriety. One girl escaped by jumping out the window but the others, aged seventeen to twenty-three, were arrested and charged with vagrancy, charges which were dismissed in court.

The matter did not end in court. 'Nude Girls in Melbourne flat orgy; Negro comedians as partners; Raid by police' bayed newspaper headlines of 27 March, which Mr Jackson read to a shocked parliament. Jackson righteously demanded, 'Does the Minister not think that in the interests of a White Australia and moral decency, permits to such persons should be refused?' The Minister agreed, the honourable members concurred, and the Negroes were forced to sail from Australia on the first available steamer. Only six were deported by government order, the other five were forced to leave by weight of public opinion. Sonny Clay attributed it to the Commonwealth Band trouble and claimed they had been framed and hounded ever since they landed: 'Why should they be nailed for something which goes on nightly in Darlinghurst and St Kilda? From the time the boys and I landed we were chased by women who popped up no matter where we hid'. The Tivoli cancelled their contracts and Carlyons tore up their contract for the band to play at the Green Mill. Melbourne lost its first chance of dancing to a Negro band.

Interestingly, Ivy Anderson, Dick Saunders and the rest of the troupe were allowed to stay and did not experience any spleen from their audiences. In August 1929, the Kentucky Jubilee Singers, eight coloured singers of spirituals and plantation songs, were warmly received by vaudeville patrons when they performed at His Majesty's Theatre. Obviously white society could accept the humble Christian aspirations of the spirituals which showed Negroes in a yielding, resigned light, but could not tolerate Negroes in the exuberant, confident and assured role which jazz gave them.

The controversy did not subside after the deportation. Overseas newspapers reported that ex-Prime Minister W. M. Hughes made it the opportunity for a sweeping offensive on the Federal immigration policy. The *Montreal Gazette* (29 March 1928) stated: 'No incident of recent years has so stirred the Commonwealth and the "White Australia" cry is loudly raised'. The *New York Times*, the *New York Sun* and even the *Rabaul Times* reported Hughes's angry rhetoric: 'Our musicians, the Commonwealth Band, were boycotted in the United States. Now the land of liberty sends us these Negroes to entertain us. Are we going to take all these things lying down?' They were going to make sure that no Australian women would.

The Musicians' Union, after pressing for protection for four years, was granted its request within two months, despite opposition from the principal theatrical houses. The new rules applied also to promoters who wanted to bring in coloured boxers. Individuals were not prevented from coming, and in the next decade more Negro artists performed at the Tivoli and white leaders were brought in to front the palais bands, but it was not until 1954 that another complete American band led by a Negro was permitted into Australia.

The deportation signalled the end of the second phase of Australian jazz. The Depression was already creeping within Australia and it struck hard at musicians particularly. The Depression forced jazz into retreat all over the world and in Australia it coincided with an authoritarian trend to restrict democratic rights and working people were obliged to accept a diminished share of the national dividend.

FOOT FOOD FROM THE MIRE

'Every now and again . . . the band would get stuck into something and we'd go mad . . . Well, that sort of blew our tops and let off a bit of steam, because we felt a little bit hemmed in with our public music . . . Now all of us want to do this all our lives, but if you want to stay alive you've got to do something else, in order to eat regularly.'—Ern Pettifer (Music Maker, Vol. 34, No. 4, September 1965, pp. 4–5)

As a general rule in entertainment, when times are good the music is hot, but when times get tough, the music goes sweet. Frank Coughlan felt that only a brave man would have launched into a chorus during the commercial mire of the Depression, and the principle still applies today. From 1936 to 1976 the ABC maintained two dance bands, one in Sydney and one in Melbourne, and it was the rôle of the Melbourne band to be the sweeter of the two, though in recent years it has become hotter under the direction of Brian May. In March 1976, during an economic recession, the government decided that one of them had to go, and the hotter Sydney band got the axe.

During the Depression, unemployment among musicians was twice as high as the national average and many were reduced to busking in the streets for a living. Hard times were compounded by the arrival of talking pictures which drove hundreds of musicians out of work. Most of the pit orchestras were dispensed with and other musicians were forced to take a cut in salary. The first sound film to be screened in Australia was 'The Jazz Singer', starring Al Jolson, which opened at Sydney's Lyceum Theatre on 29 December 1928. The talkies hit vaudeville hard too, and in 1930 Fuller's, the last big Australian vaudeville management, eliminated all activities except for four revue companies and swung over to sound films. 'Canned' music replaced live performers on stage, in ships, cafes and hotels. The Musicians' Union fought ineffectually against the introduction of mechanical music, and at a low point in the battle even the union turned against jazz. In a 1929 pamphlet, *Kinema Crisis in Australia*, the union blamed American jazz for perverting public taste to the extent that they would go to shows which played canned music. Wireless magazines apparently decided that the opportunity to give jazz a swift kick while it was down was too good to miss, so articles proclaiming the end of jazz were again written.

The union organised benefit recitals and did what it could to alleviate the effects of the Depression but the structural dislocation was immense and the popular music profession took years to readjust. The lingering unemployment explains why the Americanadians had difficulties with the union when they tried to tour Australia in 1937. A Melbourne entrepreneur and musician, Clarrie Gange, brought them to Melbourne, where they were not very successful, then to Sydney where they did well at the Top Hatter's Club at King's Cross. The union was putting pressure on them, but the end came when there was a gun-fight and murder at the club and the crowds stayed away.

The Depression was particularly hard for violinists and cellists who were not good enough to play in the symphony but passed in pit bands in suburban picture shows. Once the talkies came to the suburbs they were out of a job. Many young men who failed to find other jobs tried music, and for a while there was a rash of poorly trained musicians on the market, but the Depression weeded out the mediocre, the fainthearted, and the middle-aged players who were not going to improve. Young, talented, ambitious players snatched at the few places available.

Perhaps the only other bright spot in these bleak years was that the struggle in the brass band movement between the supporters of high and low pitched instruments was finally resolved in favour of the low pitch. Until 1929, all Australian brass bands were tuned to the high pitch (A=452 c.p.s.). Colonel J. A. C. Somerville was one of the main figures who succeeded in getting it lowered to orchestral pitch (A=440 c.p.s.).

About the time Ion Idriess was writing *Lasseter's Last Ride* and had the doomed Lasseter whistling a jazz tune to himself in the desert, a number of Australian musicians were prospecting with greater certainty among the bands of London. Frank Coughlan arrived on 20 December 1928 on the *Otranto*, armed with letters of introduction from Eddie Frizelle. A week later he was playing in Arthur Rosebery's orchestra at the Kit-Cat Club. In the following months Coughlan played with Al Starita at the Piccadilly Club and with Jack Hylton's band in Hamburg, Berlin, Antwerp, Brussels, Liege, Paris and London. In February 1929 Coughlan joined Fred Elizalde's Orchestra for six months at the Savoy Hotel, and while he was with them, the band recorded 'Singapore Sorrows'. In Elizalde's band were Adrian Rollini and Fud Livingstone, and the band was England's first experience of a resident 'hot' orchestra. It was a remarkable achievement for an unknown twenty-four year old Australian trombonist to grow up on the other side of the world from New Orleans and yet be able to learn enough about jazz and dance music by 1928 that he could walk into jobs with the top English bands. England was not America, but it was much closer to the source than Australia was. While in England Coughlan was also thrilled to meet Chelsea Quealey and Bobby Davis of the Goofus Five, and Max Farley of Whiteman's orchestra. Coughlan recorded with the New Mayfair Dance Orchestra, joined Al Collins Orchestra in August 1929 and left England on 10 December 1929 for New Zealand to play under Ted Henkel, but this fell through and he came on home.

When Coughlan got back he gave letters of introduction to Abe Romain who went to England on 22 February 1930. Romain was one of that long and impressive list of New Zealanders who have contributed so much to jazz and popular music in Australia. A history of jazz in Australia is essentially a history of

Sydney and Melbourne with the cream skimmed off the other major centres, and this includes Auckland and Wellington as much as Adelaide or Perth. The list begins with Eric Dare, of Leslie and Dare, and continues with John Robertson (trumpet), Maurie Gilman (saxes), Colin Bergersen (saxes), Jim Gussey (trumpet), Charlie Lees (guitar), Les Mitchell ([sax]—Errol Buddle's tutor), Dave McRae (piano), Julian Lee (piano), Bob McIvor (trombone), Mike Nock (piano), Barry Woods (drums), Lyn Christie (bass), as well as Judy Bailey (piano), the best female instrumentalist on the Australian jazz scene, and the enormously talented Charlie Munro (reeds, flute, cello) whose contribution ranks with Coughlan's. Many more would be mentioned if the rock and roll bands were detailed, or if the list was extended to people like Buddy Wikara who popularised Hawaiian music in the 1940s. Australian music cannot be discussed without referring to New Zealand.

Adrian August Bussy de Saint-Romain (b. 27 August 1905, Hititi, Wellington, NZ), known as Abe Romain, was of a French-Mauritian family. His grandfather owned a sugar mill in Mauritius and Abe's father stowed away on a sailing vessel to Australia after the grandfather would not allow a serious romance to continue. Eventually he settled in New Zealand and became a dairy farmer. Abe, the youngest of four boys, was discouraged from going on the land, and from the age of ten his family set him to music, whether he liked it or not. He had private tuition on violin for two years, then sax and later clarinet. He had a few lessons on sax from Harry Lazarus, an Australian touring the vaudeville circuit with 'The Peep Show'. Romain was educated at the local convent, then at the Marist Brothers and finally at St Patrick's College in Wellington. There was no music at school but he played a lot of football, and when he was with Jack Hylton's band in England he was a member of the charity soccer team. Romain had a classical training but got more fun from dance music. He had a girlfriend in a record shop who used to let him listen to records by Whiteman, Ted Lewis and the Original Dixieland Jazz Band. While still in his teens Romain worked as musician and bell-boy on the ship *Tahiti* which plied between New Zealand and San Francisco, where he heard some live jazz and bought more records. He changed his name to Abe while working at the Goring Street Cabaret in Wellington, opened in 1918 by Theo Trehsize, because he could not stand the effeminate way the manager said Adrian. Early in the 1920s he decided to try his luck in Australia with his friend Eric Ambler. Ambler knew only Harry Larsen, who introduced them at the musicians' club. Romain's first job was with the George Sorlie Show in a big tent at Balmain in a three piece band. Larsen invited Romain to rehearse with a band at the Petersham Town Hall, which went into Ambassadors under Merv Lyons's leadership until the band kicked him out and Al Hammett took over. This band recorded for Columbia in 1926. Romain listened to all the visiting American bands, and Eddie Frizelle, from Ralton's Original Havana Band, was a big influence on his life. As with Coughlan, Frizelle advised Romain to travel and improve himself. It took about six months for Romain to crack the big jobs in England but then he got the first saxophone chair with Jack Hylton's band, with which he stayed for eighteen months and made recordings. The band played at such places as Paris, Monte Carlo, Brussels and Berlin, and Louis Armstrong appeared with the band in England. Thus Romain was probably the first Australian to play with that great man. Romain also saw Jimmy Dorsey in

London with the Ted Lewis band. Romain spent most of the 1930s in England. He returned to Australia in 1933, but from 1936 to 1940 he was back in London playing and recording with the Harry Roy band.

The third musician to go overseas in the Depression who was of particular importance to the development of Australian jazz was Ben Featherstone. He was a handsome, well-built, wild personality who liked his grog but who could play up a storm on many instruments, especially on drums, trumpet and trombone but also on piano, all the saxes, clarinet, bass, euphonium and tin whistle, a five minute act which he did regularly at a frantic pace, drunk or sober, which left him and his audiences gasping. Featherstone was born in Birmingham, England, the son of a doctor, so it was unusual that he became a musician because boys from comfortable backgrounds tended not to risk their careers to the vagaries of professional popular music. The family emigrated to Australia when Ben was a child and one Christmas he was given a drum. He was educated at Melbourne Grammar School. There, on trombone, he joined 'The Footwarmers' in 1925, one of the first of the many jazz bands to arise out of the Greater Public Schools of Melbourne. They played in private homes to raise funds for charities, and Dick Bentley, later a successful Australian radio comedian, appeared with them on sax. Featherstone knew good music when he heard it and he used to go down to the Tivoli to see Traps, the Drum Wonder (Buddy Rich), do his act, which was so good that even the hardened pit musicians would stand up to look over the edge of the stage at the boy. Featherstone amassed a good collection of records in his career and his favourite drum stylist was Stan King of the California Ramblers and the Goofus Five. When he left school Featherstone joined Joe Watson at the Green Mill. In January 1930 he made a jazz record with his group, 'The Beachcombers', some of whom were from 'The Footwarmers', and in November 1932 he joined Ern Pettifer's band at the Palais de Danse.

Even before he went overseas Featherstone was becoming known as Australia's Louis Armstrong. Musicians like Featherstone helped make Armstrong's name familiar to the general public in the early 1930s. Featherstone was one of the first to do the imitation Armstrong vocal, one of the most embarrassing habits to persist in jazz, mainly in the traditionally oriented bands. In those days, when jazz was unthinkable without Armstrong and when hot records were so hard to come by, it is understandable that anything to do with Louis was seized on, but it is still regrettably easy to find jazz musicians who should know better, and not necessarily trumpet players either, who will sing in a way entirely unnatural and foreign to them, apparently convinced that this is the only way to sing jazz. Armstrong's singing was marvellous, but hearing Australians and Dutchmen and Englishmen do it is not so good.

The difficulties which Australians have with singing are revealing. Excluding professional singers for the moment, the singing by instrumentalists in the amateur and semi-professional bands is a disaster. Many players sound like an asthmatic Fats Waller, or else they shout the lyrics because this is 'authentic'; in fact they do almost anything except render a studied, skilful, and genuine vocal performance. This is quite peculiar considering they put so much passion and effort into their instruments. The moment they have to put a microphone to their lips instead of a mouthpiece they become self-conscious and uncomfortable, and are psychologically incapable of interpreting a song in public in a way which says

This is me. The Armstrong imitation, the shouting and the mugging all spring to the rescue of the stranded male instrumentalist; the imitation cloaks the personality, does not reveal it. Australian men are much more prone to this than women. To take up an instrument in their youth took a certain independence of mind, but to want to learn to sing well was to invite too much suspicion that one was a cissy. Perhaps that is why some of the best professional Australian male jazz singers were homosexuals; having made an irretrievable step beyond the straight world there were no psychological barriers to prevent them singing well, and they had to be good to survive. Women, on the other hand, have been allowed to sing and still be considered wholly female, and from the 1950s, there seem to be more good female singers than there are male. Partly this is economic —most bands cannot afford to carry a speciality singer and most bands are all-male, so a singer will stand a much better chance of getting a job if she can provide some visual contrast to the band as well. A man has to be much better than a female singer, or an instrumentalist as well, to get a place in an Australian band.

In 1933 Ben Featherstone spent about five months in London picking up all that was new in dance and jazz music and played for a short season at the Silver Slipper Club in Regent Street. Featherstone's visit prompted English *Rhythm* (October 1933) magazine to praise his and Coughlan's ability. Featherstone found that a 'hot Harlem rhythm' was played at most London dances and that coloured stars like Nina Mae McKinney and Duke Ellington were very popular. He discovered that there were more hot records available in England than in Australia, and he bought a stack of them to take home, mostly Armstrong, Ellington and the Washboard Rhythm Kings. Above all, it was his delight to observe, meet and take lessons from Louis Armstrong.

Featherstone returned in November 1933, fired with an ambition to introduce the pulse-quickening tempos to Australian dancers. Among musicians he was regarded as the most modern mind in Melbourne for dance rhythms. Featherstone never again bothered much with plain reading jobs but always tried for a position where he could push the band along all the way. He went into Art Chapman's band at the New Embassy and the management specially imported a drum kit for him which was reputed to be better than Jim Davidson's, and in June 1934 he led his own band, which included Coughlan, at the Rex Cabaret. He added a washboard solo to his multi-instrument act and made a great hit with his Armstrong imitation. Unfortunately, Featherstone could not demonstrate his rhythmic powers to the full, for Melbourne dancers were still dancing an outdated style.

Other musicians were sure enough of their ability to want to broaden their experience elsewhere, and small dance units or individuals visited countries like South Africa, America, England and Europe. In 1934 Joe Aronson, who had been arguing with his son ever since he had arrived in Australia, took Wally Portingale (piano), Keith Kingsland (trumpet), and Billy O'Flynn (sax), with him to Shanghai where he formed a band at the Canidrome with nine Americans, a Hawaiian and a Swede. After a successful season they were replaced by Buck Clayton, and went on to the Beach Café in north China, then the three Australians came home through Shanghai, Hong Kong, Manila and the Dutch East Indies. On his return O'Flynn was approached by the management of Earl's

Art Chapman's band at the New Embassy Cabaret, Melbourne, 1935.
L–R: Reg Lewis (piano), Harry Danslow (sax), Cliff Adam (guitar, vocal), Harold Moschetti (sax), Ben Featherstone (drums), Arthur Chapman (sax), George Dobson (trumpet), Don Barille (bass), Dutchy Turner (trombone), Barbara James (vocal).

Court, St Kilda, to form a band of twelve known as Billy O'Flynn and His Orientals. They all wore Chinese costume.

After leading the Palais de Danse band at St Kilda for seven years, Ern Pettifer went to England in 1936–37 where in imitation of Boyd Senter he recorded 'Memphis Blues' and 'Somebody's Wrong' for Parlophone.

A popular novelty band, the Tom Katz Saxophone Band, went to England in 1934. While not strictly a jazz band, it was an integral part of the Australian popular music scene. The conductor of the Sydney Tivoli, Will Quintrell, formed the six man saxophone band in 1927, and with the Tivoli manager, Jack Musgrove, decided that they should all perform in black-face, dressed as bell-boys. Sam Babicci was the leader for the first eighteen months, then it was Ted Case, another ex-member of the Jimmy Elkins band. Tom Katz went to England via New Zealand and topped the bill at eighty-four English theatres. They broke up in 1936; Case and Thomson formed the Tom Katz Saxophone Six, and the others formed the Kit Kat Saxophone Rascals.

There were some Australian men and women who were better known to the English public for their jazz or popular music than they were to the Australian public. These were Bill Airey-Smith and Brian Lawrence, who led their own combos, and singers Janet Lind who was with Louis Leves, Magda Neeld with Jack Hylton, Stan Patchett with Joe Paradise, Anona Winn with Billy Cotton's Savoy Orpheans, and a good rythmic vocalist, Marjorie Stedeford who sang with the 6 Swingers, Joe Paradise, Mario Lorenzi, and the New Mayfair Dance Orchestra *et al*.

While these musicians were overseas, there were many more at home who were learning the trade. Ben Featherstone returned home to be delighted by the modernity of Jim Davidson's drumming style and with his band. James Hutchinson Davidson (b. 1902) grew up in Birchgrove, Sydney, and delivered milk in the adjoining suburb of Balmain to earn money to buy dance records. He began playing various brass instruments with the Compulsory Military Training Band in the Rozelle Drill Hall in 1917. While working in the advertising and accounts branch of Lever Brothers in 1919, he joined the house social band on cornet, but after deputising for the drummer one night, drums became his sole concern. After Jimmy Elkins's band broke up in October 1928, Davidson and Gussey went into pianist Jack Woods's ten piece band at Ambassadors until February 1931 when Ambassadors was closed for good by fire.

Davidson formed his first band at Smith's Oriental in Her Majesty's Arcade in Pitt Street, the most important cabaret in Sydney for nurturing jazz talent in the 1930s. During the Depression the higher priced business drifted away from it and the clientele was largely comprised of young unemployed people, and a proportion of 'professional girls'. Jim Davidson liked to sit higher than the average drummer so he had a special enclosed stool built with a hinged seat; the prostitutes would push their handbags under the chimes behind for him to put inside his stool. Through many a performance Davidson minded a working girl's wages.

As leader of the band at the Oriental, Davidson produced what was regarded in the trade as the finest five piece band in Australia, and on 14 August 1932 he augmented his band to ten for what was Sydney's first 'rhythm' concert, at Hillier's Cafe. J. C. Bendrodt attended and was so taken with the performance that he contracted the band to appear at the Palais Royal from 5 May 1933 for the winter season. This was the first indication that the entertainment industry might slowly climb out of the slump. At the time there was only one other ten piece band in Sydney, Theo Walters and His Personality Boys at the Croydon Palais. It also showed to what extent the local music scene responded to local needs. While it is undeniable that Australian jazz had much to learn from the United States it is not true to say that it has all been a slavish copy. Neither Davidson nor Bendrodt knew that Benny Goodman was going to initiate the swing era in a couple of years, yet here was Davidson enlarging his band to ten, and more when he could afford it, because that is what his musical sense told him to do.

Another indication that Australian dance musicians were acting on their own initiative was the publication of *Australian Music Maker and Dance Band News* in Sydney in 1932, a monthly journal for and about dance musicians which lasted for forty years. Prior to *Music Maker* the attitude of all the popular and variety magazines to jazz had been, at best, ambivalent. Here at last was a magazine which consistently championed jazz. The editor and publisher was a Sydney drummer, Eric Sheldon. Like other special interest magazines it formed in its readers a sense of cohesion, made them aware of activities in all states and helped them to understand more about jazz. From the beginning *Music Maker* carried historical articles on jazz, reprints of articles about dance and jazz music from American trade journals, and essays by leading Australian instrumentalists on all technical aspects of music, from playing hot, to arranging, harmony and the finer details of practice and embouchure. The magazine resembled English *Melody Maker*, which was widely read by Australian musicians, and carried articles by pioneer jazz writers Leonard Feather and Alistaire Cooke.

Jim Davidson took over from the American Ted Henkel at the Palais Royal, and Jim Gussey was the only one he kept from Henkel's band. Davidson was an instant success there. His opening was preceded by one of the biggest advertising campaigns Sydney had seen, with the result that they packed in an average of 10,000 people per week. Not bad for a city of one million. They had to play loudly owing to the size of the place but Davidson controlled the boom by damping his bass drum and covering the floor of the sound shell with red felt. Vocals were by John Warren, Molly Byron, Davidson and a trio from the band. On Thursday nights the band broadcast over 2UE; Bendrodt announced each number in his slow Canadian drawl and listener response prompted Columbia to record 'Forty

Jim Davidson and his Australians at the Palais de Danse, St Kilda, 1933.

Second Street' and 'Shuffle Off To Buffalo' which sold 30,000 copies in 1933. This was the beginning of a recording career which over the next eight years totalled more than 150 sides. Davidson encouraged original compositions from his band and got tunes like 'Davidson Stomp', 'Perception' and 'I Love You My Dear'. In November 1933 Davidson recorded his own composition called 'Eventide', a piece heavily influenced by Ellington's 'Mood Indigo'. A lot of the arranging at this stage was done by Pete and Dudley Cantrell.

Following this recording session the band journeyed to Melbourne for a six month season at the Palais de Danse, still under contract to Bendrodt. This move was slightly risky because musical communication between Melbourne and Sydney was limited. If, say, a trumpet player went from Melbourne to Sydney, he would be welcomed by all musicians except other trumpet players because of jealousy. Davidson scored a great success on opening night at the Palais de Danse but initially his tempos were off, something which an experienced musician like Davidson would not have done deliberately. Tempos and dancing styles were a little different in Melbourne, and the band, not the dancers, had to adjust to that.

The season concluded successfully and the band went back to the Sydney Palais Royal for the winter season beginning 20 April 1934. Davidson was approached by Major Conder, the General Manager of the ABC, to sign with that organisation, so when Bendrodt's contract finished on 1 January 1935, Davidson took his band down to Melbourne, replacing Cecil Fraser's band as the ABC Dance Band. Signing the contract with the ABC made Davidson's band the most successful in Australia and ushered in a new phase of his career. He had been able to keep the band together for two years and now he enlarged it to fourteen members. With the extra work involved, Tom Stevenson was moved to the drum chair leaving Davidson free to conduct.

Davidson's visit to the Palais de Danse interrupted Ern Pettifer's Rhythm Boys' five year tenure on the place, and after Davidson went back to Sydney, Pettifer put together his most famous band, the Good Companions. The formation of the Good Companions set music at the Palais on a forward looking path, because Pettifer gave some talented young players a break. Auditions were held on a hot summer day and in the line of hopefuls stretching round the corner was a gifted alto saxophonist from Perth, Bob Gibson. The audition piece was a tough arrangement of 'Bugle Call Rag' by Frank Coughlan who was then with Pettifer. Gibson sailed through it because he had had a thorough classical training and had won many scholarships for his ability, and he knew dance work too. Gifted young players never appear out of nothing, and Gibson was no exception—Perth had its own thriving dance bands.

A trip to Perth is the best way to find out that there is an Australian style of jazz. Closer to Singapore than Sydney, Perth is the most isolated capital in the most remote continent. The only thing which makes it easier to get to eastern Australia from Perth than from New Zealand is that you cannot hitch-hike across the Tasman. Perth musicians often feel ignored, convinced that easterners still think that jazz never made it further than the rabbit-proof fence, but they look to the standards of Sydney and Melbourne as the goal to aim for. Young musicians, if they were good, were for years urged to try their hand in the east, a habit which did nothing to ease the frustration of those who chose to stay behind. Hal

Moschetti, who took over from Pettifer at the Palais de Danse in 1936, was an early musician to go east, and others include Abe Walters (piano), George Watson (drums), Billy Weston (trumpet, trombone), Keith Hownslow (trumpet), Peter Clinch (saxes) and Splinter Reeves (sax).

As in the east, dance musicians were the first to be interested in jazz in Perth. The Vice-Regal Band led by Charles Sheridan Senr. was the longest established dance band. Sheridan started it in 1903 and the band played the popular tunes of

A tin matchbox cover distributed in Perth in the late 1920s which advertised a popular band.

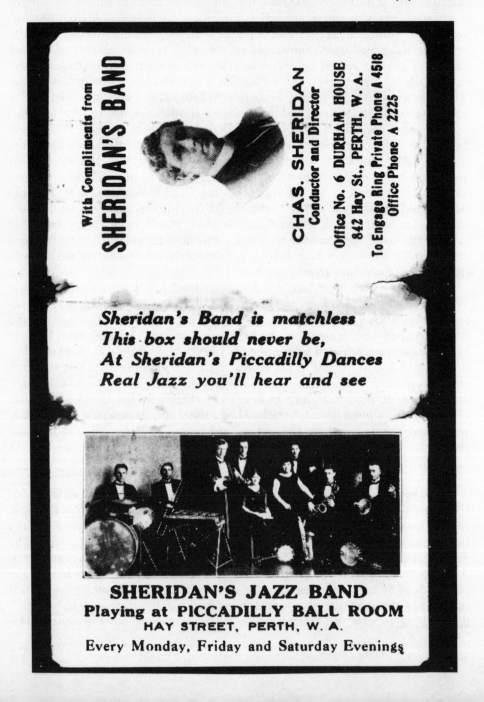

With Compliments from
SHERIDAN'S BAND

CHAS. SHERIDAN
Conductor and Director

Office No. 6 DURHAM HOUSE
842 Hay St., PERTH, W. A.
To Engage Ring Private Phone A 4518
Office Phone A 2225

Sheridan's Band is matchless
This box should never be,
At Sheridan's Piccadilly Dances
Real Jazz you'll hear and see

SHERIDAN'S JAZZ BAND
Playing at PICCADILLY BALL ROOM
HAY STREET, PERTH, W. A.
Every Monday, Friday and Saturday Evenings

the day. For the dance in honour of Field Marshal the Right Honourable Viscount Kitchener of Khartoum on 24 January 1910, the band included the ragtime number 'Old Faithful' by Abe Holzman. The Tivoli opened in 1913 to provide a suitable venue for touring vaudeville acts but it was not until 1924, when Bert Ralton's Original Havana Band stopped off on its way home to England, that Perth heard the new style of playing at first hand. Ralton did a series of tea dansants at the Piccadilly Ballroom in Hay Street. Sheridan made sure his son, Charles Jnr. (b. 1908) received some tuition on sax from Ralton. Sheridan supplied the music at the Piccadilly, which had punkahs hanging from the ceiling to stir the air, and it was the plum job in Perth until 1929 when the Temple Court and the Capitol Theatre opened at the foot of William Street.

From the mid-twenties jazz gained enthusiasts in Perth. By 1926 wireless magazines were receiving complaints that there was too much of it on the air. Perth's first important crop of jazz players were from the group of men who came into their teens during this period, and got their breaks in the established dance bands. Billy Naughton was a pianist who quickly got the right ideas and improved his style by having records, arrangements and magazines sent to him from America. Charles Sheridan Jnr. went into his father's band in 1925 and became musical director of it the next year. In 1928 he went to Melbourne to play at Leggett's Ballroom at Prahran and took lessons from Walter Beban of the Californians. Abe Walters (b. 14 March 1913), pianist, was the youngest of four musical brothers, Harry and Wally on trumpet and Izzy on trombone. Harry and Wally went over to play with Joe Aronson at the Wattle Path in Melbourne in 1924. Abe opened at the Indiana Cabaret which was a tin shed for drinks and dancing on the beach at Cottesloe. Once in 1928 at Kalgoorlie he played for 108 hours for a marathon dancer and was promised £50, but the promoter ran off with all the takings. Abe Walters left Perth in 1931 by the ship *Dimboola* to join his brother Wally in Art Chapman's band at the Rex Cabaret, Melbourne. In 1936 Abe went to London, worked with Ambrose at Ciro's and with Syd Philips, and from 1945 to 1969 under the stage name of Don Carlos, he led a successful Latin-American band. Opposite the Walters lived Sammy Sharp (born 26 August 1910) whose idol was Wally. Sharp could not get over how Wally practised all day, and when Wally went east he gave Sharp a battered cornet. Sharp went to Melbourne in the Depression to work with his brother. There he was fascinated by the trumpet playing of Joe Watson in Ray Tellier's San Francisco Orchestra. Sharp soon returned to Perth where he was heard by Colin Smith (b. 7 December 1902). Smith usually had the best band in town because he was able to pick the best men.

These young men were keen collectors of records, especially as most of the classical music teachers shunned jazz; aspiring jazzmen had no one to teach them and there was no conservatorium. Fortunately there were some classical teachers who, while they could not teach them anything about jazz, did not curb their pupils' interest in it. Professor Martin Smith taught theory to Colin Smith and Wally Hadley (b. 26 November 1908) who played guitar and banjo; Professor Nowotney gave Bob Gibson an excellent grounding on violin and Gibson became the youngest foundation member of the Perth Symphony Orchestra; George Reid, who conducted the original Perth Symphony, and his son Harold, gave lessons to Sharp, Ken Murdoch (b. 1907 Portsmouth, England) a sax player and

Merv Rowston (b. 23 April 1907). Harold Reid (drums), had been overseas with the Australian Commonwealth Band in 1927 and had stayed on in the USA for a while. The association of jazz players with good classical teachers has always been of benefit to the former, and quite often to the classical musicians also.

Because they felt they were so far away from everything, the young musicians made sure that they grabbed on to anything new which came along and quickly copied it. Murdoch and Rowston became known for their record collections, and when they read about the English rhythm clubs they decided to start their own. The Westralian Modern Music Club was inaugurated on 24 June 1934; without knowing it they had formed one of the first clubs of its type in Australia. During the 1930s they contacted record collectors around the world. Murdoch wrote to the record critic of the English *Melody Maker*, Spike Hughes, and asked him to send out a Mills Brothers and an Ellington record. Hughes sent 'I Heard' and 'Black and Tan Fantasy'. Perth musicians flocked to hear them.

Occasionally they wrote to leading musicians for advice. Harry Bluck (b. 15 June 1915) wrote to Fats Waller asking him whether he should forget his classical piano training, because Bluck incorrectly assumed that you did not need a great technique to play jazz as long as you could play rhythm. Waller straightened Bluck out, telling him of his interest in Bach and recommending the study of Bach's 'Two' and 'Three Part Inventions'. Merv Rowston went to Britain, 1934–36, and maintained a correspondence with leading English drummer Max Abrams. Abrams wrote to Rowston on 9 June 1936 advising that the Joe Daniels type of drumming was out, as was all drumming for noise; instead, the drummer should be lifting the front line by feeding them a steady swing from his drums.

Another outlet for aspiring musicians was the Young Australia League Band. A lot of professionals in the west cut their teeth on this experience; Billy Weston and Harry Bluck being prime examples. In addition to band work, the Y.A.L. provided solid performing experience by taking the boys on three vaudeville tours each year, including, in 1937, a trip to Singapore where they were guests of the Sultan of Johore.

Bluck was a scholarship boy at the Perth Modern School, a 'skull' school for intelligent boys from poor families. (Bob Hawke, the president of the Australian Council of Trade Unions, and Dr 'Nugget' Coombs, the Federal economic adviser, also went to this school.) Bluck's interest in music was not assisted at school, because his peers regarded anyone interested in music as a freak; his Welsh parents gave him the initial necessary encouragement.

But once the lads became young men, they looked for other places to blow and the brothels in Roe Street called 'the drums' were often the venue for a late night jam session. This is not to say that jazz in Perth developed the same way as in New Orleans, but, just as any industry has its sister industries, so entertainment has prostitution. Most of the brothels had pianos in the parlours and it was a good place to go after a job to have a blow, because you could get sly grog and Chinese food at 2 a.m. from the gambling clubs in James Street around the block. The brothels were tolerated in Perth until the end of World War II.

Perth dance bands reached quite a good standard; but without a large population, they did not have the punch which the eastern bands had. Consequently, whenever a good musician came to Perth, he was well received. The Depression seemed to drive a few over because, though the talkies came to

The interior of the Temple Court Cabaret and Ballroom, Perth, 1929. It was later renamed the Embassy Ballroom.

Perth not long after they appeared in Sydney and Melbourne, the bad effects were mitigated to some extent by the opening of the Ambassadors Theatre in 1929, for which Bert Howell's band was engaged from the east, and the Temple Court Ballroom, for which Merv Lyons came over to conduct the band. Harold Moschetti returned to Perth with Howell and he taught Bob Gibson sax and clarinet because Gibson needed to double on something now that the talkies had decreased violin work. Theo Walters, a saxophonist and consummate showman, came over to play in Colin Smith's band and he fronted his own five piece band, The Knickerbockers, at the Luxor, formerly the Tivoli.

The visitor who made the most lasting impression on Perth musicians in the Depression was a rising trumpet star, George Dobson. By the age of twenty-two Dobson had already worked in the Green Mill under Joe Watson and Vic Woods. Dobson admired the playing of Red Nichols, Bix Beiderbecke and Louis Armstrong and he showed Perth musicians what a well turned trumpet solo could be. Dobson was born in Berrigan in the New South Wales Riverina and grew up in Henty. Like many Protestants in country districts (because there was nowhere else to learn), his first piano lessons were from a sister at the local convent. Then an old German called Sandegreen came to Henty and persuaded the townspeople to support his efforts to form a boys' band. Dobson started on tenor horn, then became solo cornet player with the band. At the age of seventeen, on a trip to Melbourne, he convinced his parents to leave him there to try to become a professional musician. He made steady progress until the Depression hit, then a pianist friend, George McWhinney, told him of a job going at the Temple Court. Dobson was pleasantly surprised by the standard of the local bands, but was more surprised by the verve with which Perth residents threw themselves into their leisure hours. The Temple Court had loges along two sides which could be curtained off for privacy. Dobson had never seen so much high-spirited night-life. He stayed about two years in Perth, sometimes playing in Colin Smith's band, and he had a ball. When he returned to Melbourne, Dobson joined Cecil Fraser's ABC Dance Band which was formed in 1932.

Bob Gibson, armed with the new skills Moschetti had imparted, got a break with Doreen D'Arcy's Orchestra, a six piece dance band which got a lot of good work. Perth had a number of bands led by women, which were regarded as equal to the bands led by men and they got their share of the best jobs. Betsy Spiegl, Em Riley and Leoni 'Dot' Salter led their own mixed bands, and Dot's sister, May Salter, led an all-girl band, 'The Melody Girls'. Female bandleaders in Australia usually remained known to the public by their maiden names after they were married, long before there was a women's movement to encourage them to do so. In 1934 Dot Salter took a seven piece band, three women and four men, to the Mount Lavinia Hotel in Ceylon. From there they went to the Grand Hotel in Calcutta, returned to Ceylon and broke up. Wally Hadley, Sammy Sharp and Leah Waterman went on to England, whence they did not return until after the war.

From D'Arcy's Orchestra, Gibson went into Ron Moyle's seven piece band at the Temple Court, which was renamed the Embassy Ballroom in June 1933. Moyle was inspired to enlarge his band to ten pieces by the visit of Joe Aronson's Airmen in 1933. During that year Moyle's band conceived the idea of going east and they each put £1 a week towards it. Moyle, through his job at Westralian Farmers which ran 6WF until the ABC took it over, got contacts and bookings in the east. They had a good trip; they performed on 3LO in Melbourne and 2FC in Sydney, and while in Sydney, did some shorts for Cinesound. When they went back to Melbourne, Gibson succeeded in his audition for Pettifer's Good Companions and remained in Melbourne. It was the early 1960s before another complete band, the Riverside Jazz Band, a traditional group, left Perth for eastern Australia.

Back east Bendrodt, having lost Davidson to the ABC, searched for another band to fill the brightest creation he ever built for Australian dance music—the Sydney Trocadero. Bendrodt offered Davidson the chance to open it, but Davidson elected to remain with the ABC. The 'Troc' was still in the planning stage early in 1935 but Bendrodt had his eye on Maurie Gilman's six piece band at the Ginger Jar, formerly the Oriental. Gilman's band was recognised as one of the top combinations, particularly because of Gilman's ability as an arranger. The Ginger Jar was regarded as a dive in some quarters, perhaps because it was inexpensive and patronised by a widely mixed clientele. It was built underground and the air-conditioning was done by fans which, during the afternoon session, brought in all the heat from the street. There were some good fights there and occasionally pistols were drawn, but the musicians were always popular with the dancers. Mainly popular tunes were played, but occasionally they slipped in a hot one, and on Sunday afternoons musicians would congregate there for jam sessions.

In March 1935 Bendrodt took the band north to appear at the Brisbane Trocadero and he allowed Gilman to enlarge it by three pieces. Gilman chose Norm Goldie (bass), and George Dobson and Geoff 'Dutchy' Turner (trombone), from Cecil Fraser's ABC Dance Band. Dobson and Turner began their lifelong friendship at the ABC and a professional association which spanned fifteen consecutive jobs. They had similar ideas about music, listened to records together and phrased together. The other trumpeter in the band was Lyn Miller, an American from St Louis who deserted from the U.S. Navy to play music in Australia.

Billo Smith's Orchestra, Brisbane Trocadero, 1927. Notice the advertisement for Brunswick Records on the front of the bandstand.
By Courtesy of the State Library of Queensland.

The season in Brisbane was a success, but initially Gilman had the same problem getting the correct tempos that Davidson had when he went to the Palais de Danse at St Kilda. The Brisbane public were used to the tempos of the man Gilman had replaced, Billo Smith, and his audiences remained his staunch supporters. Billo Smith came to Brisbane in 1925 from the Sydney Cavalier and he held the plum jobs in Brisbane until 1957, first at the Trocadero and after the war at the Cloudland Ballroom. For all intents and purposes Billo Smith was the Brisbane Trocadero. He had a fine, old-time band, but when Gilman's band first played, the Brisbane public were not sure how to dance to it. Gilman's arrangements were too far ahead for Brisbane, and unless the dancers heard a clearly stated melody they did not think the band was playing anything.

Things settled down after a week or so and Gilman began to receive requests every night for George Dobson to play 'Stardust'. Dobson got sick of this and enquired who was asking. It was a female admirer, who became his wife. Years later, when Mrs Dobson lay dying and they realised she had only a few days left, their daughter came to George and told him he had to play 'Stardust' for his wife one last time. Unaccompanied, George gave the best performance of his life.

One of the saxophonists, Colin Bergersen (1914–1977), also found the girl he was to marry at the Brisbane Trocadero, but first he had to break off with his Sydney girlfriend, and she broke his entire record collection of Ellington, Lunceford, Armstrong and Coleman Hawkins. Bergersen began his collection in New Zealand when he was taken under the wing of Arthur Pearce, a radio broadcaster with an encyclopaedic knowledge of jazz and an enormous record collection. Pearce's would have been the first big collection in New Zealand; he had money and used to import records from the United States, which was the best way to get the real thing. It is from the early 1930s that enthusiasts in Australia and New Zealand commenced amassing comprehensive record collections. Pearce's judgment was astute and Sydney jazz musicians always tuned in to his wireless program.

Gilman's band came back to the Ginger Jar at the end of September 1935, but Gilman and Bendrodt fell out and Bendrodt looked for another leader. It was public knowledge by this time that Bendrodt was putting a new band together for his Trocadero, which was being built next to the Regent Theatre near the Town Hall in George Street. Several American bands offered their services but Bendrodt wanted Australians, and was determined to get the best. The organisers approached the cream of the available talent and told them they were wanted. When it came Dobson's turn to discuss his salary, he knew how superstitious Bendrodt was and told him he wanted £12.19.11 per week. Bendrodt went pale with fright, but the ruse worked and that was the wage that Dobson received all the time he worked for Bendrodt. Bendrodt's inspired choice for leader was Frank Coughlan, then leading his own eight piece band at the Bondi Esplanade Cabaret, and a favourite amongst musicians and the public alike.

In the next four months Coughlan moulded thirteen musicians into the finest palais band ever seen in Australia. With Dobson, Turner and Miller in the band, the brass section was very strong. Also on trumpet was John Robertson who was a marvellous technician though he had no idea of jazz. Robertson played with a non-pressure system and as part of the showmanship of the band, when they played 'The Music Goes Round and Round', the band played chords for about sixteen bars while Robertson held top C and revolved the trumpet on his lips at the same time. With Colin Bergersen doubling on trumpet, the brass could be filled out to six for swing choruses. The trumpeters also doubled on mellophones.

The sax section was not overshadowed; in it were Jack Moore, Frank Ellery, Colin Bergersen and a hot young player, Keith Atkinson. Coughlan also had a fair talent on sax and could build this section to five.

On guitar he had a man who was years ahead of his time, Charles Lees. Lees was using chromaticism before anyone else in Australia, he had ideas about interrelating keys, playing a key which was not the tonic key, and he voiced chords beyond two or three octaves when everyone else was jamming it all within one octave. Lees played an electrically amplified Gibson Super 400.

At thirty-one Coughlan was the eldest in the band; the average age was twenty-six.

The brass and sax sections of Frank Coughlan's Trocadero Orchestra under the glass sound shell, Sydney, 1936.
L–R: Geoff 'Dutchy' Turner (trombone), John Robertson (trumpet), Frank Coughlan (trombone, trumpet), George Dobson (trumpet), Lyn Miller (trumpet). Saxes: Keith Atkinson (tenor), Jack Moore (alto), Colin Bergersen (alto), Frank Ellery (baritone).

Out front were the three Rhythm Boys and three Rhythm Girls, one female and one male straight singer, and Frank's brother Jack Coughlan to do comedy in his Ish-ka-bibble costume. A featured singer with the band was Barbara James, the daughter of Will James who had given Coughlan his break into the dance scene fourteen years previously.

The real star was Frank Coughlan. His sax playing was good, his trumpet was beautiful, but his trombone was thrilling. He played in a way which made you want to play trombone too. He could be as rough as guts or as smooth as Dorsey on 'Song of India'. He was an all-rounder but his heart lay with traditional jazz. A story goes that during the war when Coughlan was up on Bougainville, and a collector and noted jazz buff, Sid Bromley, had a record of the Original Memphis Five which Coughlan wanted, Bromley would only let him have it if he played every tune that Bromley nominated. Coughlan got the record. Coughlan talked for hours about jazz to his musicians. Backstage, between sets, he had a wind-up gramophone on which he would play jazz records to anyone who was interested. He would often begin rehearsals by saying, 'Let's play the blues. Let's find out who's who'. There was never any jealousy either; if a sideman played a good chorus then Coughlan always congratulated him.

Coughlan worked hard to sell the band to the public. His conducting and playing were flamboyant, so much so that one night he fell over backwards into the audience. They even had a band rehearsal devoted solely to actions. The band was outfitted with three suits—full morning dress including spats, striped pants and double-breasted waistcoats for the afternoon matinee; dinner suits for the evening and white tuxedos for formal supper dances. The brass section also had three herald trumpets for announcements. No band has been better presented in Australia.

Critics referred to this band, and other outstanding Australian musicians, as being of 'international standard', or, 'world class'. These expressions have remained current as a form of praise, but they are peculiarly Australian—Americans do not use them. If an Australian is said to be 'world class', it means that he is considered good enough to be able to perform in the United States with credit. Americans do not know what 'world class' means because, in the home of jazz, a musician either makes it or does not: there are no outside criteria. The persistence of the term is an indication of the anxiety many Australians feel at being so far away from the rest of the western world; an anxiety which affects critics more than anyone else, for they still think it is insufficient just to say a musician is good.

The Trocadero cost about £350,000. The dance floor was made of tallow wood set in rubber and covered over 14,000 square feet. It had a capacity for 2000 people. The band appeared on a revolving stage under an acoustic sound shell made of glass which could be illuminated in many colours by hundreds of concealed lights. The Trocadero had its own kitchens and Bendrodt imported the chefs from USA.

Bendrodt's pre-publicity leaflets distributed on trams and trains emphasised 'S-W-I-N-G' music. On 3 April 1936 the Trocadero was opened. A huge crush of people choked traffic on George Street waiting to see the brilliant scenes of gaiety. At nine, Monsieur Francois Stempinski and his Silver Sextette opened with the Trocadero March, specially composed for the occasion, while the guests arrived. At nine-thirty Coughlan, immaculate in white tails, lead his band into Will Hudson's 'Cowboy in Manhattan', followed by his own composition, 'With a Sweet Melody'. During the first month more than 100,000 people attended the 'Troc'. It was common to see hundreds of men and women all in their best clothes gliding through town on the trams on their evening out, because no one could afford a taxi. At the Troc, Mayris Chaney and Edward Fox gave displays of dancing. The 'Trocadero News', a weekly pamphlet, ran a series of articles about the band members. Each afternoon, at the 'Entertainment Tea', the band played excerpts from operas and a wide range of light classical music. The band played many commercial favourites in the evening, but because Coughlan was wrapped in it, jazz remained a big feature of the program. The ABC won the right to broadcast the band live on 2BL between 7 and 8 p.m. on Thursdays.

The management was surprised when people began to attend, not to dance, but to listen. Usually the keen fans just stood in front of the bandstand but now some dragged chairs on to the floor. In March 1936 Coughlan had been elected President of the Sydney Swing Club which had been formed on 21 January 1936, and many of the fans who came to listen were members of the club. Their fortnightly Sunday evening meetings would be devoted half to records and the rest to a jam session, often with musicians from Coughlan's band sitting in. Coughlan sometimes took the band up to the Newcastle Swing Music Club where Happy Sutherland made them welcome. The Newcastle Club also invited other leading bands up from Sydney.

The keen fans were disappointed when not only did Bendrodt give up directing the Trocadero on 5 September 1936 and left the Trocadero Syndicate, but also Dobson and Turner left the band. The management dispensed with the afternoon session and introduced old time dancing twice a week. On the last swing night Coughlan chose numbers to express his feelings. The only commercial number he played all night was 'Alone'. The crowd hung breathless in front of the stand as Coughlan exhausted himself in 'It Don't Mean a Thing (If it ain't got that Swing)', and they refused to leave until 'Twelfth St Rag' was repeated. The next day Coughlan remodelled his band along the sweet lines of Guy Lombardo. The change in policy was due to poor attendance.

For some reason, this illustrious band did not inspire its members to stick together. By October 1937 there were only five originals still with the band. There was a certain amount of dissension within it, but perhaps the musicians moved on because they were young and talented. Dobson and Turner went to New Zealand with Theo Walters, and Dobson later did very well leading the Victorian Trumpet Trio, 1955–1968.

Still Coughlan managed to keep as many swing numbers as possible on the program. On 13 June 1937 he presented a concert in the Sydney Town Hall which was packed with 3,000 people. The band featured the relaxed saxophone of Harry Danslow, and one segment was devoted entirely to Ellington. The band appeared in a cabaret sequence in the film, 'The Flying Doctor', and, as part of the sesquicentenary celebrations in 1938, the band gave a command performance in Canberra.

Bearing in mind the band's popularity and ability, it is unbelievable that it was recorded only sixteen times, in 1937, and only four of those were jazz tracks. There is no more obvious indictment of the 'safe', commercial values ruling the Australian recording industry of the late 1930s than its failure to get more of the Trocadero band on to disc. The enthusiasts knew the band was good—Arthur Pearce, the New Zealand radio announcer, came to Sydney in October 1938, and was so impressed with Coughlan's outfit that he organised a private recording session—but Coughlan's efforts seemed to fall on deaf ears elsewhere. Jim Davidson had had the right idea to get out of private industry and into the ABC when he had the chance.

But Coughlan pressed on. He formed a dixieland unit from his big band in September 1938 which had a tenor sax in addition to the traditional trumpet-trombone-clarinet front line and conventional three piece rhythm section.

During 1938 Coughlan selected and rehearsed the fourteen-piece Trocadero All-Girl Band which made its debut on 22 August. Though there were other all-girl bands around, like Maggie Foster's band which played on harbour cruises and at suburban dances, the Troc band was the first attempt to put a female band into the big time. The girls assembled backstage at the Troc, and when the bandstand revolved, they came out doing their special numbers. This band was

Some members of the Sydney Trocadero All-Girl Band, 1938. They have been posed holding the wrong instruments, which in reality were:
L–R: Betty Gilles (violin), Pat White (bass), Edna Robinson (tenor), Renee Krejick (drums), Bernice Lynch (guitar).
From the original *Music Maker*, Vol. 7, No. 4, 1 Sept. 1938, p. 11, in the Mitchell Library.

never much more than a stunt but it laid the foundations for the second all-girl band formed at the Trocadero by Dick Freeman in May 1942, which played an active part in the entertainment there during the war.

A few of the girls from the first band went into an all-girl band formed in Victoria in June 1939 by a visiting American woman, Babe Egan. She had led a girls' band in America for eight years, called 'Babe Egan and her Hollywood Redheads'. In Australia Egan and her companion, Thelma White, formed another band by the same name. They opened in Geelong in July, went to Adelaide and Melbourne, but in August Egan and White left the country suddenly and the girls' uniforms, music and even the brass players' mutes disappeared.

By mid-1939 patronage of the Trocadero had fallen to a low level and the management decided that a new face to conduct the band was necessary. Coughlan finished on 31 August and went back to Roy Starfield's Bondi Esplanade Cabaret.

There were two other important dance bands playing from the mid-1930s to the war—Jim Davidson's band and the band at the Palais de Danse, St Kilda.

Jim Davidson spent 1935 with the ABC in Melbourne, then came back to the Sydney Palais Royal for the season from May to August 1936. There was a lot of publicity about an offer from London of £400 per week for the band, but this was an advertising stunt by the Palais management which also hoaxed Davidson, as he had not been told. During his year in Melbourne the band had grown to four reeds, five brass, five rhythm, three vocalists and one arranger.

One of Davidson's new singers was Alice Smith. Both she and Barbara James, from Coughlan's Trocadero Band, were influenced by Connie Boswell and later by Ella Fitzgerald. Recordings show that these women mastered an American style of singing long before the men did. It did not become fashionable for men to Americanise their singing voices until after the war.

Microphones were introduced for singers about 1932 and with them came an intimate style of singing called crooning. No longer did dancers expect to see the veins on a singer's neck, though instrumentalists were still required to make the effort. Crooning added more fuel to the campaign against jazz and the 'Deadly Dance'; crooning was supposed to be yet more evidence of how much rubbish jazz was and from what base, animal instincts it sprang. Academics had their turn at analysing it. T. Inglis Moore wrote an article entitled, 'Is It Music? The Significance of Crooning' (*Sydney Morning Herald*, 6 Jan. 1934), in which he diverted his discussion of crooning into a discussion of modern writers and poets, and decided that crooning 'is the beginning of our "Brave New World"'. If he had spent more time listening and less reading, he probably would not have made this too, too sombre conclusion. Professor Bernard Heinze, whose profession was to listen, told the annual conference of the Association of Music Teachers in 1935 that he objected to the fashion of sneering at crooning and jazz music, and again defended popular music.

On 5 October 1936 Davidson's band became the Sydney ABC Dance Band and Davidson remained its conductor until he enlisted in the war. It was primarily a radio band, though it made a few interstate tours as a stage show, unique for the thirties. Originally it used stock arrangements but Jim Gussey and David Samuels were pressed into doing originals. When the band moved into the ABC's Piccadilly Arcade studios, Wally Portingale and George Trevare became the new arrangers. Portingale was one of the best arrangers in the country at the time and his composition, 'Marmalade', recorded by the band in 1938, was one of the best tracks they made. Trevare specialised in novelty and comic arrangements. He claimed that his father had come to Australia with Sousa's band. Davidson had some of the finest soloists in Australia in his band; in particular, from 1937, Keith

Atkinson (b. 1915) on reeds, and from 1938, a hot trumpeter named Norm Litt (b. 1910), both of whom could make the band fire.

Davidson's band made recordings every year from 1933 to 1941 with substantially the same members. The records show their gradual assimilation of jazz. 'Forty Second Street' and 'Shuffle Off to Buffalo' were good numbers, but generally the early recordings had a rigid feel about them, partly because it was then a palais band. Five years later—the band was on radio and liberated to that extent from the bind of strict tempo dancers—their performances were now much more relaxed and the arrangements gave the soloists a chance to fly. The band swung. Even so, like Coughlan, Davidson had to follow a commercial policy.

Davidson's reputation grew large. A readers' poll of the South Australian *Radio Call* in 1937 voted Davidson's band second most popular behind Jack Hylton's band. The bestselling records for 1938 were Alan Jones first, Davidson's ABC Dance Band from second to fifth places, above Jeanette McDonald sixth, and Nelson Eddy seventh. There was a controversy amongst the fans around Australia as to who had the best band, Davidson or Coughlan. Both were favourites with separate and complementary audiences; Davidson with radio listeners and Coughlan with palais and jam session enthusiasts.

Davidson's band became well known through their regular Saturday night program called 'Tonight We Dance'. It ran from 8 p.m. to 12 a.m. with only a fifteen minute break for the 11 o'clock news. The last forty-five minutes were played non-stop, no script, just one number after another. The public got a chance to see them on three interstate tours. The first, in November 1937, set off for Brisbane, Toowoomba, Newcastle and Sydney. Gladys Moncrieff and Tex Morton appeared with them. Horrie Dargie, harmonica, and Bob Dyer doing a hillbilly act accompanied the band on their second tour. Before the war, the distinction between 'pop', dance and jazz bands was minimal. No Australian big band could afford to specialise. The second tour, starting on 22 February 1938, lasted thirty-nine days and took the band as far as Hobart, Adelaide and Broken Hill. The third tour, planned for Sydney, Brisbane and Melbourne, had to be rescheduled because the Sydney segment was so successful and was extended, and the trip to Brisbane was dropped. On 1 December 1939 the band gave a concert in Martin Place, Sydney, to aid the war effort. French chalk was put down for dancing, but nine thousand people jammed the place and police had to order the band to stop at 9.45 p.m. for fear that someone would be crushed. Davidson was the most successful Australian bandleader of the 1930s.

The Davidson band broadcast with the Mills Brothers during their 1939 tour. The Mills Brothers were given a tumultuous welcome at the Melbourne Swing Club. Clubs for the jazz enthusiast were not as well organised as they became after the war, because a small number of interesting Negro performers, mainly singers, came to Australia in the 1930s and passed almost unnoticed by jazz buffs. After the war they would have been made much of. The Tivoli brought out Nina Mae McKinney and her two accompanists, Yorke de Sousa and Kirby Walker, in October 1937; in 1938 Chris Gill who had sung with Ellington, and Chuck Richards who had sung with the Mills Blue Rhythm Band, Chick Webb and Fletcher Henderson. Ada Brown, who sang in Fats Waller's last film, 'Stormy Weather', performed here. One night in February 1939 at the Trocadero, Frank

Coughlan spotted Gene Rodgers and invited him to sit-in with the band. Rodgers had played with Clarence Williams and King Oliver among others, and was at the Tivoli with Frank Radcliffe. They split up in Brisbane and Rodgers continued with George Sorlie filling the other half of the act.

When Davidson went back to the Sydney Palais Royal in 1936, the ABC was left without a Melbourne dance band. They experimented by importing a conductor to lead a band especially formed for him. After considering every big-time leader in England they chose Howard Jacobs and his arranger, Cecil Norman. Jacobs was from Boston, Massachusetts, USA, but had been in England since 1922, conducting at places like Claridges, the Berkeley and the Savoy hotels. Jacobs liked Whiteman's band, Ray Noble and Rudy Vallee; Australian musicians might have learned more had Jacobs's ideas been more progressive, but the ABC wanted to win over some conventional music fans and did not want anyone too adventurous. Jacobs's programs comprised mainly tunes by leading British and American arrangers and by Cecil Norman, and though they featured some Ellington and Gershwin, they tended to be 'sweet'. Still, Jacobs played alto sax very well, and he concentrated his efforts on a persistent problem in

Jay Whidden's Palaise de Danse Band, St Kilda, 1938.
Top Row: George Watson (drums), Max Jordan (bass), Ted Foster (guitar).
Middle Row: Chas. Thompson (trombone), Geoff 'Dutchy' Turner (trombone), Frank Arnold (trumpet), George Dobson (trumpet), Bernie Duggan (piano, piano-accordian).
Bottom Row: Vin McCarthy (tenor), Syd French (tenor), Reg Lloyd (alto), Bob Gibson (alto), Jay Whidden, Theo Walters.

Australian bands—there have always been good individuals but the difficulty has been to get them to play together. Jacobs worked on the dynamics of the band and brought out more variety from the rhythm section. Australian musicians enjoyed working for him. Al Hammett, assisted by Abe Walters from Perth, selected the sixteen musicians for Jacobs from Sydney and Melbourne. From June to October 1936 Howard Jacobs's ABC Dance Orchestra toured all states of Australia, appearing at town halls and theatres, and picking up about six extra string players in each state. The tour was so successful that Jacobs's original contract was extended for six weeks and at the end of his stay the ABC announced that they would form two permanent dance bands, one in Sydney (Davidson's) and one in Melbourne. Hammett took over the band after Jacobs left.

Overseas bandleaders were tried by other organisations in Australia. The Palais Royal in Sydney tried a Hollywood leader for six months in 1935. Sunny Brooks and his arranger, Maurie Paul, liked sweet, Guy Lombardo style music, but their season was not a success and they returned to America. The Trocadero employed a Canadian, Bob Lyons, for four months after Coughlan left. He brought out many arrangements in the style of Artie Shaw and Woody Herman, and his arranger was Rupert Dumbrille who had arranged for the Americanadians.

The most interesting experiment with imported bandleaders occurred at the Palais de Danse, St Kilda, where the band was conducted first by an American, then by a 'kind of Englishman', and then by the American again. The American was Jay Whidden, a tall, fine looking, well-dressed man who had been to Australia before, in vaudeville in 1925 with a 'laughing violin' act at the Tivoli. Theo Walters helped put the band together for him and they began on 1 October 1938. Where the previous leaders, Pettifer and Moschetti, had been stilted and unable to throw off the rickey-tickey phrasing, Whidden introduced a relaxed, broader style, holding notes in easy, swinging phrases. The bass player was pleased that his part had four beats to the bar and not the normal dance routine of two to the bar. Whidden was not cowed by the dancers, so he chose tempos to suit the numbers. He had good arrangements sent to him from San Francisco, and many were in the Glenn Miller style. Then Roy Fox, 'The Whispering Cornetist', came from England and replaced Whidden on 28 February 1939. Fox was born in California and had played in Abe Lyman's band, but he had been in England for eight years prior to visiting Australia and had become a typical English hotel conductor. He brought English arrangements out and returned to the stiff, stilted, rushed style that Whidden had worked hard to eradicate. Fox proved to be less popular with the dancing public and Whidden was brought back in June. Whidden was unhappy that he had to do his work over again but he soon had the band playing in the style he wanted.

Of all the bandleaders who came to Australia in the 1930s, Whidden aided Australian musicians most to come to understand modern styling. He encouraged arrangements from Dutchy Turner, George Dobson and particularly Bob Gibson. Gibson began to use more sound colours and provided room for soloists to move, and some of his arrangements went so far ahead that half the musicians did not know what he was aiming at. Whidden gave Gibson opportunities to shine on lead alto, featured a hot tenor player, Tom 'Red'

Crowe, and gave Wally Norman (b. 1919), trombone, his first important professional position. Whidden returned to USA in April 1941.

1938 and 1939 were the transition years out of the strict tempo era, though the grip of the dancing schools was not finally broken until rock and roll came along. The transition was assisted by growing numbers of jitterbugs, young swing fans who wanted to do more than the staid ballroom steps. The jitterbugs met with a cool reception in the palais from the other dancers, and in many halls jitterbugs were only allowed in roped-off sections of the floor. One place in Melbourne where the jitterbugs loved to dance was the Sunday afternoon jam sessions at the Fawkner Park Kiosk, run as a dance hall from early 1937 by two champion ballroom dancers, Micky Powell (said to know the gangster Squizzy Taylor) and Bill Panter. The brakes were off there and over three hundred enthusiasts regularly turned up, and 'jazz hounds' like Graeme Bell and his friends would sit on the floor, starry-eyed and spellbound by the band. The music was strictly modern, the mainstream of the day. The audience would have booed if they had played anything from the hit parades. It was the place where all the interested professionals from the palais bands around Melbourne sat-in and exchanged the latest ideas about jazz. Hardly anyone got paid.

Bob Tough led the regular band there. Tough (1911–1949, b. Hobart, Tasmania) was the first real tenor sax player in Melbourne; he did not play it like a euphonium but with guts and a tone similar to Coleman Hawkins. The others in the band were Bob's brother Ern Tough, guitar and bass; Don McFarlane, bass; Alf Warne, piano; Mick Walker, drums; and naturally, Ben Featherstone, trumpet and trombone. Bob Tough's style and harmonic sense were attributable in part to his association with Featherstone, for whom he had played the previous year when Featherstone was leading the band at the Forty Club.

Featherstone was a major figure at the Kiosk. Even if he was too drunk to stand up he could still play excitingly if someone put an instrument in his hands. He was idolized by Wally Norman and had a profound influence on Billy Weston. Weston, then on trumpet, considered that Featherstone played things on trombone that any trombonist would have been proud of. Featherstone and Coughlan, who sat-in when he was leading the Forty Club band from 1940, were the two who turned Weston to trombone.

Melbourne has been particularly strong in its brass players and Featherstone was a contributing influence, but whereas this can also be explained by the strength of the brass band movement in the city, it is less obvious why Melbourne should produce so many good drummers. Again, Featherstone and the Fawkner Park Kiosk are important. In any discipline, be it mathematics or music, the presence of one brilliant individual will attract and inspire others. Featherstone's hard driving style of drumming influenced Billy Hyde (1918–1976), who assimilated what Featherstone was doing and then went further ahead technically and stylistically. Hyde gave Don Rankin's Forty Club band unusual drive and kick, and he was one of the first drummers to phrase with the brass section. Hyde was also a competent exponent on vibraphone, xylophone and timpani. Featherstone directly influenced Charlie Blott (b. 1925, Melbourne). Featherstone spent hours playing records to Blott and talking to him and Blott was old enough to catch the tail-end of the sessions at Fawkner Park. When Hyde left Coughlan's Melbourne Trocadero Orchestra in 1942, Coughlan was having trouble replacing him until Blott got the chair on the strength of his knowledge of traditional jazz, and the bassist, Frank Walsh, helped Blott with his reading so he could cope with the rest. But Blott was not a second Hyde. Blott played with a lot of ride cymbal and drummed independently against it with the rest of the kit. The rhythm section of Hyde, Frank Walsh and Bernie Duggan, piano, was the first in Melbourne to 'cook'; the pianist was freed from supporting the bass to be able to do fill-ins. But where this section was driving, the section of Blott, Lyn Challen, bass, and Don Banks, piano, was a looser, Basie style. From Featherstone, Hyde and Blott come the Melbourne drummers, who include Ron Sandilands, Len Barnard, John Sangster, Laurie Thompson, Stewart Speers, Graham Morgan, Ted Vining, Chris Karan and Alan Turnbull. Each learned as much or more from records as from each other, but for drummers especially, being able to see how a phrase is executed is an important part of learning, and Melbourne drummers would not have been the same without Featherstone, Hyde and Blott.

Big time leaders were not slow to recognise the calibre of musicians who frequented the Kiosk. Coughlan, leading the Melbourne Trocadero band from November 1941 to June 1943, leavened his band with younger, less experienced players, like Tom Crowe, or Neville Maddison, clarinet, who was good at cooking up riffs with Larry Keane, sax, or Billy Weston, because they had fire and Coughlan could get them to play the way he wanted them to.

William James (Billy) Weston (b. 1922, Sydney) came from a similar 'respectable' background to Featherstone, and Weston disappointed his family by going into jazz instead of nice music. When he was twelve, growing up in Perth, he heard on the crystal set, 'Solitude' by Duke Ellington. By virtue of his family upbringing, he thought how delightful it was that a member of the royal family should write music like this. Weston was shocked to find that it was written by an American, and a black one to boot. Later, Weston found his way to Armstrong via Nat Gonella who was played much more on the radio. Weston was a good student until music got him; he left school at fifteen to work for an insurance company, and then at Goldsborough Mort until the manager took exception to his practising in the stationery department and dryly suggested that in view of the enormous musical talent he was displaying the company was holding him back. So Weston got a job in the band on the coastal steamer *Duntroon* and had a look at what he would have to beat in Melbourne and Sydney. In May 1939, aged seventeen, he landed first trumpet with Clarrie Gange at the Forty Club. Weston stayed there under Don Rankin and Coughlan. Coughlan had them playing the Americanadians' library which involved some very high parts and Weston had trouble with his embouchure. Coughlan suggested he swap over to trombone, which he finally did when he moved to Bob Gibson's band at the Palm Grove in Earl's Court.

Gibson had become discontented in Whidden's band at the Palais de Danse and booked his passage to England, but war broke out and he could not go. Claude Carnell and Buddy Wikara opened the Palm Court and Gibson was given the chance to lead his own band there from November 1940 to March 1947. Gibson also chose some men who had jammed at the Fawkner Park Kiosk. Bob Tough was Gibson's tenor star, Alf Warne on piano, and on drums he had Billy Hyde for several seasons, and Keith Cerchi. Gibson had one of the best trumpeters Melbourne has produced, Freddy Thomas (b. 1920, Melbourne). The band—four reeds, four brass, three rhythm—was larger than Coughlan's at the Melbourne Trocadero and by the end of the war Gibson had built it to sixteen. Morale was high and about half a dozen of them would go round to Gibson's place just to practise and develop a style. Gibson wrote about half the arrangements, many in the Glenn Miller style. Billy Weston furthered his interest in arranging which he had begun with Coughlan, and received progressive advice from the New Zealand guitarist Charlie Lees, and from a saxophonist, Syd French. Gibson had the most advanced swing band in Australia at the time.

In the early years of the war the focus of jazz development swung from Sydney to Melbourne. In the mid-1930s, with Jim Davidson's band and Frank Coughlan at the Trocadero, Sydney was where it was all happening. But now that Coughlan was in Melbourne, Gibson at Earl's Court, Whidden at the Palais de Danse and the Fawkner Park Kiosk sessions had been going for about three years, Melbourne was jumping.

Australian jazz progressed a lot between the Depression and World War II. The good bands pulled themselves out of the rickey-tickey era and there were soloists whose style could only be described as 'hot'. The leading arrangers assisted the soloists and voiced bands in more interesting ways. Dance musicians gained a sense of identity, particularly through the magazine *Music Maker*. Newspapers still gave a lot of space to people who wanted jazz to go away, but they were coming across to the idea that jazz could be discussed seriously, and in 1939 a cadet journalist and saxophonist, Merv Acheson, on the staff of the Sydney *Labour Daily*, began the first regular jazz column in an Australian newspaper.

A chair in a leading palais band remained the top job in the dance profession, but there were regular places where a musician could jam and experiment. The general public were still content with ballroom dancing, but enthusiasts helped to loosen the straitjacket of strict tempo music, through their swing clubs and jitterbugging. Records, while still not freely available, were there if you searched for them, and a general awareness of who was the best to listen to had increased markedly.

Then the war began; musicians were drafted or manpowered; but the progress had been solid, and the war did not stop it.

AUSSIES ON PARADE

DURING the Second World War it might be thought that all social and intellectual endeavour was suspended and that normal life resumed in 1945 where it left off in 1939. For Australian jazz the contrary was true. The war invigorated it by bringing many Australians into personal contact with large numbers of Americans.

Jim Davidson enlisted on 30 May 1941 and was made a lieutenant, in charge of all music in the special AIF Entertainment Unit directed by Lieutenant-Colonel Jim Gerald. Also from the ABC Dance Band came Sergeant Wally Portingale, Corporals Keith Atkinson, Bob Atkinson, Chic Donovan and Lawrence Brooks. The ABC Band carried on under the direction of Jim Gussey. Davidson's 'All In Fun' 6th Division Concert Party was sent to the Middle East in November 1941 where they toured Egypt, Syria and Transjordan. In the crucial battle of Bardia, Australian troops stormed the town singing a song Davidson had taught them, 'We're Off to See the Wizard'. Davidson returned to Sydney in October 1942 as a captain and became leader of the unit when Gerald retired due to ill health. In February 1943 the unit was sent to New Guinea but Davidson was there only a month before he was appointed Superintendent of AIF Concert Parties at headquarters in Pagewood, Sydney. Until April 1942 the army provided entertainers from its ranks on a part-time basis. Full-time bands were sent only to those locations and camps where it was undesirable to admit civilians. By early 1942 circumstances had changed enough to warrant the formation of full-time performing units to tour all camps. The men were getting sick of amateur shows; there were many more men in uniform; many professional entertainers had enlisted; and the arrival of American troops, with their well-organised back-up services, prompted the Australian Army Amenities Service to put entertainment on a better footing.

The performing units were comprised of musicians who had been professionals before the war. The amateurs, many of whom were active in the revival of traditional jazz after the war, served in all sections of the services, though a proportion of them were put into signals or related areas because the forces considered that their sense of rhythm helped them master morse code more

Conditions of service for the forces' musicians were often arduous. Members of the swing band of the 'Tasmaniacs'—the Tasmanian Lines of Communication Concert Party—rehearsing in a jungle clearing in preparation for the evening performance, December 1944, Bougainville Island.
L–R: Pte Ron Stevenson, Cpl Billy Weston, Pte George Batson, Cpl Eric Saunders, Pte Eric Madden, Pte Edward Cockman, Pte Bruce Redhouse, Sgt Don Denholm, Staff-Sgt Noel Judd, Cpl Jack Duffy.

Photo per courtesy of the Australian War Memorial.

quickly. Tony Newstead, now a planning executive with Telecom, spent a lot of the war playing his trumpet in the hills behind Port Moresby, and on Manus Island while installing and maintaining isolated radar beacons. An English drummer and radio officer in the merchant navy, Eric Child, arrived in Perth in March 1942 after his vessel was torpedoed in the Java Straits. He stayed on in Australia teaching signals in the R.A.N. and went to New Guinea. Since 1952, the ABC has broadcast his highly informative and much appreciated jazz programs which have established him as a leading authority on jazz. For the non-professionals in the camps the Army Education Service set up a program of musical education and put together groups like the 116th Rhythm Ensemble which performed anything from light classical to jumping big band swing.

Organising the entertainment from Pagewood was a big task because musicians were often an intractable lot and to get things moving it needed a man who was not afraid to make himself unpopular. Pagewood was crawling with actors, make-up artists, managers, female impersonators, jugglers, dancers and everyone who was needed to form a show. Musicians were assembled from all over Australia and it was an opportunity for lesser musicians from interstate to rub shoulders with the big names of Australian music. Arrangers like Eddie Corderoy from the Melbourne ABC Dance Band, and Billy Weston, worked at

Pagewood and were given their own bands to lead: Corderoy led the 1st Australian Entertainment Unit Concert Orchestra, and Weston the 'Tasmaniacs'. Colin Bergersen from the Sydney Trocadero was made a Staff Sergeant and put in charge of the 6th Division Concert Party—'Aussies On Parade'—which accompanied Gracie Fields on her three month tour of Australia, New Guinea and Borneo in 1945. Frank Coughlan left the Melbourne Trocadero in 1943 to enlist and was given charge of the 9th Division Concert Party which toured camps in Queensland and New Guinea, sometimes so close to the front that the Japanese could listen to them.

Playing in the tropics was difficult because the heat and humidity affected the instruments, especially woodwinds and pianos. War restrictions created other problems for musicians. From 1 October 1940, the Federal Government totally prohibited the importation of all band and orchestral instruments from non-sterling countries in order to save valuable currency. Brass players were affected less than others because their instruments were manufactured mostly in England, but professional musicians were hard put to secure accessories such as reeds, mouthpieces and other small essentials. Don Burrows (b. 1928, Sydney) often had to use a sanded-down toothbrush handle instead of a reed, which was like playing with a surfboard. Burrows also experimented with the material used to make dental plates. If a clarinetist or saxophonist did manage to get a reed that worked, he painted it with red nail polish to stop the moisture getting into it. Everything was much harder to obtain because shipping was interrupted and there was a ban on the importation of records, though the monthly release of locally manufactured records continued.

During World War II over one million American troops passed through Australia, including a small percentage of Negro GIs. In the initial strategic plan, Australia was regarded primarily as an air command, but this was discarded because of Japanese advances. In December 1941 the first US troops were landed in Australia and in January 1942 US Headquarters was transferred from Brisbane to Melbourne. US divisions brought their bands with them and most had a dance unit with them. The twenty-eight piece band led by Warrant Officer E. L. Huffman which toured camps in Australia in mid-1942 could be divided into a jazz band, a salon quartet and a fifteen piece dance orchestra playing harmonies similar to those of Claude Thornhill or Glenn Miller. The following year the eighty piece American Armed Services Band toured South Australia, Tasmania and Victoria for several months. This too had a swing combination. Many of the small American units performed free at charity functions, an act which pleased the lady committee members of patriotic organisations but one which slightly irritated officials of the Musicians' Union who were trying to keep jobs open for the few musicians who had not been manpowered.

The most exciting American band to come to Australia in the war was Artie Shaw's Navy Band. It arrived via the islands and New Zealand in September 1943. Sydney musicians had prior notice of its arrival when one of the trumpeters from the band, Johnny Best, asked Abe Romain at the Trocadero if he could sit in. Best was in Sydney on recreation leave; all bands let their members go on leave but only in one's or two's so that the band could still function. The Shaw band was particularly hardworking and in the end, they were all sent home for

Christmas after being medically examined in Brisbane and found to be suffering from fatigue. Romain refused to believe Best because by this time a lot of Americans were giving Australian musicians 'the screaming horrors'. Every second GI who wanted to sit in to impress a girl claimed to have played with Goodman or Dorsey. Australians eventually found that the good players usually were quiet in their approach to the band, but meanwhile they had to be wary of all the indifferent players who clamoured for a turn. Watching Romain's and Best's conversation from backstage was Betty Smythe, a tenor saxophonist in Dick Freeman's girl band, and she recognised Best. The pianist and leader, Dot Hubner, called him over and invited him to join the girls. Wally Norman frantically pulled out some trumpet parts for him, and when the stage revolved the girls came out with Best looking like the cat that swallowed the cream. Romain realised his mistake and asked Best to join the male band. Best courteously declined, saying that he was very happy where he was. The girl band was not a stunt but an integral part of the show. Because of manpower planning, many of the male musicians had to work at day jobs and could not play for the whole night. The girls played for half the evening six nights per week and did the Saturday matinee. They played the swing music of the day with special arrangements by Wally Norman, because the band had no brass but a string section instead. The sax section, as a section, was admired by musicians as one of the best in Sydney. Dot Hubner was a good jazz pianist who could lift any rhythm section. After the Americans moved north, the British centre opened and the girls worked there for two and a half years.

When the Shaw band reached town the word spread quickly amongst musicians. In Melbourne, Splinter Reeves rushed into Suttons music store where the musicians congregated, almost incoherent with excitement. Most of Shaw's concerts were for American servicemen only, so Blott, Hyde and the rest sensibly scrambled along to the US Army Public Relations Office, showed their union cards and got in. Sydney musicians took more devious routes. Duke Farrell got into the concert by hanging around until he met an American servicewoman who would take him. The only one of the teenagers in Don Burrows' crowd who succeeded was Arthur 'Yank' Christian who was a member of the Navy League and put his uniform on and conned his way in. Burrows stood outside in the alley and listened. Wally Norman gained admission by applying a pair of bolt cutters to the back door of the Trocadero.

The effect of the band was immediate. Its depth of tone, precision, phrasing, attack and release, and the sheer physical presence of so many good musicians all blowing superbly knocked out everyone who heard them. The following week all the bands around town were playing twice as loudly as they had before, and horn players knew that they had to extend their range higher. For years musicians had suppressed their blowing for fear of offending someone. In the first flush of excitement after Shaw's visit musicians could not care less about the public, and strangely, the public enjoyed it more too. It took a few more years for Australian musicians to discover that hard blowing in itself was insufficient to produce the big sound, and that a lot of attention had to be paid to the finer details of tone production, breathing and the knack of projection. Shaw's drummer, Dave Tough, was an influence on Charlie Blott. Tough was the first leading overseas drummer Blott had met and it was through seeing him—because Blott had already studied him on record—that Blott realised how much ride cymbal Tough employed, and Blott modified his style accordingly.

Shaw's visit also gave a boost to the musicians interested in traditional jazz because Tough and the trumpeter, Max Kaminsky, were fine exponents of that style. While Shaw's band was in Mackay in Queensland, Kaminsky stayed with Graeme Bell who was playing piano for the American Red Cross. Bell organised an introduction with his brother Roger and other interested musicians in Melbourne. Kaminsky recorded two tracks which were released, 'That Da Da Strain' and 'Oh That Sign', with an Australian band comprised of half of the Bell band and half of Splinter Reeves's group. Tough was scheduled for the session but he was having an unhappy trip and was indisposed at the time.

In other theatres of war Australians were getting the chance to hear and play with Americans. In New Guinea, Alan Nash and Charlie Munro were among those in the orchestra of the 50-50 Army Show, a show with half American, half Australian personnel. Nash and Munro also broadcast in Queensland with the United States Army Base Section 2 Band. Billy Weston heard Bob Crosby's Marine Band in the islands. Perth musicians were inspired by Johnny Turk's fifteen piece band. Some of the value of fraternising with a lot of Americans was that Australians met a number of musicians who were not good players. America was a magic word then, the home of a huge amount of good music, and many Australians, especially younger musicians, went in awe of anyone with an American accent. They soon found that this did not necessarily mean that the American had greater musical ability and they concluded that there was about the same proportion of good jazzmen in the American army as in the Australian.

On the other hand thousands of Americans on leave perceptibly altered the musical climate, especially in Sydney. Pitt Street took on some of the aura of 42nd Street. Standards were lifted because Australian musicians felt they had an audience that was interested and discriminating and they never knew when a good American musician might be listening. Bob Rodin, who had played trumpet with Bob Crosby, sat in with Abe Romain's band, and Andy Seacrest, who had played next to Bix Beiderbecke in Whiteman's Orchestra, served in the Pacific area. The public's taste shifted through association with Americans. They wanted the latest pop tunes and the ban on the importation of records was circumvented through getting records, 'V' discs, and arrangements from the Americans who had them flown out. The war added to the favour of big bands. GIs were pleasantly surprised when they arrived in Australia because they thought they were being sent to a barren island in the South Pacific, but instead they found some bands as good as the ones back home. Bob Gibson's band at Palm Court in St Kilda worked with the Australian Red Cross and the American Special Services Entertainment Department and proved to be a drawcard for thousands of American troops. At the Melbourne Trocadero Frank Coughlan had them crowding around the bandstand listening with amazement. On nights like that Coughlan would forget about the program and give them everything they wanted. Those who were not staring at the band were teaching Australian girls to jitterbug and truck, which gave Australian musicians more freedom in their playing. There were many objectors to the jitterbug craze; some were shocked at the apparent abandon and exhibitionism of it, and there was anxiety lest these young dancers grow up to be unstable adults. From overseas came reports of dance halls which banned jitterbugging because it interfered with other dancers, and occasionally jitterbugging was linked to American race riots. The NSW Jitterbug Championships were promoted by an American, Bill Ferrier, in February 1944 at Leichhardt Stadium.

Between ten and twelve thousand Australian women married Americans during the war, compared to about four thousand Australian men who married while serving overseas. The indirect influence of Americans on Australian music through the female public was almost as important as the direct impact of American musicians on Australian musicians.

Australian men realised that this change in musical likes was not due only to cerebral communion and there was some friction between American and Australian troops caused by the lavish way Americans were able to spend money and the general difference in the standard of rations, supplies and living facilities. The most notorious incident was the 'Battle for Brisbane' on 26 November 1942, a riot which lasted for three hours and resulted in one Australian shot dead and eight wounded. In Perth, whenever there were Americans in town and a shipload of Australians or New Zealanders arrived from the jungle, the nurses at the hospital prepared as a matter of course the material to stitch cuts and wire broken jaws. Underage musicians playing in the nightclubs, like Club Cabarita or the Coconut Grove in Hay Street, had their eyes opened wide by the goings on. For many troops Perth was as far away from home as they were going to get and they could all die tomorrow, so life was lived at a reckless pace. While there were blemishes in the relationships of troops *en masse*, individuals found that some of the worst, and some of the best people, were Yanks.

Thousands of troops in town at one time put a strain on entertainment facilities. In Sydney, officers were advised to leave the Trocadero to the other ranks. This was not simply a class distinction but a tactical avoidance of the trouble which might result from tension between the ranks. Officers escorted their friends to the nightclubs, like the Roosevelt which was managed by Sammy Lee of the Americanadians. The American Warrant Officers' Club took over the Swan River Rowing Club in Perth and called it the 'Swan Dive'. No Australian male civilians were allowed in except for a few musicians who saw bulk ice-cream and Coca Cola for the first time. In Melbourne Myers Emporium opened in May 1942, a club for Australian and American servicemen and women called 'The Dugout'. A seven piece Australian band played. What to do on a Sunday was a big problem because most places were shut by law. This was remedied in April 1942 by the War Cabinet recommending to the State Premiers that entertainment venues be opened on Sunday afternoons and evenings for Allied and Australian personnel.

Radio stations endeavoured to broadcast programs and music which would interest their new American listeners. In April 1942 the ABC contacted Major Lynn Cowan, the Officer-in-Charge of Entertainments, to ask him what would be suitable to put over the air for Americans. Cowan had been to Australia some years before as a vaudeville artist at the Tivoli. He was pleased with the co-operation being extended to him and replied that US troops were accustomed to very high standards of entertainment of all kinds, from symphonies to vaudeville. The ABC and commercial stations broadcast transcriptions flown in from America, which provided another opportunity for Australians to hear American jazz. By May 1943 there was opposition to this practice from the Musicians' Union, supported by the managers of Stations 2UE, 2KY and 2UW, the Australian Journalists' Association and Actors' Equity. An order from Washington restricted the use of transcriptions to centres where American troops were congregated, thus eliminating Western Australia, South Australia and Tasmania. Americans brought juke boxes to Australia, which did much for popular music but little for jazz.

Working closely with the forces were semi-civilian organisations which provided entertainment for the troops. Bob Dyer, 'The Last of the Hillbillies', was stranded in Australia when the war started and he joined the United Services Organisation. When military authorities took over the Palais de Danse at St Kilda and made it the postal headquarters, Bob Lyon and the band went under contract to the Special Services Section of the American Army, performing throughout Victoria at American and Australian army camps, hospitals and hostels. The Red Cross Comforts Fund provided a lot of entertainment for servicemen. At their canteen and hostel in Exhibition Street, Melbourne, Gren Gilmour led a nine piece band which played for half the program when Shaw's band appeared there, and played for Mrs Roosevelt during her visit in 1943. In Sydney, Les Welch worked for the American Red Cross at their centre in Pitt Street, and at places like GI Paradise at the Australian Golf Club, the Navy Base Hospital at Merrylands, or the Lido on the promenade at Bondi. Welch was ahead of his time, not in any great creative way, but in the sense that he would have made a good rock and roll artist. He was self-taught on piano so everything was played in the key of C and built mainly around the blues. Asked what the band would play for a bracket, Welch would nominate a fast blues, a slow blues and a bit of boogie. His strength lay in his singing and his ability to present a song. He endeavoured to bring out a negro timbre in his voice, and Helen Humes mistook him for a black man until she saw him in the flesh. Welch could take a flimsy tune like 'Cigareets, Whusky and Wild, Wild, Women', which was his first hit after the war, and spin it out on stage into a twenty minute act which held the audience's unwavering attention.

Welch had a few young musicians in his band, teenagers like Don Andrews (guitar), Don Burrows (clarinet) and Ron Falson (trumpet) who were getting their professional opportunities early in life because so many older musicians were in the forces. They were underage in the nightclubs they worked at, and one night Burrows was caught by the manpower officers at the Roosevelt. He would have been sent to work at the munitions factory if a pianist, Reg Lewis, had not fixed him up with a job in the 2GB music library.

Don Burrows's musical potential was evident even at this early stage. His father was a bread carter who played the ukulele a little and showed Don elementary chord progressions when he was about five. At the Bondi Public School Burrows took up the B flat school flute and progressed so rapidly that he was made Captain of the Metropolitan Schools' Flute Band. The Director of Music in Schools, Vic McMahon, who started Burrows on flute, must have been disappointed to find that this natural flautist wanted to play the clarinet, but he wangled a good clarinet for him at a reduced price. Sydney professionals became aware of the youngster at jam sessions they had at Palings on Friday nights and Saturday mornings. Burrows wormed his way into these sessions playing softly in the corner and gradually got known and was encouraged. He received invaluable advice on clarinet from Les McGrath. Burrows and his friends used to follow the musicians all over town to informal blows at the weekend on the esplanade at Bondi, and to cinemas which still had pit orchestras because that was just as important to them as the films. Most of the films which featured star American musicians were shown in Australia. When he was fourteen Burrows played twice over the air on the Amateur Hour, the first time leading a contingent from the Metropolitan Schools' Band and the second time in Wally Wickham's Hawaiian band. Other radio shows then which helped to introduce talent to the public were 'The Youth Show', 'Over to Youth' and 'Star Parade'. Burrows went into the Roosevelt band when Bert Mars was leader. Mars came to Australia in 1929 with the Canadian Cowboys. Mars ran a 'hot-plate-taxi' after the Roosevelt closed at night for American airmen who wanted to get back to the Bankstown aerodrome. He charged £10 each, which was expensive and illegal, but if Burrows sat beside him it looked innocent, like a father and son with their American guests. Mars occasionally slipped Burrows a few quid for his time. Burrows learned to read music at the Roosevelt because Monte Richardson promised him a job with the Bob Dyer Show Orchestra if he did. Jim Gussey noticed Burrows and invited him to join the ABC Dance Band in 1944.

Burrows and Don Andrews kicked around together and often went to Sunday afternoon jam sessions at the back of the Parisienne Milk Bar at Campsie, the suburb where Ray Price was born. One evening Les Welch and Duke Farrell were jamming when a cheeky kid in short pants said he could play boogie-woogie better than Welch could. Welch did not want to know, but they had a rule that anyone had to be allowed to prove himself, and the kid could play better. He was Terry Wilkinson, who became one of Sydney's best modern pianists.

Often Negro GIs came to the Parisienne because there was a small Aboriginal community at Campsie and Negroes were on strict instructions not to be seen on the streets with white women. Negroes comprised about eight per cent of the American forces in Australia and by tradition they were segregated into the quartermaster and service divisions, not the combat units. Large scale operations against Japan by the USA from Australia and the implementation of a construction program of essential aircraft defences and aerodromes faced Australia with a potential labour shortage. On 2 January 1942 the manager of an American steamship company, the Matson Line, operating between the west coast of USA and Australia, enquired whether civilian coloured work gangs from USA might be employed in Brisbane to handle the increased traffic in goods caused by the war. Ray Tellier, who brought his San Francisco Orchestra to Australia in the 1920s, was musical director for this line for a number of years. The Department of Labour and National Service regarded the proposal as 'most dangerous', and were only prepared to allowed coloured labour in when all available local civilian labour had been absorbed, and then it was to be US Army labour, not black civilians. In the same month the US War Department wanted to know the Australian government's reaction to the proposal that Negro forces be sent to Australia. Initially the Australian War Cabinet was against it but soon relented because they had little choice in view of the advancing Japanese threat, and said that, while the Australian reaction would not be favourable, they would let the US government determine the composition of the forces they would despatch, though they assumed that the Americans would also be mindful of Australian susceptibilities in the numbers they sent. By August 1942 there were over 7,000 coloured US troops in Australia. General MacArthur hoped to minimise any friction by deploying Negroes in the front zones away from the great centres of population, so nearly half the Negroes in Australia were stationed in the Mt Isa area. Many of them were drivers for convoys from Mt Isa to Tennant Creek and Birdum. Throughout 1942–43, Negroes could be seen daily in such northern Queensland towns as Cairns, Ingham and Charters Towers, but not all of them were stuck out in the bush. Townsville, Brisbane and Sydney developed as large leave centres for Negroes. It was in these centres and in New Guinea that Australian musicians made rewarding contact with US Negroes.

Segregated in action, Negroes were also segregated while on leave: even the American Red Cross blood plasma banks were segregated. Recreational facilities were limited to those provided by the American Red Cross but these were below the standard available to white servicemen. The North American Club, called that because the Negro committee did not want a name which would be identified with blacks only, was opened in Townsville in October 1942. In the competition for the attentions of girls, Negroes were handicapped because they had no

The Fifth Air Corps Orchestra playing for a dance at the American Red Cross Dr Carver Service Club, wh was for the use of coloured American troops on leave in Brisbane.

Photo per courtesy of the Australian War Memorial.

facilities to hold dances. If all else was denied them, then they were forced to associate with prostitutes. The American authorities set up several brothels near Townsville for the use of Negro troops, much to the disgust of local civilians. The brothels were medically supervised and seemed to be entirely successful. In Brisbane and Sydney, Negroes were restricted to certain parts of the city. Before the Negro club was opened in Brisbane, an Aboriginal ran a dance from mid-1942 at the Protestant Alliance Hall in the suburb of Red Hill. The Dr Carver Club opened at 100 Grey Street, South Brisbane, on 7 May 1943, on the site of the Blue Moon Roller Rink. The club was named after George Washington Carver, a Negro agricultural scientist who did much to improve the economy of the South, who had died in January 1943. Some members of the Queensland parliament objected to the proposed site but the co-operation of the American Red Cross, the Brisbane City Council and local business people broke down the opposition. The club provided a place where Negro troops could sleep while on leave, and activities included dances, talent shows, athletics and excursions. About two hundred Negroes were on leave at any one time and there would have been more except that Negroes were given leave every eighteen months instead of every nine like white soldiers.

The Booker T. Washington Club at 207 Albion Street, Surrey Hills, Sydney, was in what was formerly the German Club, but it had become vacant when all its members were interned. It began in July 1942 and was named after a leading US Negro educator and reformer of the nineteenth century. The first Negro club in Sydney had been near the Parramatta race track where the men were billeted, but because Negro troops were more generous than white troops in their payment of prostitutes, the club had been a constant source of trouble. It was discontinued and the Booker T. Washington Club opened. Prior to the arrival of American Red Cross Negro personnel in Australia it was necessary to staff the clubs with Australians, and they were largely ignorant of American racial patterns. Most officers in the US Army were southerners, and they and the white southern enlisted men did not want Australians to continue their easy fraternisation with the blacks. Most racial disturbances involved the southerners and Negroes, not Australians. Mr Homer Smith, representative of the American Negro Press in the USSR, mentioned to Mr Crawford of the Australian Legation there that he had seen letters from Negro soldiers in Australia to their folks in America which praised highly the treatment they had met among Australians and contrasted it with the treatment they received from white Americans. Smith said such letters were important in defeating Japanese propaganda in the Negro community which played up the White Australia Policy. In 1962 John Killens, a Negro who had served in the Pacific during the war, wrote a novel called *And Then We Heard the Thunder*. He composed an episode which was probably based on the 'Battle for Brisbane', but which he converted to a race war within the American Army. Killens made a point of including a truckfull of Diggers who fought on the side of the blacks. Presumably relations between Australians and Negroes were such as to make this fictional episode seem not too far-fetched. At dances in Melbourne, where there were not enough Negroes on leave to have their own club, if there was any trouble the Negro servicemen were always thrown out first, no questions asked. But sometimes Australian men and women walked out in protest, and a few white Americans too, who made sure that blacks got taxis and were not harassed by other white US servicemen. The opening of the Dr Carver and Booker T. Washington clubs lessened the incidence of street fighting. Negroes were allowed to bring white guests, mainly Australian soldiers who enjoyed the famous chicken dinners, and white girls who liked to get on the hostess roster because Negroes were masters of jitterbugging, though at the Booker T. Washington Club the girls were nearly all coloured, being either Islanders, Maoris or Aboriginals.

There were many instances, though, where Australians adopted the same attitudes as the southerners. Women were 'advised' that Negroes were inclined to rape and it became common to blame the Negro for any sex crime when no assailant could be traced. The Sydney Victuallers' Association proposed to close hotel bars to Negro soldiers and in 1943 and 1944 the Surry Hills and Belmore branches of the Australian Labor Party, and other local citizens, made complaints to F. M. Forde, the Minister for the Army, desiring the removal of the club. Nothing came of this except a little heavy-handed tightening up of control over the club by the military police. The Australian and American military authorities investigated the complaints and the NSW Commissioner of Police, William J. Mackay, assessed in his report to Forde that the conduct of coloured troops compared favourably with that of any of the Allied soldiers and sailors who had passed through Sydney.

Most Australians were content to let the US Army manage its own affairs, except for the Communist Party of Australia. The Commonwealth Investigation Branch reported in May 1942 that the CPA was distributing circulars urging the Australian people to fraternise with Negro soldiers and to take up every instance of discrimination against them. The party was trying to create feelings of friendship between the Australian armed forces and the Negroes and to stamp out all expressions of racial prejudice, not only against 'niggers' but also 'chows', 'dagoes' and 'pommies'. Many young men in the forces became interested in communist theories and sometimes pondered the question of whether civilisation was worth saving.

There were never any reservations about jazz though; it was always referred to with enthusiasm. The Army Education Service seemed to attract many people with left wing sympathies and its fortnightly magazine, *Salt*, carried many articles on jazz. In articles like these pop tunes were denigrated as one of the opiums that Karl Marx forgot about, whereas jazz was simple and pure, raising its voice against industrialisation and the bourgeois morality, and it was a symbol of the free individual and of real human values. These opinions were being voiced at a time when the USSR had banned jazz as another expression of western decadence. The Communist Party of Australia might have been a more powerful force in politics if it had extended its independent attitude on jazz to other issues.

The CPA attempted to take over certain key positions of the Musicians' Union, starting with a move to unseat the Victorian District Secretary in 1943. This activity petered out after the war. Why any organisation would want to gain control of the Musicians' Union is a puzzle, because the union frequently bears more resemblance to Meals on Wheels than to a step towards assuming the reins of government. Jazz has continued to be associated with left-wing politics in Australia, particularly in street marches because a jazz band does not depend on electricity, but there is no intrinsic relation between the two. Jazz bands have been hired for rallies of both the major political parties in the 1970s. The relationship between developments in music and politics is tenuous. Certainly a jazz fan is more likely to have an enlightened attitude to race, but the left seems to have embraced jazz, especially traditional jazz, as much for the image it evoked of a pure freedom struggle by the suppressed Negro masses as for the sound itself. Once the pure suppressed masses got into bop it became much harder for the left to appreciate the same connection.

The band at the Booker T. Washington Club was comprised of Australians, led by a drummer, Giles O'Sullivan, who was an honorary colonel in the US Army. Sydney musicians could not believe their luck—they had the exciting opportunity to play at a club for American Negroes. It was basically a five piece band but many came to sit in because it was a genuine jazz job, never any thought of a barn dance, everything could be played to the tempo the song demanded because the Negroes were good dancers. Musicians were thrilled by the dancing and often found that the visual stimulation was enough to lift the band. The music played was small group swing; arrangements by Basie, Andy Kirk or Don Redman that were obtained from the US Army. Musicians who played at the club included Jim Somerville (piano), Ray Price (guitar), Mischa Kanafe (guitar), Jack Baines (tenor), George Fuller (trumpet), Don Burrows (clarinet), 'Slush' Stewart (trombone), Billy Weston and Rolph Pommer (alto sax), Pommer being the first Sydney musician to play the alto saxophone with guts, and Merv Acheson, a strong tenor saxophonist. A couple of artists, Donald Friend and Cedric Flower, were taken there by musicians and drew some pictures recording the atmosphere at the club.

The club acted as a catalyst and helped Acheson to fire. Acheson was influenced by Chu Berry and Coleman Hawkins, and his big style was much admired by the Negroes who handed up reefers as tips. MPs patrolling the club did not take any action because marijuana was not illegal then and no one knew much about it. Musicians knew what it was because they had discovered the meaning of the titles of songs like Fats Waller's 'I'se a Viper' or Teagarden's 'Tea From Texas, Tea From Tennessee', but they were not interested in it and saved it up and swapped it for alcohol. Indian hemp was not made illegal in Australia until the Poisons Act was passed in 1952, but the Drug Squad was formed in 1927 to combat the razor gangs and the cocaine and opium trade trafficking through prostitutes and crooked dentists. It was alleged that cocaine tablets had been found in the possession of one of the girls arrested in the raid on Sonny Clay's Colored Idea in Melbourne in 1928, but it was not brought out in court, probably because the charges of vagrancy were dismissed. *Music Maker* in 1932 explained why Armstrong served a gaol term and briefly described the effect of marijuana. Marijuana was not widely used until the late 1960s when some more naive musicians tried harder drugs too. The musicians still playing today are the ones who never got heavily involved or who woke up to themselves soon enough to stop in time. But alcohol is the drug that has done the most damage. Perhaps musicians are vulnerable to it because much of their working lives are spent in social situations where everyone else is drinking, and many musicians and fans are in love with the idea of the bohemian life.

In coming to the style he did, Acheson fell between two stools in Sydney, for while the professionals pursued modern developments after the war, the dixielanders did not grow to appreciate what he was doing until the last decade. Merv Acheson is the son of Bob Acheson, a professional classical violinist who worked with the Sydney Symphony Orchestra, the Colgate-Palmolive radio show and various theatres. Bob started Merv on violin when he was about five, but when Merv was eleven he had both arms broken playing football and when the bones knitted the muscles were stiff, so when his father asked him what he wanted to play, Merv nominated the tenor sax. Acheson was very thin then and was never concerned with becoming a millionaire. He really knew his way around Sydney as Duke Farrell (bass) found out when Acheson was seeing to Duke's jazz education. They went to play at the dive in town, Ziegfield's, in King Street. Strange women asked Farrell if he wanted to go home with them, which Farrell thought was a nice gesture until they told him he had to pay. Acheson served with the infantry, then with the 116th Rhythm Ensemble, and he replaced an ill saxophonist in Artie Shaw's band for part of the tour. Once he accidentally shot a man at the 2KY Radiotorium in George Street. The 2KY Jazz and Swing Club, formed by Ron Wills and Eric Dunn, met there from 1943 on Sundays. Merv was having a stand-off backstage with another gunman when a peacemaker jumped between them and copped it in the leg. Acheson did thirteen months for that.

All American and Australian musicians visited the 2KY Club when they were on leave. Two Negroes who made a lasting impression were Jesse Martin, who played drums with a stick in one hand and a brush in the other, and Wilbur Wilson, who had been first trumpet for Andy Kirk and his Clouds of Joy. The band really swung when they sat in, and they excited visitors like Ade Monsbourgh, on leave from the RAAF, and Tom Pickering, doing Army Education training in Sydney, and both became leading reed players in the traditional revival after the war. Lee Young, Lester Young's younger brother, went there and played good drums and sang. As with the white Americans, the war enabled Australians to realise that not all Negroes were potential Louis Armstrongs. If there were any Negroes in the audience the band would search them out, hopeful that they would know something about jazz or play, but frequently the Negroes' knowledge of music extended no further than corny hit parade songs or else their upbringing had been so strict they had hardly even heard of jazz. Negroes who wanted to sit-in, fabricated the same stories as their white countrymen, but instead of having played with Goodman or Dorsey, it was Ellington or Henderson. It was a salutary experience for Australians to discover that there were many Negroes who simply did not appreciate jazz.

But it was the good players who impressed. At the Parisienne Milk Bar, Aaron Bell, who later played bass with Ellington, sat-in. Up in New Guinea Frank Ellery, who had played at the Sydney Trocadero, came across the swing section of the 415 AEF Band, the 'Quartermaster's Caravan', and was nearly blown out the back wall by them. The leader was Jimmy Coe (alto and clarinet) with Ernest H. Phipps (piano), Joseph Johnson (bass) and Bryant Allan (drums, vocal) among others. All Australian musicians who served up north made a point of seeking out Negroes to talk and play with. Jazz hounds like Tony Newstead, Willie McIntyre, Cec Davidson and Sid Bromley formed the Port Moresby Jazz Appreciation Society and when they shifted to Bougainville they renamed it the Bougainville Jazz Appreciation Society. In Melbourne, Roger Bell and friends met Morris Goode, a trumpeter from Harlem with a fiery and masculine style, and they made a record of Goode's own composition, 'I'm Going But I'll Be Back'.

The Musicians' Union continued to press the government to abolish 6 p.m. closing and to grant wine licences to restaurants. Radio stations became subject to new regulations in 1942 requiring them to play a $2\frac{1}{2}$ per cent quota of Australian compositions over the air. The ban on the importation of records was effective in providing employment for musicians, but as the war drew to a close the union was concerned that, because of manpower difficulties and the shortage of materials for the manufacture of records, the Australian market was wide open to capture by USA, but the government took little heed of the warning.

The government rewarded those servicemen with the ability and interest with Commonwealth Reconstruction Training Scholarships and some, like Ray Price, Ian Pearce, Don Banks, Harry Bluck and Ed Corderoy, took them in music. Others like Tony Newstead decided to keep music as a hobby and did a degree in another discipline.

From the end of 1944, as the front advanced nearer Japan, fewer Americans came on leave to Australia and the clubs began to close. The war uprooted thousands of people and brought them many new musical contacts and experiences. The American presence was stimulating for the Australian public and musicians and helped to dispel many misconceptions and exaggerated notions.

THE HIGH PART FROM
'THE GOLDEN WEDDING'

THERE was a short break in professional popular music after the war, during which musicians left the armed forces and returned to jostle for positions in the re-forming bands. There had always been more musicians than outlets available for them, but demobilisation brought a sudden surplus. Some of the older musicians sought to recapture the mood of before the war, but there was a new generation of dancers who had learned new steps from the American troops, and who did not necessarily want what their parents had had. And there was a new development in jazz—bop—a radical departure from all previous styles, which no one could dance to. The advent of bop meant that some forms of modern jazz would slowly, very slowly in Australia, be recognised as an art music. Bop demanded an almost schizophrenic dedication from the adventurous professional musician who earned his living by commercial gigs and in big bands, but often played bop in situations where the band outnumbered the audience. Bop was the thorn and the spur in the side of post-war modern jazz in Australia, and the story of the musicians involved with it is one of ceaseless search for someone to listen to them do it.

Wally Norman first heard bop at the Roosevelt in Sydney on records which the Americans had. After the war he was lucky enough to get some imported records of Dizzy Gillespie, Charlie Parker, Howard McGhee, and Charlie Ventura and he invited all interested musicians to record sessions at his house at Bondi Junction. Norman also transcribed them and his Roosevelt band performed the new changes with enthusiasm. Charlie Munro, then one of Norman's sidemen, was particularly impressed with bop and immediately switched to it.

The musical community knew that bop was an important innovation and *Music Maker* (20 Aug. 1946) invited Norman to write a guest editorial on the topic. Norman's brief description of bop was accurate and incisive, unlike the fanciful stories which circulated about jazz when it had appeared twenty-five years earlier. Communications had improved to the extent that Australians were aware of all subsequent major changes after bop within a year or so of their development, and even that time lag has continued to decrease. A problem with bop was that most of it was on independent labels like Savoy, Blue Note or Black and White which had no representatives in Australia. Local record companies did not want to release anything that was not commercial and it was a couple of years before the wartime restrictions on currency outflow were lifted to permit musicians to purchase, by bankdraft, American records for their own use. Australian musicians knew something important was developing in America but the problem was to get sufficient records to find out about it. There was a good deal of frustrated floundering around in the new idiom, and a lot of what passed for bop was watered-down. But at Sydney jazz concerts in the late forties, there appeared good bop-oriented groups such as Billy Weston's Bop Cats, Wally Norman and his Be-Boppers and Ron Falson's Harbour City Six, performing transcriptions of records such as 'Ornithology', 'Salt Peanuts' and some original compositions.

The situation in Melbourne was similar. There was a group of musicians who were not satisfied by commercial work who found bop refreshing and a challenge. Charlie Blott was at the centre of the progressive jazz movement, partly because he had one of the most up to date record collections. Stewie Speers also had an imported bop collection. After gigs, he, Splinter Reeves and friends used to sneak in through the back window so as not to wake his mother and stay up until breakfast trying to work the records out. Blott and Don Banks heard their first bop records before the first Australian Jazz Convention in 1946, but the convention was unswervingly directed towards traditional jazz and they felt out of place. Blott organised modern sessions on Sunday nights at the Katherina Cafe, St Kilda, which were always being closed by the police for being Sunday night entertainment. Banks caught on to bop straight away because of his sound theoretical knowledge and classical studies at the Melbourne Conservatorium. He wrote charts and formed the Don Banks Boptet with Ken Brentnall (trumpet), Eddie Oxley (alto sax), Joe Washington (guitar), Charlie Blott (drums) and John Foster, an able bass player from Adelaide. The Banks Boptet was the best of the early bop groups because Banks was able to set a style for his band whereas some other young musicians, who were feeling their way to bop by imitating their favourites, were not always able to resolve the conflict of styles when they played together.

At one stage the musicians jamming at the Katherina could not find a guitarist who could cope with modern chord progressions. Blott received a call from a young man with a bad stammer who had been recommended to him by Vern Moore, Horrie Dargie's guitarist, but Blott was dubious about letting him come because he said he played at the Hawaiian Academy. But when Bruce Clarke sat-in he was immediately accepted by them. Clarke (b. 1925) became a guitarist because he was not outgoing as a child and his mother answered an advertisement by Buddy Wikara's Hawaiian Academy which said that your child would become the life of the party if he learned music. Clarke learned quickly and became a teacher there. While he was serving an apprenticeship as a plumber on a housing commission development in Coburg he had lots of spare time, and studied music with a manuscript book and a torch in the ceilings of new houses while waiting for the pipes to be handed up. He first became aware of jazz in 1944 at a record store when, from the next booth, he heard someone listening to Charlie Christian, which at first he thought was Hawaiian music played at an incredible speed. Hawaiian music was finished for him when he heard Dizzy

Gillespie's 'Anthropology' on the radio. Clarke had taught himself modern chords and the first tune he played at the Katherina was 'How High The Moon', then the boppers' anthem, and everything gelled marvellously. He was invited to join the Splinter Reeves Splintet and the Banks' Boptet for which he wrote his first arrangements.

The Splintet came into its own when Banks went to England in 1950 to continue his studies. Reeves, nicknamed Splinter because he was so skinny, was a leading bop tenor saxophonist. He was an erratic character and no one could be sure that he would turn up for a job, but he played harder than most until he drifted out of jazz in the early 1950s into novelty acts playing motor-car pumps and other oddments.

In 1950 the boppers moved their sessions to the Galleon Coffee Lounge, St Kilda, calling themselves the Boposophical Society of Australia. Terry Wilkinson from Sydney joined them there.

Fred Thomas Big Band, Sunday afternoon jazz concerts at the New Theatre, Flinders Street, Melbourne, 1948.
Fred Thomas (trumpet), Frank Arnold (trumpet), Ron Ferrier (trumpet), Ted Hellier (trumpet), Ken Coburn (trumpet), Colin Williams (trombone), Des Blundell (trombone), Jack Williams (trombone), Wally Barton (trombone), Ken Weate (alto), Eddie Oxley (alto), Errol Buddle (tenor), Bob Limb (tenor), Neil Randrup (baritone), Ron Loughhead (piano), John Foster (bass), Charles Blott (drums), Joe Washington (guitar).

Apart from jam sessions, jazz concerts were the main opportunities to present bop to the public. The Rex Stewart tour of 1949 was a high point. At his concerts, for which Banks wrote some of the arrangements, Stewart played in the way he was renowned with Ellington but, though he was not an out and out bop man, at after show sessions he would demonstrate to the boppers what he could really do.

The boppers, not sidetracked by the call for 'purity' as the traditionalists were, were usually the key players in the big bands, which retained their popularity for dancers into the late 1950s. Established leaders like Bob Gibson and Frank Coughlan continued with the styles for which they were known. Bop made little impact on them. Gibson finished at the Palm Grove in early 1947, became musical director for the Shell Show on radio and went to England in 1948 for two years, where he toured with Tommy Trinder's show and worked with some of the leading dance musicians. Coughlan performed his share of the new Kenton numbers but felt they were too brassy and were blowing the people out of the dance halls. He thought the traditional jazz revival was in part due to the public looking for the danceable beat which rock and roll was later found to possess. It was a good period for arrangers such as Don Rankin, Ron Loughhead, Bob Young, Syd French or Joe Washington, because the big bands were performing a percentage of originals, especially for radio shows. The bands were good enough to try other things besides cover versions. The advent of rock and roll in the mid-50s ushered in a period of non-adventurousness where all that was wanted was a live copy of the record sound.

The public were ready to sit and listen to the bands in concert. The most dynamic of the new post-war progressive bands was formed by Gibson's star trumpeter, Freddie Thomas. Blott had been up to Sydney on the Bell band's farewell tour when he heard the Ralph Mallen band playing Kenton arrangements which were the big sound of that time. Blott found out where they could be bought and blew his wages on two dozen arrangements which he brought back to Thomas whose band made its debut before a packed house at Melbourne's New Theatre on 21 September 1947. The band had a gutsy authoritativeness about it that previous bands had lacked. From September 1949 to 1954 Thomas led his band at the Palm Grove with a progressive policy, tempered with pops.

Many town halls and suburban ballrooms had resident dance bands, mainly on weekends. Usually they were not as progressive as Thomas's band, but they often served as a training ground for aspiring young modern players. The most popular of these suburban bands in the early 1950s was led by an irrepressible trumpeter, Paddy Fitzallan. He began on cornet in the Westmead Boys Brass Band in Sydney. After serving with the RAAF he came to the public's eye when he took over the Bruce Kennett Orchestra in Melbourne and won a readers' poll of the *Listener-In* magazine in 1951. Technically he was an able player but his improvisations were limited. He was the only Australian to play on stage with Louis Armstrong in 1954. They had fourteen trumpet battles which Armstrong won every time. Fitzallan played lead trumpet in Dennis Collinson's band for Sinatra's 1955 tour, was musical director for the Downbeat concerts for many years and portrayed the last musician on earth in the film 'On The Beach'.

Another initiative of Charlie Blott resulted in the Australian Rhythm Festivals of 1952 at the Melbourne Town Hall, designed to demonstrate to the public the

MEL. LANGDON

presents

THIS CONCERT

at the

ASSEMBLY HALL

MARGARET STREET, SYDNEY

NEXT MONDAY NIGHT
11th APRIL 1949

the
RALPH
MALLEN

★ O
R
★ C
H
E
★ S
T
R
A

and
EDWIN
DUFF

THE
and SUCCESS STORY
BAND

DUKE FARRELL
with the
Illawarra
JAZZ GANG

PLAN and BOOKINGS
NOW
at J. STANLEY JOHNSTON
NICHOLSON
PALINGS

4/- and 3/-

Plus Tax

Compered by
BILL McCOLL

ability of Australian musicians in jazz and light music, and to enlist public support for the Musicians' Union's plea to the Federal government for a measure of protection from imported recordings. Blott talked Bruce Clarke into doing a big band concert and Clarke approach the Musicians' Union to back it. Clarke organised arrangers, Loughhead and Bob Gibson, and put together a seventeen piece band, the Melbourne Rhythmaires. Also on the program were the Melbourne ABC Dance Band and smaller groups, including a sextet led by Don Harper, Australia's leading mainstream violinist. Harper was bandleader at the St Kilda Town Hall from 1945 until he left for England in 1955. He enjoyed a professional association with, and was influenced by the fine guitarist Doug Beck, and did a lot of duet work with Len Williams, the father of world renowned guitarist John Williams. In England, Harper became a successful composer of mood music and wrote the themes for such television programs as 'Champion House', 'Sexton Blake' and 'World of Sport'.

In Sydney there was more scope for big bands because there was more money for entertainment; radio shows and nightclubs were more successful than they were in Melbourne. The pioneer progressive band was led by trombonist Ralph Mallen (b. 1926, Campsie, N.S.W.). Mallen learned trombone at the Conservatorium from Harry Larsen, who had helped Coughlan years before. During the war Mallen was associated with a group of young modern musicians who later played in his band—Dick McNally (trumpet), Ron Gowan (tenor), Johnny Cerchi (alto sax), Andy McIntosh (baritone sax), Ron Falson (trumpet) and Terry Wilkinson (piano). Mallen jammed at the 2KY Swing Club and served his time with various suburban bands such as Cec Williams' Albert Palais Orchestra on Parramatta Road. The sixteen piece Mallen band made its debut in mid-1947 at Bill McColl's Sunday night Swing Sessions at the Radio Theatre. Mallen had all the Kenton Artistry series, some Les Brown material and other good jump music. Accordingly, the line-up was eight brass, five saxes and three rhythm. Their signature tune was 'Leave Us Leap'. Wally Norman helped to coach the band. It made a series of successful concert appearances, lunch-time performances at the 2GB auditorium, played at Sydney University and, from mid-1949 at its most successful venue, the Gaiety, a milkbar with a ballroom out the back in lower Oxford Street, Darlinghurst. The atmosphere was excited and relaxed, both for musicians who actively enjoyed the advanced arrangements, and for the hundreds of 'hep' enthusiasts who came to jive. Musicians were still buzzing from having had the Americans living amongst them. In addition to those above, the band had with it at various times Billy Weston, Norm Wyatt (trombone), Alan Nash, Frank Smith (alto sax), Clare Bail (tenor sax) and Jim Shaw (drums). The band continued its Sunday performances until 1956 when they came to a tragic end. They survived a setback in June 1954 when the Gaiety burned down and destroyed Mallen's library of music and a new amplification system. Mallen took his band to a ballroom in Newtown and acquired a financial interest in a trucking firm, hoping to buy a new library. On 14 December 1956 Mallen was killed instantly when he jumped out of a runaway truck.

Early in 1949 Billy Weston formed a progressive band. While playing with Mallen, Weston was asked by a musician called John Ferguson to rehearse his Kenton-styled band, and Weston ended up taking it over. Weston continued to form bands into the 1970s and has mainly used keen young musicians, leavened

Bob Gibson's band, Earl's Court, Melbourne, 1947.
Back Row L–R: Alan 'Chan' Redding (sax, flute, clarinet), Bob Limb (tenor, clarinet), Bob Tough (tenor, clarinet, flute), Keith McDonald (trombone), Bob Trenberth (trumpet), Bob Storey (alto, clarinet), 'Pappy' McGlade (trombone), Alan Hill (trumpet).
Front Row L–R: Bob Gibson (clarinet, alto), Keith Cerchi (drums), Alf Gardiner (bass), Fred Thomas (trumpet), Jack Wilson (guitar), Ken Weate (clarinet, baritone), Charlie Thompson (trumpet, trombone), Bob 'Beetles' Young (piano), Pam Corrigan (vocals).

with experienced players in the key positions. So in 1952, Doug Foskett in Weston's sax section was playing alongside Frank Smith on tunes like 'Collaboration' and 'Scuffling'. In the 1970s Foskett himself was a key performer in the Daly-Wilson Big Band, forging solos of great drive and swing. Before Weston's band finished in 1955 it had had such good players through it as Dave Rutledge (tenor sax), Ken Flannery (trumpet), Ron Falson and Alan Geddes (drums). The band was based at the Gaiety and did concerts at the Assembly Hall, and occasionally at the Sydney Conservatorium.

Weston took every opportunity to talk to visiting artists from overseas, especially drummers, with whom he had an affinity, because he wanted to know why everything Australians played never seemed to sound like the music which Americans played. Australians played loudly rather than fully. When in rehearsal with Kenton and his sidemen, Weston and other Australians expected to be exhausted after three hours, but only once did they blow hard; the rest of the time they were holding back against the Americans, yet the Americans could blow a passage at *forte* and fill the Stadium, but the Australians could not fill it at triple *forte* because their tones were thinner. They tended to be shy of dynamic contrast, but this was not confined to musicians. As late as 1972, *Music Maker* (Feb.) ran an editorial lamenting the prevalence of sound mixers at Australian concerts who seemed to feel that climaxes were basically impolite, who turned down the volume on soloists and generally distorted the sound of the whole band. But Australian and foreign mixers went to the other extreme in the 70s, amplifying even big bands to physically painful levels. Sheer loudness became a mystique but all it did was make audiences' ears ring. Continuously high volume impedes dynamic contrast more than no amplification at all.

The leading commercial big band of the era was led by Bob Gibson. He returned from England in 1950 and moved to Sydney, and a number of Melbourne musicians moved up at the same time. Though its repertoire was a little conservative, Gibson's band held its place in the jazz concert scene because he had some of the best soloists: Ken Brentnall (trumpet), Johnny Bamford and Wally Norman (trombones), on saxes Charlie Munro, Don Burrows, Dave Rutledge and Errol Buddle, and on piano, Bob Young. The Gibson band played the suburban dance circuit one night a week at the Surreyville Palais for six and a half years and did the Ford Show on radio 2GB for six years. Gibson made a successful transition to television, working on the Bobby Limb shows. He formed his own company in the 1960s to make commercials and jingles for TV, and since 1970, has led the twelve piece band at the Eastern Suburbs Rugby Leagues Club. It was Gibson's honour to be musical director for the first concert to be performed in the General Assembly of the United Nations, on 12 December 1976.

The suburban dance circuit was a steady source of employment until rock and roll came along. Three of the better known circuits were Paradance, High Hat and Metronome, each employing forty or fifty musicians at town halls, Masonic and memorial halls around Sydney. The Metronome circuit was a co-operative run by musicians, which had some of the big names of the jazz concerts playing with them—Frank Smith, Billy Mannix (tenor sax) and Ron Mannix (alto sax), Ron Webber (drums) and Jim Shaw (drums). Their arrangements were a little further ahead than others, the Kenton influence was strong, and they sent two bands to a job, one of which was a girl band. The girls did the donkey work— they were the old-time band while the men featured the modern sounds.

The Sydney ABC Dance Band reached one of the peaks of its career in the late 1950s, particularly in a weekly programme called 'Streamline' in 1957. The seventeen piece band was regarded as the best job in the profession and attracted a wealth of talented performers and arrangers. The sax section, led by Charlie Munro on first alto, produced the most tightly knit and richly ringing sound of the band, despite the remarkable brilliance of the brass.

After helping to promote bop in Sydney, Wally Norman also led bands in the jazz concert era of the late 1940s and 1950s, usually of about fourteen pieces—six brass, five reeds and rhythm—and he made his name backing overseas artists at the Stadium. Norman's first was for Artie Shaw and Ella Fitzgerald in 1954, which was followed by such greats as Armstrong and Buddy de Franco.

Norman was musical director for Les Welch, one of the top popular entertainers of the early 1950s. Welch was accused of copying American records, and this was true for a period, but there was an explanation for it. After the war,

EMI had a stranglehold on the recording industry and were determined to maximise their profit by releasing only one hit from overseas per month, and blocked the release of others for up to six months. Welch and Norman stymied EMI's programme by obtaining a copy of the hit, writing-out the arrangement note for note and had a local artist do the vocal. For example, Larry Stellar would do the Nat King Cole records and Edwin Duff the Frankie Laine ones. The records sold well, broke EMI's grip and forced them to release their hits.

Norman had good business sense and was rarely stumped by any new development. When rock and roll came in, he featured a series of 'Rock and Roll Vs Dixieland' concerts at the Sydney Town Hall; the lineup of his band was nearly the same as it had been in the early 1950s.

Music Maker (Vol. 49 No. 6, Jan. 1954, p. 19) made a prophetic insight into the future of popular music when it reviewed Charlie Lees' contribution on electric guitar at a Brisbane concert—'One can almost visualise, with the coming of television, the tremendous appeal of the guitar player of the future'.

The jazz concert era of the decade following the war saw the consolidation of Don Burrows's expertise. In 1945 he played clarinet on six dixieland recordings by George Trevare's Australians which engulfed the musical communities of Sydney and Melbourne in one of those silly controversies which periodically characterise relations between the two cities. EMI made some unjustifiable claims about the records which understandably raised the hackles of traditional jazz musicians in Melbourne, where dixieland had its best exponents and strongest following. This did not concern Burrows directly, because he did little playing in that style, being employed full-time in Jim Gussey's ABC Dance Band and making appearances with other small modern groups like the Gus Merzi Quintet on radio and Jack Allen's Katzenjammers at concerts.

Burrows resigned from the ABC band, and with musicians Merzi, Jack Lander and Mark Bowden, went to Canada via the USA in June 1950. Burrows met some important musicians and gained confidence from their acceptance of him. It is a pity that more Australians have not been allowed to perform in the USA over the years because of the American 'alien actors regulations'. Well into the 1960s there was a great imbalance in the number of entry visas granted to American and Australian artists.

In Los Angeles Burrows jammed after hours with Tal Farlow and Charlie Mingus of the Red Norvo Trio. He befriended Dave Brubeck, then unheard of in either Australia or America and became his keen admirer. Burrows had a session with Wardell Gray of the Count Basie band where some people mistook him for Buddy de Franco. Unknown to Burrows, Gray was engineering for Burrows to take de Franco's chair on de Franco's departure, and Gray was going to surprise Burrows with it, but because he did not know, Burrows left for England. Gray's letters chased him across the world but did not catch up with him until he got back to Australia.

Burrows found that good American musicians had the knack of complete relaxation, particularly rhythm sections which 'cooked' from the word go, whereas Australian rhythm sections usually sat back and waited to be inspired by the soloist. Burrows was surprised though by how few tunes the top players knew, compared with himself and his colleagues. Australian musicians of those days were expected to play a wider variety of tunes than their American counterparts. A top American could specialize and develop his certain style to an unsurpassed degree. Burrows lamented the fact that he could not specialize on clarinet or alto as he might have in America, without having to play anything and everything from barn dances to modern jazz. No matter how fluent any musician might be at bop, how advanced his knowledge of harmonics, none of it was worth anything if for example he could not play the high part from 'The Golden Wedding'.

Ironically, Burrows's versatility came to work in his favour years later when he took his own quartet back to the USA to appear at the Newport Jazz Festival at Carnegie Hall, New York, in 1972. They presented their normal program which involved a variety of styles. The *New York Times* jazz critic praised them saying, 'The Don Burrows Quartet covered a remarkably wide range of territory in their short programme . . . refreshingly free of stylistic stigmata . . . a strong sense of musical direction . . . never losing sight of the fact that they are a jazz group'.

Bryce Rohde, one of the most adventurous Australian jazz pianists and possibly the least willing to compromise, has lived most of his life in the USA since 1953 and thinks that the broad musical background of the Australian popular musician then, though generally different to the average American's, did equip him well for a musical career. Johnny Hawker (b. 1935, England), a good balladist on trombone, agrees. He was educated at the Trinity College of Music, London University, from the age of eleven, but his training had been so insular that, until he migrated to Sydney and got a job with Wally Norman's band, he did not know who Artie Shaw and Ella Fitzgerald were. The Australian modern jazz musician, and to a fair extent the traditional jazzer too, is likely to have a broad spectrum of ability at and appreciation of, not only different styles of jazz, but also other music from classical to country and western.

Burrows showed that he had benefited enormously from his overseas experience and stole the limelight at many jazz concerts. He worked in the Sydney Trocadero band under Colin Bergersen until 1953, at Joe Taylor's Celebrity Club in a six piece band, 1953–55, at Club 11 and won the *Music Maker* readers' poll of 1957 for clarinet.

The decade up to the mid-1950s saw the movement of talent from Adelaide to Melbourne and Sydney. Like Perth, this was a product of Adelaide's own dance and popular music scene.

Commercial dance palais had opened in Adelaide in the early 1920s: the Floating Palais on the lake of the River Torrens (which used to leak, once caught fire, and about 1929 had a pontoon collapse and it sank); the Maison de Danse in Colley Terrace, Glenelg; the Palais de Danse opened in North Terrace in 1924 and the Chinese Garden, Moseley Square, Glenelg. Other ballrooms which began in the 1930s were the Palladium in Pirie Street, the Bondezvous in Currie Street and the Embassy in Grenfell Street. There was dancing during the day at the Railway Dining-room on North Terrace, and at the restaurants of two department stores, Myers and John Martins. Nightclubs opened in Adelaide in the 1930s, the first real one being the Plaza in North Terrace, then the Blue Grotto in Grenfell Street, and the Tuxedo in a lane off Hindley Street.

Adelaide was close enough to the eastern capitals to receive regular injections of talent. It was the practice to import the first sax and first trumpet from Melbourne to lead the sections of a palais band. The largest dance hall, the Palais de Danse, opened as a variety show, which went broke, went through a pay-as-you-dance period and was taken over by Hugh Carmichael and renamed the Palais Royal. The band was led first by an American drummer, Joe Aronson, followed by Paul Jeacle from Melbourne via a stint at Broken Hill, then an Adelaide trumpeter, Les Sims, who went to the Melbourne ABC Band. Harry Boake-Smith (banjo) had the longest reign. He began at the Palais Royal in 1932 leading an eight piece band which had eighteen year old Alf Holyoak, a pillar of dance and jazz in Adelaide, on sax. While Boake-Smith was popular with dancers and encouraged his musicians, he lacked definite ideas about what he wanted from the band. He led the band at the Palais Royal until 1943, spent a couple of years conducting at the Palladium and eventually died of a heart attack working on a pearling lugger off the Northern Territory.

In 1932, Alf Holyoak (b. 1913) was also playing in the Maison de Danse band which had Tinker Wallace on drums, who had been with Tommy Dorling and His Red Hot Peppers at the Floating Palais. Holyoak's interest in jazz progressed when Harry Bloom visited Adelaide with Howard Jacobs's ABC Dance Band in 1936 and told him to buy all Benny Goodman records and memorise the solos, which he did. Later his other favourite artists were Benny Carter and Johnny Hodges.

The Palais Royal band sharply raised its standards in the years 1947–50 when Hugh Carmichael offered Colin Bergersen the leadership. After the war Jim Davidson wanted to form a thirty-six piece orchestra to tour the world. Harry Wren backed Davidson and a smaller show opened at the Cremorne Theatre in Brisbane, with Bergersen in it, but Wren kept putting Davidson off. Davidson took the show, 'Meet The People', starring Evie Hayes and Wil Mahoney, to Adelaide, but there he quit Wren, so that Bergersen concluded the season as conductor and accepted Carmichael's offer. Davidson went to England, became Assistant Head of Variety (Music) for the BBC and later headed that section, responsible for initiating such programs as 'The Goon Show'.

Within a short time Bergersen had revolutionised the bandstand and the style of playing. There was now plenty of muted brass like Kenton and the band played in tune without blaring. Cynics in the eastern states were favourably surprised by his ABC broadcasts, which paved the way for regular sessions on the air. Two seventeen year old finds he brought into the band were Charlie 'Chook' Foster (trumpet) and Johnny Bamford (trombone). Ten years later, leading his own big band at the Sydney Ironworkers' Club at the foot of George Street, Stan Kenton heard Bamford and offered him a place in his band in America. Bamford won the 1957 *Music Maker* readers' poll for trombone and big band. Bergersen was a quiet, genial man who had a way of making his band work for him; every night musicians tried to make him pleased with what they were doing. He had musicianship, developed during his years at the Sydney Trocadero, and was able to put his finger on weaknesses but in a way which made his musicians want to do it correctly. Bergersen played many instruments, all above average. He had a teaching clinic for band members and interested people on Sundays, teaching them correct embouchure, how to blow for the best volume and drive, and how to get teamwork in the sections. He encouraged Bamford, Wally Lund (piano) and Doug Swanson (sax) to write arrangements for the band. Bergersen continued at Ciros nightclub in Melbourne, his next job, urging Bruce Clarke to write properly for the band. Clarke matured a lot under Bergersen. The Ciros band were so keen on Bergersen that they would do breathing exercises out the back during breaks.

Maurie Le Doeuff, a fine Adelaide reedsman, took over the leadership of the Palais Royal. Geoff Williams (trumpet) was the last conductor before the hall closed.

There were close parallels between Adelaide and Perth in the first post-war decade. The counterpart to Colin Bergersen was Sammy Sharp who returned to lead the Embassy Ballroom band in August 1946 after twelve years in England. In England Sharp had played trumpet with the bands of Ambrose, Geraldo, Lew Stone and Harry Roy, and had lived and worked with Max Goldberg, one of the best English trumpeters before the war. Sharp came back with a new regard for big bands and set about putting Perth music back on its feet. Perth saxophonists left him cold; he called their style, or lack of it, the 'Perth moo', and worked them hard until they could play together. Sharp was a perfectionist and a taskmaster, and elicited the sound he wanted on the new orchestrations he had brought back with him—arrangements by Miller, Herman, Basie, John Kirby and Kenton, before Kenton records had even been released in Western Australia, and before the locals had heard of anyone playing Kenton in the east. Sharp directed Perth's first jazz symphony concert in 1948 using twenty-five musicians—four violins, seven brass, five saxes, flute, clarinet, guitar, two pianos, bass, vibes, drums and tympani. The public gave it a great reception. Sharp's leading tenor sax soloist was Horrie King, much admired by younger musicians during the 1950s.

Adelaide and Perth had their own series of jazz concerts. Bill Holyoak produced the Adelaide Swing and Jazz Shows at the Tivoli Theatre to benefit the Henley Life Saving Club. Sharp initiated Perth's Jazz Jamborees in 1947, with the assistance of Harry Bluck and Wally Hadley. It raised money for the Musicians' Benevolent Fund and still continues irregularly today. Both shows featured a widely mixed program, from traditional jazz through dance bands to modern combos.

The upsurge of young jazz musicians in Adelaide in the late 1940s was the fruition of a unique training scheme begun in the 1930s. Adelaide probably had a greater emphasis on music then for young people than any other capital. The core of it was the Adelaide College of Music, founded in 1932 by J. E. (now Sir Ellerton) Becker. If ever there was a man who epitomised the central character of the film 'The Music Man', it was Becker. In the middle of the Depression he convinced the parents of Adelaide to buy instruments for their children which he imported from the USA so that he could form the Adelaide Drum and Fife Band and the Adelaide Banjo Club. Not surprisingly, Becker is now a millionaire, living on an island in the south Atlantic. As the children grew older it was necessary to form, in 1937, the Adelaide College of Music Military Band. Eventually, the organisation became the Music League of South Australia. The military band was enormous. It had ten sousaphones and the other sections were correspondingly large—thirty clarinets, twenty-six saxophones, thirty trumpets, ten trombones, ten french horns, eight oboes, eight bassoons and percussion. Upwards of two hundred schoolboys participated in an annual music camp in the Adelaide hills, and made a concert tour to Melbourne and Sydney, from Christmas 1936 to January 1937. The band memorised four or five long pieces, wore uniforms and had steps worked out while they played. The College of Music was the focus of teaching in Adelaide, bringing together military, brass, orchestral and dance musicians to tutor the students. Its alumni followed equally diverse paths—Bill Munro, Bruce Gray and Bob Wright went into traditional jazz; Bob Limb, Errol Buddle, Syd Beckwith, Ian Drinkwater and later Bob Jeffery went into dance music and modern jazz.

Limb (b. 1924, Adelaide) and Buddle (b. 1928, Renalla, SA) were taught by Les Mitchell who played in small dance bands around Adelaide from the early 1930s. Mitchell had a beautiful smooth tone on sax, a love of which he instilled in his pupils. Mitchell never tied his students to rules which might result in an uncomfortable embouchure. At fourteen, Limb began sitting in at the Bondezvous and met Maurie Le Doeuff. With him and Mal Badenoch, Limb formed The Jive Bombers. Limb's first fully professional band was for the Supreme Bootpolish radio show, Bobby Limb and the Shoeshine Boys. In December 1941 he met Bob 'Beetles' Young, pianist, the start of a lifelong personal and professional association. Young (b. 1923, Adelaide) did not attend the College of Music, but had lessons from Brewster Jones and George Trenery, a classical pianist and cousin of Alf Holyoak. Trenery taught some of the best of Adelaide's jazz pianists—Lew Fisher, Bryce Rohde and Ted Nettelbeck.

The Palais Royal was closed down in the war and utilised as a canteen by the Red Cross, but Limb and Young got into Boake-Smith's band at the Palladium. At the time Limb was indentured to the South Australian Railways as an apprentice fitter and turner, and formed his seven piece 'Roctette' to play for apprenticeship dances.

Jazz failed to get to Buddle until he went to a swing night at the Astoria Ballroom, run by pianist and dance promoter, Hedley Smith. Some of his friends from the College were performing. Jazz 'happened' for Buddle that night when Limb's tenor knocked him out. Buddle had sold his soprano for an alto sax for country dance gigs, but he was always playing it in the bottom register. He bought his first tenor in January 1946. The robust type of player influenced him on record—Coleman Hawkins, Ben Webster and gradually Stan Getz.

Limb, his indenture completed, and Young left Adelaide for Melbourne on 7 February 1946 to join Bob Gibson's band which they had sat-in with the previous Christmas holidays. Buddle took over all of Limb's jobs in Adelaide except at the Palladium. The Gibson band gave 'Beetles' Young his nickname after they all saw a film about alcoholics, 'The Lost Weekend', with which the band identified. Young was named after a character with the DT's and it stuck. Limb learned of bop in Melbourne, and took lessons from an American Mormon saxophonist, Elder Jackson. Musicians would attend service at his church in exchange for lessons afterwards. Limb developed his talent for comedy with a nightly song with Gibson's band, 'Right in Der Fuehrer's Face', complete with blurts. After Gibson left for England, Limb and Young led a band at Ciros, bringing Bamford over from Adelaide. Limb and Young went to Sydney in 1950, working on radio, in nightclubs, making records and appearing at jazz concerts with Gibson and leading his own band. Though Limb was increasingly performing as a comedian, he received constant praise from critics for his tenor playing until his departure overseas in 1954.

Singing at Ciros was Georgia Lee, more of a cabaret artist than an outright jazz singer, but she is also significant because she is one of the few Aborigines to rise high in the entertainment profession. Lee (b. 1922, Cairns, Qld.), and her sister, Heather Pitt, a good jazz singer in her own right, were taught the songs of the Torres Strait Islanders by their mother, and listened to popular records at home. They started singing for church charity shows and had their chance when Bob Lyons came to Cairns with his US Red Cross Army Show. They came to Sydney with their brother Wally at the end of the war to sing in Tivoli shows. Lee went to Melbourne in 1949 to sing at Claridges, then Ciros. She studied at the Sydney Conservatorium and went to the United Kingdom, securing a one year contract in 1954 with Geraldo's orchestra. Lee and Pitt are still performing in Australia today.

In the 1930s and '40s there were few Aborigines in towns where they might have joined brass bands and learned instruments. White Society never encouraged them and the Aborigines showed little motivation to master western instruments. Since the mid-1960s, Aboriginal communities have sprung up in the poor areas of big cities, but that period coincided with the height of the Beatle era when a whole generation grew into their teens not knowing what a horn looked like. Black Australians, like most white youngsters, were only interested in rock and roll, or country and western. There are still no signs of Aborigines taking up acoustic instruments with the intention of playing jazz.

At the time Limb was making his first records in the 1950s, sound engineers were experimenting with the echo chamber, which, in those days, was a speaker and a microphone at opposite ends of a men's toilet. The inevitable occurred while Limb's wife, Dawn Lake, was recording 'How Deep is the Ocean'.

The Limb troupe—Young, Lake, Johnny O'Connor and Nola Lester—went to the UK for two years. Like Harper, the violinist, who arrived a year later, they learned a lot about professionalism, how musicians there worked and thought, and about their dedication, and Young discovered that he wanted to compose and arrange. They returned in time for Limb to make a successful move into TV, with his Mobil Limb Show, for which Young was musical director and then 'The Sound of Music' show. Television was a boon for arrangers—it ate material. After fifteen years on TV Limb gave all his music to the Rockdale Town Hall Musical Society and it needed a ten tonne truck to take it all away.

As good as he was on tenor, Limb gave warning of the brilliance of Errol Buddle. An Adelaide quartet—Jack Brokensha (drums and vibes), Ron Lucas (piano), John Foster (bass), and Clare Bail (sax)—had an offer of a job in Melbourne, but Bail stayed behind. A few weeks later Buddle received a call asking if he would join them at the Plaza Coffee Lounge, which he did at Easter 1947. He was fired after two weeks but got the job back because every time he played 'Buddle's Bebop Boogie' the audience went wild when he changed key. Buddle had not heard bop until he came to Melbourne. Brokensha was an attraction on such numbers as 'Flight of the Bumble Bee' or Chopin's 'Minute Waltz'. The group was not strictly a jazz group, but mostly played their own arrangements of the standard modern tunes of the day.

Brokensha (b. 1926) was the son of Claude Brokensha, a drummer with dance bands and percussionist with the Adelaide Symphony. Taught by his father, Jack started early on xylophone, drums and piano, and was leader of the Nailsworth Primary School Drum and Fife Band. He made many stage appearances, played over the radio and became a percussionist with the Symphony at fourteen. Brokensha joined the RAAF in 1944, touring the SW Pacific with the 'Gremlins' of the Entertainment Division under the leadership of Ken Wooldridge, who is now a clarinetist with the Adelaide Symphony Orchestra.

The group at the Plaza was called 'The Rockettes' with vocalists Marie Morely and Edwin Duff. Though no one was the real leader, they changed their name to the Jack Brokensha Quartet, which soon became the most popular modern quartet in Melbourne. They performed in the modern jazz concert at the New Theatre on 21 September 1947, played at Sammy Lee's Storkclub and at the Galleon Coffee Lounge. They made a tour of the eastern capitals and some country centres in 1948 and were an overnight success in Sydney, even eclipsing the Mallen band.

Duff was born in Scotland and grew up in Melbourne from the age of four. By 1946 he was singing with a vocal trio called the 'Tunetwisters' and was a featured soloist at Leggett's Ballroom. He was labelled as a Sinatra fan when most other vocalists were Crosby styled singers. But Duff was not a copy of Sinatra, for he was also characterised as a pint-sized Danny Kaye. Duff had his own twinkling personality. He would perform at a concert attired immaculately, if gaudily, in red trousers, green tuxedo, multi-coloured bow-tie, pink socks and black shoes, and his showmanship would bring the house down. Duff and Buddle were doing unison bop choruses before they had heard them on American records.

Ron Loughhead (b. 1929, Gawler, SA) replaced Ron Lucas in 1948. He was one of the best maturing jazz pianists of the time, a good arranger and an excellent accompanist for Duff.

The group planned to go overseas, not to the USA, because they thought they were not good enough, but their plans were shelved when Brokensha had a nervous breakdown at the end of their eastern capitals tour. Buddle returned to Adelaide until Brokensha recovered, extending his versatility by studying clarinet and bassoon with the respective principals of the symphony. The quartet returned to the concert scene in mid-1949 with a new bass player from Melbourne, John Mowson. Mowson has since played with every symphony orchestra in Australia and recorded the recognised concertos for double bass with the Melbourne Symphony. Brokensha organised a twenty piece big band for concert appearances, performing Loughhead's compositions: 'Fantasy in Orchestration', 'Fantasy in F Minor' and his arrangements of Cole Porter and Jerome Kern tunes. Some of these were recorded. They also recorded with Rex Stewart. Loughhead left the group in July 1950 to further his studies in Melbourne. In 1952 one of his songs, 'The Thrill of Your Kiss', was awarded first prize on the American CBS television show, 'Songs for Sale', and Bud Shank recorded a Loughhead composition, 'Dead is the City', when he was in Australia with Sinatra in 1955. Loughhead went to England the same year as musical director for English singer David Hughes, returned to work in TV in Melbourne and then radio in Sydney.

By April 1951, Brokensha and Buddle had decided to go overseas and Brokensha began a round of farewell appearances. Buddle worked in Sydney in Mallen's, Gibson's and Weston's bands. Big band gigs were often hard work, but developed a player in his reading, interpretation, tone and ability to play in tune. Before he left for Windsor, Ontario, Canada, in April 1952, Buddle was *Music Maker*'s popular choice of Musician of the Year.

Buddle played second bassoon in the Windsor Symphony Orchestra and led a quartet in the city. Across the border was Detroit, and Buddle visited Klein's, the top jazz club, a few times before sitting in with Yusef Lateef's group, using his own mouthpiece but borrowing Lateef's sax. The club owner made him the unbelievable offer of taking over the band. Naturally Buddle accepted the invitation and Lateef was fired. There were no signs of bad feelings and later Lateef, Billy Mitchell and Buddle had a battle of the saxes. For the next few months Buddle felt like he was playing in a dream, leading a group which included Alvin Jackson, Frank Gant, and Tommy Flanagan, which later changed to Pepper Adams, Barry Harris, Major Holley and Elvin Jones. These were top American jazz musicians, particularly Jones, who joined Coltrane in 1960 and was a major figure in the evolution of free jazz drumming. Other big names in American jazz sat-in with them. Though American jazz musicians were extremely good, Buddle felt that a good Australian could hold his own, though, like Burrows, he found that American rhythm sections had a different feel, enabling him to think and play entirely new things. Buddle achieved one of his musical goals in Detroit, that of being able to play what he heard in his head. Woody Herman asked Buddle to audition for his band, and though he did not get in it, he often sat-in Herman's band when it was in town.

Meanwhile Buddle had been writing back to a pianist friend in Adelaide, Bryce Rohde (b. 1923, Hobart, Tas.), suggesting he come over, which Rohde and Brokensha did in February 1953. Rohde's real interest in jazz began when he heard Raymond Scott on 'V' Discs while recuperating from an appendicitis operation in an American hospital in Moratai. Back in Adelaide, working as a pastry cook with his father and already with seven years classical training, he took a couple of jazz lessons from Hedley Smith, though his main development came through playing with Alf Holyoak's band at the Tramways Ballroom, Hackney, which was playing Benny Goodman Sextet and Artie Shaw Grammercy Five tunes. Rohde also led a trio at the Swing and Jazz Tivoli shows and broadcast as a soloist on the ABC's program, 'Handful of Keys'.

Rohde and Brokensha took local work in Windsor and were joined by an American, Dick Healey (reeds, flute, bass). By December 1954 they had almost given up the idea of an Australian group because of visa difficulties, when the owner of the Rouge Lounge and manager of Chris Connor, Ed Sarkesian, needed a band to back Connor, and took them on. Buddle had also written to Burrows, but there was not time and the Australian Jazz Quintet (AJQ) was formed. Edwin Duff came over but by then they were established as a jazz group and could not take on a singer. Rohde and Healey wrote their first arrangement which used flute, bassoon, vibes and piano, an unusual combination which lent them an original and successful sound, and elicited a lot of interest from jazz and symphony enthusiasts. Buddle made the bassoon swing as few others could and was the first to use it extensively in jazz. Sarkesian became their personal

manager, helped them organise a contract with Joe Glazer of the Associated
Booking Corporation in New York and Connor brought them to the attention of
the Bethlehem Recording Company, for whom the AJQ made several records
over the next few years which were released world wide. Their first concert was
in Washington DC with the Dave Brubeck Quartet, the Modern Jazz Quartet
and Carmen McRae. They often backed McRae on club dates in the first few
months until they were well enough known to branch out themselves, touring
major cities across the USA playing at the foremost clubs, including Birdland,
New York, and Carnegie Hall, where their versatility was remarked upon by
critics. They backed Billie Holiday for two weeks in Miami, and appeared on
Steve Allen's 'Tonight Show' on TV. The AJQ played on the recording of 'Porgy

The Australian Jazz Quintet, 1958.
Back Row L–R: Ed Gaston (bass), Errol Buddle (tenor, bassoon), Dick Healey (flute, alto), Jack Brokensha
(percussion).
Centre: Bryce Rohde (piano).
From the original *Music Maker*, Vol. 4, No. 5, Oct. 1958, cover, in the Mitchell Library.

and Bess' which featured Mel Torme, Frances Faye, Duke Ellington and Russ Garcia. Each November for three years they did one-nighters in a Jazz Package which included Count Basie, Gerry Mulligan, Miles Davis and Errol Garner. The AJQ had the fifth highest earning capacity in the USA, behind Armstrong, Shearing, Brubeck and Mulligan. Buddle was favourably placed in the tenor sax and miscellaneous sections of the *Down Beat* magazine poll. After twelve months they added Jimmy Gannon on bass, allowing Healey to concentrate on flute and alto. Jack Lander, the Australian, took over from him for a year in August 1956, and was followed by Ed Gaston.

The AJQ were at their peak in 1958, but were homesick too, and the quiet and unobtrusive Buddle wanted to settle down. They met Clem Semmler who was on a world tour for the ABC, who made arrangements for the quintet to tour Australia in November 1958. Apart from Buddle, the group intended to return to America, but Healey and Gaston met girls on the ship and those ideas disappeared. Only Brokensha went straight back and is now a studio musician for Motown Records, Detroit.

The Australian Jazz Quintet won audiences with their rapport, self-assurance and smooth delivery, but in Melbourne there was a small group of primarily young musicians who, though they acknowledged the virtuosity of the playing, were disaffected with the light, cool, comfortableness of the style. Australian jazz had been captured by 'cool' in the 1950s. By the time the controls needed to finance post-war reconstruction had eased, allowing more records in from overseas, bop had been overtaken by cool in America. Bop was designed to be non-commercial and initially succeeded (though thirty years later Charlie Parker records enjoy quiet, but steady sales), so bop records remained scarce while cool conquered. In the late 1950s, the circle of young Melbourne musicians whose activities focussed on the Jazz Centre 44, were finding their way out of cool back to bop and into its successors, hard and post-bop. Before they are discussed, there was a mature musician in Melbourne who was playing harder than anyone— Frank Smith.

Frank Smith (1927–1973) was a fat, gruff, argumentative, shy, outstandingly talented alto saxophonist. He was an original thinker with an unusually broad musical horizon who did a lot to get Australian jazz out of the doldrums. He also played the tenor, flute and clarinet well, and enthusiastically passed on his knowledge to his students. Smith began on tenor in the Sydney suburb of Canterbury, doing his first gigs accompanying his father who played piano. He did not know that tenor did not quite suit him until he made the acquaintance of Rolph Pommer, the leading alto of the day, and then he began to turn many heads. Smith quickly learned more on alto than Pommer could teach him. At about twenty, Smith began to lay his foundations, gaining experience in most of the name bands in Sydney—those of Coughlan, Mallen, Weston, Gibson, Kanitz, Craig Crawford and lesser known ones besides. Smith performed at most of the jazz venues—the Roosevelt, the Australian Jazz Club, Club 11, Club 7 under the State Theatre, the El Rocco, and won the 1957 *Music Maker* readers' poll for best alto. Sometimes though, Smith's personal life was disorganised, and the young musicians were saddened to see him driving taxis for a living. With the exception of Charlie Munro, no one played the way Smith did. For a young Bob Bertles, now himself an internationally experienced saxophonist, hearing Smith play 'All the Things You Are' on an old silver alto with rubber bands on it so the keys wouldn't fall open, was like listening to Charlie Parker. That inspiration has stayed

Cover photo of the winners of the instrumental sections of the Music Maker *1957 Readers' Poll at EMI recording studios.*
L–R: Freddy Logan (bass), Frank Smith (alto), Ron Webber (drums), Dave Owens (tenor), Johnny Bamford (trombone), Ken Brentnall (trumpet), Terry Wilkinson (piano), Don Burrows (clarinet, holding flute), Mal Cunningham (flute, holding baritone).

From the original *Music Maker*, Vol. 3, No. 4, Sept. 1957, in the Mitchell Library.

with Bertles. Smith, like Weston, was not a person to hang back if he thought something was musically wrong and would try to correct it politely, but if that did not work then he would find some other way. He put many noses out of joint because he was constantly questing to improve his own playing, but he never failed to encourage anyone who had aspirations and ability.

Smith was the first jazz musician to discover Raymond Hanson at the Sydney Conservatorium, and through Smith, Hanson became a key figure behind the jazz scene. Hanson taught the Hindemith method of composition, a twelve tone system, the rules of which forced jazz musicians to think in new areas. He taught counterpoint and construction, making musicians aware of the relativity of intervals and helping them to learn to arrange. The Sydney Conservatorium was not run by the university, so anyone with musical ability could study there. Many found that half an hour with Hanson left no time for any other thoughts the rest of the week. In the fifteen or twenty years after Smith went to him, Hanson's pupils included Bob Young, Don Burrows, Clare Bail, Billy Weston, Ron Falson, Neil Thurgate and Graeme Lyall. Charlie Munro had the lessons secondhand through Don Harper in exchange for lessons on modal music. Hanson was a musician's dream. Hanson loved jazz, and after work he occasionally sat-in with jazz bands around town. His repertoire of ballads was limited but he performed advanced chord changes on them. Smith once talked him into writing an arrangement for the Gaiety band, 'Moonlight Becomes You', which was harmonically exciting but did not swing—as if Stravinsky had written for Woody Herman's band.

Smith would have liked to teach at the Con, but they were not interested; a pity, because he was probably the best sax teacher Australia has had. The evidence of it can be heard in Graeme Lyall, Doug Foskett, Tony Buchanan and to a certain extent in Bernie McGann.

Smith improved his tone by corresponding with teachers at the Paris Conservatorium, and got clues about production techniques through endless talks with Harry Larsen. There was enough experience in Australia for a rare individual to build on and create his own style which compared favourably with standards in America, without having gone there himself and before many Americans had come here.

Smith's chance to lead his own band came at 'The Embers', a nightclub opened in August 1959 by Jimmy Noall, a man who periodically had his name in the papers when one or another of his acquaintances bombed his house. That sort of tension was sometimes felt in the club; the Negro musicians imported especially from San Francisco to complete the five piece band, Wilmus 'Steak Eyes' Reeves (piano) and Carl Brown (bass), refused to play commercially (variously known in the trade as 'Craven A' or 'Mickey Mouse' music), the management returned them to the USA as their contract stipulated, but only as far as Hawaii. Though Noall's other activities were questionable, he did have a genuine interest in jazz. The Embers was an expensive jazz restaurant in Toorak Road, South Yarra, part of the international jazz circuit, and was theoretically a coffee and cola venue only. Frank Thornton, an American saxophonist who had been in Australia and New Guinea during the war, led the band until fire destroyed the club on 7 November 1959, whereupon Smith took over, fronting Billy Weston, Mike Nock (piano), Peter Robinson (bass) and Chris Karan (drums).

Robinson's chair was soon taken by Dutch bassist, Freddie Logan, and the rhythm section, also known as the 3-Out Trio, was then the best and 'hip-est' small group in Australia. Nock taped four of his compositions and sent them to *Downbeat* in 1961, who awarded him a scholarship to Berklee College in Boston. Since then Nock has worked with the Yusef Lateef Quartet, the John Handy Quartet, Art Blakey, the Mel Lewis-Thad Jones Big Band and was musical director for Dionne Warwick. He co-led a band in the USA called the Fourth Way which was a pointer to the fusion of jazz and rock. Karan, born in Melbourne of Greek descent, became drummer for the Dudley Moore Trio in England and Logan played there with Tubby Hayes.

Smith was rhythmically innovative with The Embers band, exploring interactions within the melodic, harmonic and percussive aspects of music. Many Australian drummers used to drag, or play 2 and 4, and rhythm sections played straight up and down, without an edge. Smith tried to change this. When the band was Lyall, Nettelbeck, Wright and Turnbull, once a week Smith wrote exercises for them; they would have to phrase together rhythmically but each would have his own melody as well. Wright and Turnbull would have their own sessions together, just playing time for hours on end. After months of this they were very 'together' and still click today. Smith made sure they were all playing their instruments the right way and treating the music seriously. He wanted them to convey not just rhythm, but the beauty and drama of music, to create something. The easy way out was to play what they knew they could play well, what they were accustomed to, what their record collection was about, but Smith wanted them to create, to express themselves. Smith did not sound like Ornett Coleman or Coltrane, his style and sound were his own, though he could give a first rate imitation of Paul Desmond, or anyone else. His harmonic thought was original, and he used his sax to approximate the human voice, crooning, howling and jibbering through it.

Being self-taught, Lyall had learned the wrong way and had reached the point where he could go no further. Smith made him start all over again, spending the first three months getting Lyall's production correct. Fingering and harmonics came later. Smith used to finish at The Embers about 3 a.m., Lyall would wake him at 10 a.m., and the lesson would continue for up to ten hours, Smith never taking any money for it and becoming so involved that Lyall's attention never wavered. Smith wrote all the exercises himself, difficult, every note different and unexpected; weird leaps without sequence. Once Lyall could play them he was totally familiar with his instrument. Lyall is a wizard of the tenor sax.

Smith had a finely developed ear, as Bob Sedergreen (piano) discovered on his first gig with him. After The Embers, Smith went into jingles and studio work with Bruce Clarke, who wanted him because he played with such authority that any band gelled with him in it. Sedergreen arrived to find Smith hiding behind some curtains, embarrassed because he had not done a job outside the studios in so long. He asked Sedergreen for a chord to warm up on and, in a moment of devilry, Sedergreen bashed out the most difficult chord he could contrive. Smith silently looked him up and down, as if to say 'You're a smart little boy', and proceeded to run up and down every note he was on. Sedergreen suddenly realised how good Smith was. Much of the drama in Sedergreen's playing with the Brian Brown Quartet reflects his contact with Smith.

The 1960 tour of the Oscar Peterson Trio, with Ray Brown (bass), and Ed Thigpen (drums), was the first clear example of what Smith was getting at in relation to 'time'. Brown gave Thigpen a terrible trip, leaning over him and between smiling teeth, constantly ordering him 'up' or 'back'. One Sunday afternoon session at the Embers, Smith was playing 'I Could Have Danced All Night' and had his eyes closed. The Peterson Trio crept in and swapped over with the band, and created the most exciting music Lyall had ever heard. Peterson was impressed too, because when the next act arrived, the Benny Carter Quartet, Carter walked in asking where Frank Smith was, and when he found him exclaimed, 'So you're the one who's going to blow my arse off!'

Smith was a hopeless businessman and spent the last two or three years of his life paying off the debts he had incurred when he went into business for himself. Except for money, he was close to mastering everything that he did—children's stories, TV scripts, drawing cartoons. He was as near to jazz genius as Australia has produced.

A characteristic present in all societies, but one which Australians think is more prevalent in their own, is that of being scared of doing something which might not be accepted by one's fellows, which, for a musician, results in a 'safe' and usually uninspiring level of performance. Frank Smith's playing appealed to young musicians who did not want to play safe, who desired to extend themselves. For them technical fluency was not an end in itself, but desirable only in so far as it enabled them to say something.

The Jazz Centre 44 in the old Katherina Cafe, St Kilda, was run from 1955 to 1960 by a stocky Berliner, Horst Liepolt. It was a centre, not only for modern jazz, but also traditional jazz, folk music, and poetry and jazz recitals. When Liepolt moved to Sydney in 1961, his wide ranging and sure business touch took him into the management of discos and rock bands, musical direction of films and art galleries, and production, promotion and publicity for all types of modern jazz. He was turned on to jazz in 1944, hence the name of the jazz centre and his record label, started in 1975, '44 Records'. He was a tour manager with bands in Europe before coming to Australia in 1951. Liepolt's wide experience and dedication to music have gained him the confidence of all his musicians.

An important band at the centre was the Brian Brown Quintet. In the 1950s there appeared to be a black and a white approach to jazz. The black approach, emanating from the east coast of the USA was the stronger of the two, though it was less available on record to the Australian listener. Brian Brown (b. 1933) was the prime mover of the group of musicians interested in the black school. Brown enjoyed the traditional jazz of the Bells, Barnard and Johnson bands at the Brunswick Town Hall and tried to play cornet with the Coburg Central Brass Band when he had to do his National Service because he had heard he could get out of marching that way. The army said, 'No son, you just march'. At Northcote High School, which has produced a good number of musicians, Brown was friends with Johnny Fordham (drums) who, though never a big name himself, encouraged others by his openness and enthusiasm. He helped Graeme Morgan, Peter Martin and Alan Leake get into jazz. Fordham took Brown to a Downbeat concert and pointed out the tenor sax that Splinter Reeves was playing. Brown bought one at age nineteen and practised like mad, because he was labouring during the day and needed the escape. He had gigs with Fordham, John Martin

Russell's big band, William Flynn's Orchestra at the Caufield Town Hall and at the Melbourne Trocadero in Mick Walker's band. Early in 1955, Brown and three friends went to the UK. Brown bummed around, studied theory and composition with Eric Gilda of the London School of Music and discovered Miles Davis on record. The jazz climate was healthier there, with many visiting Americans, and there was a greater diversity of records. Brown returned in March 1956 and found musicians who were immediately receptive to the black way—Keith Hounslow (trumpet), and Stewie Speers (drums) who swung. Speers (b. 1928) had beautiful time, especially on cymbal, hard and straight ahead, with the message on his kit, 'Art Blakey for Pope'. Each took his turn to have a birthday so they could get a liquor licence for the jazz centre, but there was little money in it, so Speers also worked in trad bands and Brown in the palais. Brown's quintet began with John Shaw (piano) and Dave Anderson (bass), but soon settled down to Dave Martin (piano), still a schoolboy, and Barry Buckley (bass). Brown had a bank draft with an American distributor who sent out new records as they were released, enabling Brown to introduce pieces by such innovators as Miles Davis, Charlie Parker, Sonny Rollins and Benny Golson. Brown also began to compose in the same vein; tunes such as 'Warm Up', 'Diggers Rest' and 'Hilltop'. The quintet broke up in 1960, and Brown got married and worked as a musician in TV.

Of the new drummers, Graham Morgan (b. 1937) was the foremost. In the early 1950s, he was one of the first to read a book by Jim Chapman, with whom he studied twenty years later in New York, which helped him refine his practical experience and gave him a basis for expressing himself. At age seventeen he led a quintet at Downbeat concerts, performing bop numbers, and turned professional the next year. Charlie Blott gave him his first job at the Savoy Plaza. Morgan was another who practised for long hours. He went to California in 1962 to live and work with American musicians, and studied under Murray Spivak, Louis Bellson's teacher. Reading and independence, the ability to play different rhythms simultaneously, came easily; endurance and speed he had to work at. The end result was a drummer with the best hands in the profession, a top studio musician much in demand by visiting artists. Morgan backed Cleo Laine and Johnny Dankworth on their 1972 Australian tour, and they took him on their tour of the USA in 1973, culminating with a concert at Carnegie Hall which was recorded and released by RCA.

The vibraphonist Alan Lee (b. 1936) led a quartet which played regularly at the Jazz Centre 44. He bought his first vibes while doing his National Service at Puckapunyal, but the motor was so noisy that he could hardly hear himself play. He did not obtain a decent vibes until the import restrictions were lifted and he could get one from the USA. He went through various stylistic stages, wanting to play like Lionel Hampton, then Milt Jackson, and at the same time gaining equal pleasure from playing guitar in dixieland bands. Lee and drummer Ted Vining played with Frank Gow, a traditional pianist, and Lee spent three years with Ken Jones's Powerhouse band until he was fired for throwing up on the bandstand. There was always a smattering of modern musicians amongst traditional bands because there were few places to play modern. Lee had an aggressive attitude to music; he once broke the whole keyboard of a vibes, made of aluminium alloy, because he played so hard. Lee needed someone to complement his style, and in

Ted Vining (b. 1937, Sandringham, Vic.) he found a loud, exhilarating drummer who shared his approach. Vining had had half a dozen lessons from Morgan and was a cool stylist until he heard the Brian Brown Quartet and immediately changed direction.

The seat of the action in the late 1950s was in Melbourne; the new generation of Sydney musicians knew it and made efforts to get down there often. Australian society was more mobile by then and it was possible for a young man to hitch-hike from one city to the other in a day. With television studios flying artists interstate and Lee Gordon bringing out overseas acts which needed musicians to back them, the barriers between the musical communities of the two cities were coming down.

The main spot for modern jazz in Sydney was the El Rocco, a plumber's workshop and boiler room at the top of William Street in Kings Cross which was converted into a coffee lounge in October 1957 by Arthur James. Initially it operated as a jazz cellar only on Sundays; everyone watched the Steve Allen 'Tonight' show on television, then they would switch it off and jam until twelve. Television made big changes in entertainment. The Paradance at Lidcombe advertised that it was the first ballroom to install a TV set for its patrons to watch between brackets. They did not even dance during commercials.

At first the El Rocco was for established musicians. The new ones were gaining experience at the Mocambo Lounge in Newtown at a scene started by John Pochée and Dave Levy.

It is immediately obvious that John Pochée (b. 1940) is not an average drummer. Though he is right-handed, he unconsciously learned to play left-handed because he had a weak wrist, but his kit is set up as if for a right-handed player. He was one of the first to play with both hands downwards which, before rock, was considered wrong. Allan Geddes assured him that whatever was most comfortable was correct. Pochée is the son of an undertaker and his father's aunt played drums. His mother and elder sister used to go to jazz concerts at the Sydney Town Hall and Pochee would lie awake waiting for them to tell him who was on or what colour suit Edwin Duff was wearing. At eleven he used to lie about his age so he could be in the studio audience to watch the band doing the Bobby Limb radio show. The drummers around town that he liked were Lennie Young, Geddes, Jimmy Shaw who was more aggressive than the Sydney average, and Cyril Bevan, an Englishman who played with finesse. Don 'Slick' Osbourne had returned from England with bop techniques and was dropping bombs on drums at the Club 11, where Pochée met a slightly-built pianist, Dave Levy (b. 1936, Hobart).

Levy discovered what it meant to be Jewish while doing National Service. One thousand men on Sunday parade, the Catholics fell out, Church of England, Presbyterian, Methodist and so on until a solitary figure remained, drawing unto himself the complete and undivided attention of the officer in charge who, when he found that Levy's Sabbath fell on a Saturday, left him to his own devices: music. A pianist in the entertainment band showed Levy some chord progressions.

Some friends of Pochée's sister opened the Mocambo Lounge in 1956 and invited him to jam on Saturday nights. Pochée and Levy were playing material like Brubeck's 'Jazz Goes to College' record—very cool, a lot of brushes. Pochée was offended by hard players like Bob Bertles. The word gradually spread and more musicians came to the Mocambo to sit-in, including Bernie McGann (b. 1937, Kogarah), an apprentice fitter who played alto like Paul Desmond, which was great for the prevailing Brubeck mood. His practising was driving everyone mad and the neighbours threw rocks on the roof, (these days they send in requests).

Pochée attributes his progression out of cool to an unusual bop singer who burst in from the street at the Mocambo, scatting, Joe Lane. Lane always had a briefcase with the latest 'Bird' records and some sticks, because he was also a drummer. He once hitched to Melbourne in three days carrying a complete drum kit. Lane was forever knocking on people's windows at 4 a.m. with the latest releases, sleeping on the floor for three days then off again, shaving in railway stations. He gave Pochée a thorough grounding in bop, Rollins, Blakey and Miles Davis.

Pochée went to the El Rocco and convinced them to turn off the TV on Friday nights too, so that he, Levy and McGann could play. Gradually they built up an audience and started to get paid. Kings Cross was an exciting place; people would sit in the family car to see the bohemians and wicked types stroll by; Pochée enjoyed playing to the strays from the suburbs because he could see them getting involved without knowing anything about the music. He became discouraged with drumming in Sydney and took a job on a ship plying between Sydney and Melbourne, and eventually moved down there in 1959. Joe Lane lived at a place called Muttering Lodge and then they moved to a place in St Kilda with cabins out the back they called Junior Muttering. Many musicians stayed there, including Keith Stirling (trumpet), Graham Morgan and Mike Nock who slept on a roll of underfelt next to his schoolcase with Onehunga Marist Bros. written on it. Anyone visiting from Sydney dropped in. Life was a nightly hunt for somewhere to play. They might set up on the lawn or ask Lane what was on and end up driving around at 3 a.m. with some sly grog looking for a mythical party. Failing that, they would go down to the beach and set up on the promenade.

One day at Junior Muttering, a teenage lad whom nobody knew asked if he could play with them on sax and nearly blew them to pieces. Graeme Lyall had a lot going for him even before he met Frank Smith. Lyall (b. 1942) first heard the sax when his father was an innkeeper in Bairnsdale and an all-girl band came to town. He played in a couple of brass bands and then joined an instrumental rock and roll band, The Thunderbirds. Lyall, Bob Bertles (b. 1939, NSW) and Col Nolan (b. 1938) were the first serious jazz musicians to have a solid background in rock. Bertles played baritone sax with Johnny O'Keefe and the Dee-Jays for four years from 1958 and Nolan played piano with them 1961–62 and led his own Soul Syndicate from 1961 into the 1970s. Rock was good experience, professionally and musically, if only in terms of developing stamina and volume. In the early days only the guitars were amplified, and Lyall and Bertles had to play so loudly that they finished the night doubled-up in pain and vomiting because of cramps in the diaphragm. But it developed a reserve of power in them which lends a certain strength to everything they play. The other musicians in the Dee-Jays were not as ignorant as the general public or their own stage act made them out to be. Musicians in leading bands of any type rarely are. They were interested in Miles Davis and Coltrane, and appearing on Lee Gordon shows gave them a chance to meet good overseas musicians. Bertles was surprised by the competent trumpet playing of Frankie Avalon who was a fan of Clifford Brown. Graham Morgan avoided early rock, but paid his dues in the mid-1960s in Sydney, and in the 1970s played the funky rock of George Benson and Billy Cobham, a style which demanded substantial experience in both rock and jazz, because rock has its own distinctive feel.

Pochée was briefly a member of a forgettable rock band called Barry and the Planets at the Coburg Town Hall. Unemployed musicians worked as bouncers and Joe Lane was the Pepsi-Cola man, until a rival promoter sent in a bunch of thugs who beat up everyone except the band—end of rock for Pochée.

JAZZ DAGS

AFTER the Pacific war a different element appeared in the Australian jazz world, the dixielanders or revivalists, musicians who wanted to play only traditional jazz. They were not a breakaway group because most of them had never been part of the established jazz and dance scene, nor did they have any desire to become part of it. They were a new and separate community of amateurs and semi-professionals devoted to one type of music, and their aims, their stories and their heroes were different. They succeeded in creating their own scene.

The event which gave a focus and an identity to the traditional jazz community was the Australian Jazz Convention, first held in North Melbourne, 26–30 December 1946. It was so important to the traditionalists that they have held one every year since, making it the oldest jazz festival in the world. About fifty people, mostly men in their early twenties, gathered to meet and play together in a casual atmosphere. There were four bands, whose members have become the veterans of Australian traditional jazz—the Barrelhouse Four led by Tom Pickering from Hobart, the Southern Jazz Group led by Dave Dallwitz from Adelaide, and two Melbourne bands, Tony Newstead's band, and the band which was the backbone of the convention and of traditional jazz, Graeme Bell's Dixieland Band.

Graeme Bell (b. 1914) and his brother Roger (b. 1919) came from a musical family. Both their parents had been on the stage: their mother, Elva Rogers, was a contralto who had toured Australia and New Zealand with Melba, and their father had been in musical comedy. The boys were steeped in classical music and studied piano. Graeme studied for six years, taking honours in piano and theory for the Intermediate Certificate at Scotch College in Melbourne. Roger began playing popular songs on ukulele with a friend he met in the Scouts, Ade Monsbourgh (b. 1917) who played piano, banjo and mouth-organ. They interested Graeme in light music and together they did their first job as Gay's Swing Gang at the Deepdene Scout Hall (Graeme's nickname was Gay). When Roger was sixteen the brothers pooled their money to buy Roger a drum kit. In 1936 they were engaged as a four piece band and they asked Tom 'Red' Crowe to play with them.

Crowe, on tenor and alto, was associated with them for the next three years, and also with a trio led by a photographer friend, Cy Watts, on piano, and John Parker on drums. There was no one they could approach to learn about jazz, but Crowe had an instinct for improvisation and was an inspiration to his friends. His ambitions were different as he wanted to join bigger bands, so he worked on his reading and technique, became a member of Mick Walker's fourteen piece band and was the only member of it to be asked to join Jay Whidden's band at the Palais de Danse.

Monsbourgh's strict Baptist family frowned on his going to the Palais so he went to Melbourne University to study metallurgy. With his friends from Scotch College, Sam Benwell and 'Spadge' Davies, Monsbourgh formed the Melbourne University Rhythm Club in June 1937 to promote interest in 'the cultural worth of hot rhythm and modern music'. Their band was called the Shop Swingers. This involvement of university people with jazz was a major departure from previous patterns in popular music, because few professional dance musicians had university training, musical or otherwise, and university students have been a solid core of support for jazz ever since.

While Monsbourgh was deepening his knowledge of Negro jazz, particularly the records of Clarence Williams and the alto saxophonist Jimmy Shine of the Washboard Rhythm Kings, Roger Bell became interested in the lyrical cornetists and trumpeters, especially Bix and later Bobby Hackett, and he switched from drums to cornet in 1938. Through Roger, Graeme finally caught the jazz bug when he was twenty-two and was elected to the committee of the 3AW Swing Club. Graeme was influenced by pianists such as Joe Sullivan and Jess Stacy. Graeme knew a pianist, George McWhinney, who had a quartet which used a double bass, an innovation at the time because most groups would not use a bass until they had about seven players. The Bells thought it lent swing to the whole sound, so they advertised for a bassist and Billy May answered. May went on to become the maker of the high quality Maton guitars. The bass in the quartet gave bounce and proved to be a novelty with their audiences.

Still they did not know if they were heading in the right direction. The Muggsy Spanier Ragtime releases of 1941 were a source of reference for them and they met an American ship's carpenter, 'Chips', who had a record collection which impressed them. The Bell brothers opened an account with a record store in New York. The person who helped to set them on the right track was a Melbourne lawyer, William H. Miller, whom the traditionalists call the 'Dean' of jazz critics. He was educated at Melbourne Grammar and went to Oxford in 1933, where he won blues for rowing and law. Jazz was his hobby. He attended rhythm clubs in London and returned to Australia in 1938 with about six hundred jazz records. In 1939 he broadcast a weekly program over 3UZ called 'Jazz Night', using his own record collection. Miller wrote the show and Johnny McMahon, a singer in the Palais, presented it. The Bells made contact with Miller when they heard the program and Miller invited them around to his home for cakes and ale evenings to listen to his collection in sombre earnestness.

That year the Bells, with Monsbourgh on banjo, Spadge Davies on clarinet, Tom Crowe on tenor and Keith Wathen beating a suitcase, made a private recording of 'Ain't Misbehavin'' and 'Tin Alley Ramble' at a local studio under the name of 'The Original Tin Alley Five'. Tin Alley was a small lane in the university grounds. Things began to move for them and they were saving up to go overseas when the war put a stop to their plans. This was one instance where the war retarded the growth of Australian jazz, though by holding them back, the Bells were much better at jazz by the time they finally did leave for overseas. Don 'Pixie' Roberts (b. 1917), clarinet and alto, joined them in 1940. He had been playing a weekend gig at Saul's Coffee Lounge with a small group. Initially he leaned towards a more modern style but came round to the Bells' way of thinking. Russ Murphy joined soon after on drums.

1941 was a fruitful year. In March, Graeme Bell secured a three months' engagement to play on Sunday nights at St Leonard's Cafe at the St Kilda Baths on the Lower Esplanade. They attempted to play strictly hot music with no concessions to commercialism. During intermissions Don Banks and Charlie Blott played modern jazz. In October at the Hotel Australia, Graeme Bell's Jazz Gang played for the third annual exhibition of the Contemporary Art Society. The society was a breakaway group from established art schools and was creating a stir in Melbourne. The Bell band was at the exhibition to present modern music, as dixieland was then known: the term 'traditional jazz' did not come into general use until the 1960s. This was an important show for them because they were heard by the right people, that is, other intellectuals. It was a minor coup to get them on side because the Bells' music then gathered an intellectual aura about it. What the Bells were doing was no more and no less 'intellectual' than what Frank Coughlan had done years before, the difference being that it was now seen to be 'intellectual'. Professional musicians were bemused by the way the Bells turned their refusal to play any other music to their own credit, because it has never been shown that playing diverse styles of music hinders the execution of any one of them, but their determination to stick to their favourite was admirable and good publicity.

Among other tunes the band played 'Muskrat Ramble', 'Royal Garden Blues', 'Jazz Me Blues', 'Dippermouth Blues' and 'Chinatown'. This was two months before Lu Watters's Yerba Buena Jazz Band cut its first recordings and shows that quite independently the Bells had reached back to the same source of inspiration as their San Franciscan contemporaries. Much has been made of the debt the Bells owe to the Watters recordings, but it is obvious that the Bells were mature musicians completely familiar with the genre for years before they heard Watters in the mid-1940s.

The first of the little magazines devoted to the interests of traditional jazz enthusiasts, *Jazz Notes*, began publication in January 1941, before American journals like *The Record Changer* and *The Jazz Record*. *Jazz Notes* was the organ of the 3UZ Jazz Lovers' Society. William H. Miller was the editor. *Jazz Notes* was concerned only with 'righteous' or 'strictly hot' jazz. The first issue included a biography and part discography of Wingy Manone and an article on New Orleans by Tom Pickering. George M. Avakian, a Master Sergeant in the US Army, contributed a regular article called 'Backdrop to Jazz' during the war. Unlike *Music Maker*, *Jazz Notes* and other magazines for the jazz buff such as *Australian Jazz Quarterly* (1946–56), *The Beat* (1949), *Quarterly Rag* (1955–67, 1976–), *Jazzline* (1968–), or *Jazz Down Under* (1974–), rarely had technical articles; their concern was history and criticism. An Australian, John Kennedy, published the first sixteen issues of *Matrix* (Oct. 1954–May 1957), a magazine for record collectors which is published in the United Kingdom today.

1942 was a quiet year for the Bell band. Graeme sometimes played with Gren Gilmour's band when it played at the Geelong Palais. Like many swing bands it would do a dixieland bracket, but it was pseudo-dixieland because they had not studied the style as deeply as Graeme had. He was medically unfit for active service because he suffered from spondylitis, but he played for the American Red Cross.

While Graeme was in Queensland, Roger Bell secured one of the best engagements the band ever had, Saturday nights at the Heidelberg Town Hall, from July 1943. This was the first venue at which they built up a loyal following and it helped them to blow out more. Cy Watts was on piano, and Monsbourgh, who had played piano and banjo through university, was on valve trombone. In September the band began a two year stint on Thursday nights at the Palais Royale, playing opposite the swing band. The Bell band provided a contrast because they did not read from music and they were more animated. Fans would stand watching all night. Graeme returned in 1944 but Monsbourgh joined the RAAF, so it was not until the end of the war that the band was reunited at the Uptown Club.

Though the Bell band was central to traditional jazz in Australia, they were not alone at the fountainhead. This they shared with the Barrelhouse Four from Hobart. The formation of this band paralleled the experience of the Bell band. Tom Pickering (b. 1921, Burra, SA) was the son of a bank manager and both his parents had an active interest in light opera. Pickering's first musical experience was playing fife in the Burra Drum and Fife Band. There was no musical outlet for him when the family moved to Albury, but this changed when they moved to Hobart when he was twelve. Pickering made friends with Ian and Cedric Pearce, who lived in the same street, and began comparing notes about the tunes they heard on the radio. Together they started the slow and exciting task of compiling a record collection, occasionally pooling their lunch money to do it. They swiftly dismissed schmaltzy dance numbers and bought records like Goodman's 'Walk Jenny Walk', Teddy Wilson's 'You Turned The Tables On Me' and Crosby, Waller and Armstrong discs. Pickering was so interested in music that his father promised him a clarinet if he passed his exams. He had his first taste of audience excitement when he performed an unexpected jive item at the school break-up concert. The Pearce brothers learned classical piano. Ian bought a trumpet from a secondhand store and Ced had a Chinese tom-tom which he covered with newspaper for a snare effect. The rest of the kit was a collection of tin lids on which he did his best to emulate Dodds, Bauduc and Singleton with two canes. Pickering met a pianist at school, Rex Green, and played jazz records to him until he became interested and joined them, making the Barrelhouse Four in 1936. Their first job was for a twenty-first birthday party and their second at a show for girl guides. They played anywhere for anything. Pickering had a few lessons on clarinet and seized any opportunity to play, even at the rehearsals of a military band. Relations with dance musicians were amicable though their interest in pre-swing forms of jazz was viewed with amused tolerance. Pickering and Ian Pearce often played with local dance bands. Pickering was regarded as the hot player of

This band became The Barrelhouse Four with the substitution of Ced Pearce on the drums. Hobart, 1938. Tom Pickering (tenor), Rex Green (piano), Ian Pearce (trumpet), Michael Maxwell (drums). Ced Pearce's caricature appears on the drum.

Max Humphries's band. He also took up tenor sax and had some lessons from Rick Coulson from Melbourne. As the Barrelhouse Four achieved greater public acceptance, the dance bands incorporated more jazz numbers into their repertoire.

Though their own generation liked what they were doing, Pickering and the Pearces sensed that they were considered to be rebels; it took some independence of mind to play jazz. Hobart's social atmosphere was very close for boys from respectable families, as illustrated by a friend who played with them occasionally and who committed suicide because he could not stand the shame after being arrested for drunken driving.

The Barrelhouse Four had jam sessions at Fouché's Stage Door nightclub and performed in a variety show in 1939 called 'Red, Hot and Blue', with music by Darryl Miley who became head of light entertainment for the ABC. The band made its first ABC broadcast about the same time, possibly the first Australian traditional band to go on air. Still they were feeling their way and did not know about the Bells or Watters. Then they heard of William H. Miller and sent him a private recording of 'Memphis Blues', upon which he perceptively commented, sometimes favourably. This put them in touch with a wider jazz community.

The war split up the Barrelhouse Four; Ian Pearce and Rex Green were sent to Darwin where they heard American musicians in the flesh for the first time; Ced Pearce served with the medical corps and edited *Jazz Notes* from 1941 to 1946 while Miller was serving. Pickering was sent to Melbourne and met Miller who took him to hear the Bell band at Heidelberg. Tom can still remember the thrilling sensation he felt when he walked through the door and saw the first jazz band other than his own that he had heard.

There was an immediate and lasting rapport between Pickering and Roger Bell. Like many others in the jazz world, they appreciated the humour of the jazz decades—Thurber, Wodehouse, W.C. Fields, Chaplin—and in their conversation, a penchant for the spontaneous, deliberate misinterpretation of intention. Pickering's interests ranged broadly. He had attended art school for a year and still dabbles in paint, and he had a flair for literature. In 1967 Pickering won first, second and third prizes in a short story competition run by the Tasmanian Fellowship of Australian writers. He is Tasmania's parliamentary librarian, and not surprisingly, the parliamentarians can find in their library a representative selection of jazz records.

After the war the Barrelhouse Four reassembled and made a few recordings at a local radio station, some of which Miller released on his label, Ampersand. In 1946 when news came to them of the proposed jazz convention, and though Ced could not make it, they decided to go; they were the smallest band there.

The origins of the South Australian jazz band which attended the convention do not go back as far as the Tasmanian or Melbourne groups. On average, the members of the Southern Jazz Group were ten years younger then the Bell band. The jazz scene began in Adelaide in 1941 with the formation of the Adelaide Jazz Lovers' Society. Clem Semmler, later deputy general manager of the ABC, was its president. During the late 1930s he had what was probably the first jazz program on ABC radio in South Australia. Bill Holyoak, the secretary, also had a jazz program on radio, 'The Real Swing', for about fifteen years. He owned an impressive record collection which he built up through correspondence with collectors around the world. The society brought together a diverse array of talent: musicians who were to go into palais and mainstream/modern jazz like Alf Holyoak, Errol Buddle, Maurie Le Doeuff or Bob Limb, and musicians whose interests lay with traditional jazz, like Dave Dallwitz, Bruce Gray or Bill Munro. There was not the same clear separation between modern and traditional in the early days in Adelaide as there was in Melbourne—one of the first rehearsals of the Southern Jazz Group was held at Errol Buddle's home—though as their careers developed they went their different ways.

The house band of the Society was Malcolm Bills's Dixieland Group. Bills (b. 1925, Peterborough, SA) was a dental student at the university. He was a friend of Bob Limb who had a band of young musicians which played big band arrangements, and Bills took lessons in modern chords from Walter Lund for a year before Lund joined the army. Boogie-woogie was all the rage and Bills gained a reputation for it. At a welcome night for new students at the university in 1943 he was told of three musicians playing at the Adelaide Technical School.

They formed a band—Bill Munro (b. 1927) on a Harry James kick on trumpet, Bruce Gray (b. 1926) on clarinet, and Bob Wright on drums. As in Melbourne, the university crowd was a mainstay of the band; they did the faculty balls and private parties though Bills was the only student. They rode their bicycles to their gigs, a difficult task for Wright who negotiated each journey with his kit strapped all over his body and his bike. The band made a recording, played on the Australian Amateur Hour and on Bill Holyoak's show. They had not heard about the Bell band in Melbourne. Bills liked Teddy Wilson, Waller, Stacy and Hines, but he had not heard much of Jelly Roll Morton or similar artists, so he did not lead the band to the early styles of jazz. Some influence in this direction was given by Nick Stefakis, a trumpeter and mechanic who raced motorcycles in Melbourne, who came over late in the war and played with them. Bills often listened to a US Airforce band in Adelaide during the war which played Glenn Miller tunes, and a small group from it played dixieland.

Some time in 1945 Bills rang Gray and Munro saying he had a tall, skinny trombonist, Dave Dallwitz, who wanted to come out and practise with the band. Dallwitz (b. 1914, Freeling, SA) was a painter and art teacher. Many musicians apply their manual dexterity in other ways, and by profession or as a hobby they are artists, dentists, fitters and turners, mechanics, printers or architects. Dallwitz had private tuition on violin when he was nine, heard his first jazz record, 'Mississippi Mud', when he was fifteen, taught himself piano at sixteen and

The Southern Jazz Group from Adelaide at the 1948 Australian Jazz Convention in Melbourne.
L–R: Joe Tippet (drums), Dave Dallwitz (trombone, leader), John Malpas (banjo), Bill Munro (trumpet), Bruce Gray (clarinet), Bob Wright (tuba), Lew Fisher (piano).

became fully interested in jazz at Teachers College when he heard Ellington's 'Mood Indigo'. He took up trombone at twenty-eight and later classical cello and bassoon, and studied composition, harmony and counterpoint at the Adelaide Conservatorium. Dallwitz began playing in a band called the Southern Jazz Group led by Dave Jenkins, trumpet. Over the Christmas holidays in 1945 Dallwitz went to Melbourne to meet the Bells and other 'jazz dags' as they called themselves. There happened to be a few visiting from interstate and what occurred was a spontaneous convention. They agreed it would be a good idea to organise one the next year. During 1946 Dallwitz took over the Southern Jazz Group, made some personnel changes and made it a well-schooled strictly traditional band. Dallwitz was good at transcribing parts from records and working out chords, and he introduced to his band a lot of the early jazz they had missed.

A curious aspect of traditional jazz in Australia was the absence of a Sydney band from the first convention and the domination by Melbourne of that scene for the next twenty years. The history of amateur and semi-professional music-making in Melbourne goes back a long way; Frank Coughlan, who spent a good part of his working life in Melbourne, observed in 1933 (*Music Maker*, 1 March 1933, p. 12) that there were many more keen amateurs of a high standard there than in Sydney. There were fewer opportunities to become professional musicians in Melbourne and it was a conservative city: the Methodists, Presbyterians, Baptists and other Protestants considered it was not entirely respectable to frequent palais for dancing. If a few more Catholics had been in power there might have been horse racing up and down Swanston Street on Sundays. A lot of entertaining was done at home in Melbourne, perhaps because of the colder climate, and many Melbourne homes were built for this, especially in the south-eastern suburbs where there are houses with rooms that are virtually small ballrooms. Customs of entertainment were slightly different in Sydney: there were more commercial ballrooms and because there was more money for music, especially during the war, if a musician reached a professional standard on his instrument then he had a good chance of earning his living by it, if he played the music that was popular. Because of this, dixieland was despised as something you rose above. But Melbourne, because it was a tough town for musicians, forced many good players to remain amateur, and because they were amateur they were free to pursue their own interests. Melbourne's conservatism, in part a desire for the best of any particular thing, had a positive result. Dixieland musicians researched their subject thoroughly, they knew more tunes than their Sydney counterparts, they sharpened their talents, their bands stayed together longer because there was nowhere else to go, so they developed their own style and eventually created their own jobs. The traditional jazz revival was focussed in Melbourne after the war because more of the new generation of jazz musicians remained amateurs, while in Sydney they were sucked into the mainstream. Melbourne musicians, because they were good, rid dixieland of its inferiority complex.

Jack Parkes formed the first traditional band in Sydney. He began to collect jazz records in 1939 and was a member of the Sydney Swing Club run by Ron Wills at the Blue Tea Rooms in Rowe Street. Visitors to the 2KY auditorium, like Monsbourgh and Pickering, often stayed at Parkes's home. Parkes and Ken Olsen sneaked through the grounds of Sydney University one night to listen through a broken window to Monsbourgh and Pickering play with a band which included Kelly Smith, clarinet, and Jim Somerville, piano, and Clive Whitcombe, drums. Parkes bought a trombone and got together on Saturday afternoons with Don Burrows's circle—Yank Christian, Joe Singer, Ron Falson—but felt they were too jivey. He met Jack Petty, clarinet, at the 2KY sessions, and with Harold Kellet, trumpet, Alf Feeney, piano, and Mal Cooper, drums, they began practising at a hall in Rockdale. Parkes met a trumpeter with similar ideas, Ken Flannery, who was playing with a small swing group at the Bondi Esplanade, and he and a banjo player, John Sweeney, joined the band. The Port Jackson Jazz Band was underway in 1944. With Duke Farrell on bass they cut their first acetates in January 1945, 'Guzzlin' Blues' and 'Darktown Strutters Ball'. Flannery went into the army and while he was away Parkes and Falson formed the Darlinghurst Dixielanders. After Flannery returned from the war there were a few changes in the band. Bob Cruikshanks, who replaced Petty, learned of Parkes and the Bells while serving with Tony Newstead at the RAAF Base at Tocumwal. Also the pianist and drummer were changed. The Port Jackson Jazz Band sent acetate recordings to the first convention, which were favourably received, but soon afterwards Parkes was eased out. Flannery was the outstanding member, a hot inventive player, and he attracted musicians of a similar calibre. Parkes had had tuberculosis in his youth and did not really have enough wind. He had not kept pace with the improvement of the rest of the band.

In Queensland and Western Australia traditional jazz was only just beginning in 1946. Sid Bromley organised a jazz club in Brisbane and a band called The Cane Cutters. For Ellis Blain's Swing Session on ABC radio it recorded such songs as 'Who's Sorry Now', 'Moonglow' and 'Rehearsin' for a Nervous Breakdown', but the band was not as traditionally minded as the southern groups and was primarily a broadcast group. There were not enough interested young people to form a jazz club in Perth, but Keith Hounslow and friends formed the Westside Jazz Group. Neither of these bands attended the first convention.

When the four bands from Melbourne, Hobart and Adelaide assembled at the 1946 convention, it was the first time many of the players had heard another jazz band and they realized that each had a slightly different approach to the music they loved. The Southern Jazz Group had the strictest attitude, eschewing a piano and using washboard instead of drums. The rhythm section had a lighter feel than the Melbourne bands, primarily because Bob Wright played a smaller tuba than that generally favoured, and he was one of the few bass players who could successfully negotiate a solo on tuba. Gray and Munro were evenly matched in the front line: Gray, a perfectionist who was respected by all Adelaide musicians, traditional and modern alike, and Munro, a highly creative trumpeter with Bix influences but who displayed his own strong directions in his playing. Tom Pickering and Ian Pearce rejected the exclusive 'trad' label and aimed for a looser style; they retained traces of the small swing groups of the thirties which inspired their love of jazz and they have been noted for using tunes which are rarely played by others. The Newstead band was a collection of strong, independent personalities, particularly George Tack on clarinet and Willie 'The Lion' McIntyre, a showman on piano and when singing the blues. They favoured the Chicago style because it gave each individual freer rein to express himself.

Graeme Bell's Famous Dixielanders (later Graeme Bell's Australian Jazz Band) at the first Australian Jazz Convention, Eureka Youth League Hall, 104 Queensbury Street, Melbourne, 1946.
Back Row L–R: Ade Monsbourgh (trombone), Roger Bell (cornet), Don Roberts (clarinet), Lou Silbereisen (bass).
Front L–R: Jack Varney (banjo), Russ Murphy (drums), Graeme Bell (piano).

The star band was the Bells'. They used a two trumpet lead and the Watters influence was noticeable, though it was more a gel for their ideas than an inspiration. The musical impetus of the band came from Graeme and Roger Bell and Monsbourgh, and the fusion of their different interests gave them their own ensemble sound. Individually, they felt they could not equal the early greats, but collectively, by not trying to sound like any other band or trying to reproduce an old-time atmosphere, they created a genuine sound that reflected who they were. Monsbourgh was the outstanding player of the band, though as yet he was not playing alto on which he expressed himself best. He did not touch the sax until he was over thirty. In 1946 he was playing trumpet and valve trombone, but with an intensity, simplicity and spontaneity of invention that made him an influence on all front line players at the convention. Monsbourgh liked slow tempos and had the Bell band playing with a loping, buoyant pulse which has come to be known as the 'Melbourne bounce'.

The Bell band and one of the second generation of Melbourne bands, Frank Johnson's Fabulous Dixielanders, were most closely identified with the Australian style of jazz in the decade following the first convention, but there was a characteristic which was not dependent on the two trumpet lead which was shared by the other bands at the first convention and which has kept cropping up in subsequent decades in bands of diverse line-ups and styles, which makes jazz as played in this country distinct from jazz played elsewhere and recognizable as 'Australian'. It is a spirited, uninhibited, uncontrived, guileless excitement which comes out most strongly in the vigorous ensemble sound. Often it is heard more in front lines with two reeds than two trumpets. The Australian sound is more readily distinguishable in traditional than in modern bands. Perhaps this is because traditional players all begin by studying the same fixed body of recordings from the 1920s. They collect an essential library of the early works, study and absorb them, and then whatever is Australian about them begins to show through. Not all Australian trad jazz musicians play 'Australian' jazz. If they have not fully assimilated the early works, but remain copyists, then the distinctive flavour is absent.

This process has been aided by the conventions. For more than thirty years an annual interchange of ideas has occurred. The early conventions were like a small brotherhood of musicians so involved with one another they did not need anyone else. The conventions quickly achieved their aim of increasing the popularity and prestige of jazz, and as they succeeded, so more musicians and fans attended. Records by Australian bands sold well and were heard on the radio, which reinforced the development of an Australian sound. The influence which Australian records had on local groups is illustrated by the dismal frequency with which 'Ugly Child' has been re-recorded by various bands. 'Ugly Child' is a witless, bludgeoning song of no credit to performer or composer, which retains a place in bands' repertoires seemingly because the Bells did it, while a song by Fats Waller, 'Your Feet's Too Big', which treats the same subject, non-love, with more humour, does not appear as often, seemingly because the Bells did not. 'Ugly Child' was popular with audiences too, and bands will usually play what they know will be well received.

Traditional jazz in Australia is, to a certain extent, the product of purely local factors. Jazz is found mainly where there were palais and brass bands before the war. This can be shown by comparing the history of Newcastle with Wollongong, two heavily industrialised coastal cities to the north and south of Sydney respectively. In 1971 the population of Newcastle was over 146,000 and Wollongong's over 161,000, but Newcastle's jazz scene was much stronger and had been so for decades. This is explained by the fact that all of Wollongong's expansion occurred after the war; in 1947 Wollongong's population was about 18,000 whereas Newcastle already had a population of 127,000. The seeds of interest in traditional jazz must have been sown by Newcastle's Swing Club, its own palais bands and by the visits of Sydney dance bands, and not just by records. This suggests that the separation between the professional dance musician of the 1930s and 1940s and the budding traditional scene was not as distinct as might first be supposed. Newstead took some lessons from Coughlan, Warwick Dyer and Doc Willis took some from Roger Smith, Flannery from John Robertson, Jack Parkes from Harry Larsen and so on. The connection should not be ignored. Australian traditional jazz is in part an outcome of local factors which can be traced back to the beginning of professional dance music in Australia.

The first convention was held at the Uptown Club at 104 Queensberry Street, North Melbourne, in the premises of the Eureka Youth League. The Eureka Youth League in Brisbane also made its premises in the Rationalist Hall available to a jazz club. The Eureka Youth League, which began in 1941, was a left wing society with strong communist affiliations which took up jazz as a cause of the proletariat. They thought jazz was the Negroes' protest at the conditions of life and felt it could be related to Australian working class traditions. The Eureka Hot Jazz Society was formed in mid-1944. If the organisers had really wanted to make jazz a part of working class life they should have gone as cadres to where the working class took its leisure, in the palais and old-time dances in town halls, but since they rather wanted to run their own jazz club, their audiences were comprised of jazz enthusiasts who came from all classes. The middle and upper class fans who had the gift of the gab dominated the league and were disliked by some of the factory girls who resented being called 'workers' as if this meant 'mascot'. Music and politics have little bearing on each other. The appeal of jazz is wide, and from a performer's point of view the only important thing is to have people filling the seats; it does not matter what their consciousness is as long as they are enjoying the show.

Because they took an interest, the Eureka Youth League have the credit for sending the first two Australian traditional bands overseas, the Bell band to Czechoslovakia in 1947, and the Southern Cross Jazz Band from Sydney through Mainland China to Moscow ten years later.

Most Australian jazz musicians are practically apolitical. Only in exceptional circumstances, such as the 1975 constitutional crisis when only one Sydney band would accept an engagement with the Liberal Party, do they take an interest. Yet Graeme Bell was actively involved with the EYL and sympathised with their youth work. Bell came from a family of independent thinkers. His grandfather was an engineer and an Eight-Hour Day pioneer. Bell's band started at the Uptown Club in November 1945, though Monsbourgh, Kelly Smith, Jack Varney (piano, banjo) and Bill Rogers (drums) had been there since September 1944. The club became the centre of jazz in Melbourne.

Before he became fully engaged with jazz, Graeme Bell had studied art with Max Meldrum, and he had connections with Melbourne's art world. When war broke out and prevented them from going overseas, Graeme and Roger invested their savings in a block of land at Eltham near the artists' colony. On Sundays the jazzers would go there, help clear the land and make mud-brick houses.

Traditional jazz was affiliated with the intellectual foment occurring in the art and literary world. Avant-garde artists, film makers and writers frequented the Uptown Club. Max Harris edited and the Angry Penguins literary group printed the souvenir program for the first convention. Dave Dallwitz was among the artists who broke away from the Royal Society of Arts when it was set against Modernism and he was elected president of the new Contemporary Art Society in 1942. The artists viewed their paintings as a weapon of protest and felt a common bond with jazz because they saw in jazz freedom of expression and revolt against the accepted and conventional.

Cover of the souvenir programme of the first Australian Jazz Convention, Melbourne, 1946.

But though Sidney Nolan was a personal friend of Graeme Bell, though jazz bands played at artists' exhibitions and Clem Meadmore designed covers for the Bells' record label, none of the big names who emerged at that time, such as Tucker, Boyd or Percival, painted anything about musicians. The subject of a piece of art lies deeper than the object being represented, so there is no more reason that artists should portray musicians than they should paint plumbers or butchers. The absence of anything to do with jazz was because artists and musicians were off on different tacks in defining what it was to be an Australian. Australia was a society which felt it had few traditions and, consequently, there was a tendency for people to attach themselves to what they saw as 'authentic' or 'real'. The results of this could be seen well into the twentieth century: the educated classes fawned on England and were content to import culture like consumer goods, but this produced an automatic disbelief in local endeavour. Artists were in the forefront of intellectuals who broke out of this alignment and began looking to Europe, but if you accept that jazz and popular music have been one of America's major cultural contributions to twentieth century life, then the professional dance musician's shift of his focus of interest from European popular music to the musical culture of the American Negro was even greater. However, artists seemed to retain the idea that the locale of authentic experience was somewhere other than where they were. When two world wars convinced them of a malaise in European civilisation, they wanted to reject it. They turned their sights on the Australian countryside; the bush became a dominant theme of as great a cultural significance as it was to the writers of Lawson's time. Artists repeatedly portrayed stark figures against a dry landscape, almost transmuted into a part of that landscape. Ultimately, the land of Australia may well be the determining factor which gives Australians unique national characteristics, but the reality is that Australia is still very much an urban society. The significant expressions of cultural activity have been made in the towns and cities. By saying that 'real' experience lies 'out there', artists failed to come to grips with that. Jazz musicians were different; they were an expression of life in the city; they are what they play and they play what they are.

Only one musician, Dave Dallwitz, who is also an artist, has applied himself to many of the same themes that have occupied the painters and writers, e.g. Ern Malley, Ned Kelly, scenes of the gold rushes and the bush, but Dallwitz has also written a Melbourne suite. It is good that Dallwitz has tackled these themes through jazz—someone would have had to do a tune on Ned Kelly sooner or later —but his tunes have a significance in themselves quite apart from their titles. The question of the origins of inspiration is a vexed one. Few tunes have the same identity between sound and title as say, Ellington's 'Solitude', yet if all Ellington's pieces had just been given consecutive numbers as titles, his work would still have had as much importance for the jazz world. So too with Dallwitz: quite apart from whatever has inspired him, his tunes have a life of their own because they are well written, and they contribute to the literature of Australian jazz tunes.

John Sangster has composed many tunes directly inspired by the bush, but his message is very different from the artists'. His aim on the album 'Australia and All That Jazz' was similar to, though not directly comparable with, the work of John Gould, the ornithologist. Sangster loves the bush and attempted to depict musically its various aspects—the animals, their movements, the colours and the sound of the vegetation—which is not what the artists were using the bush to convey. Sangster has also drawn extensive inspiration from J. R. R. Tolkein's books, 'The Hobbit' and 'The Lord of the Rings', and a young modern composer, Craig Benjamin, has written suites inspired by the poem 'The Wasteland' by T. S. Eliot and the book by Joseph Conrad 'The Heart of Darkness'. Are these any less 'Australian' for not having an Australian title? What you hear when listening to Australian jazz is the expression and fulfilment of men with a passion in life, which is not mindlessly happy nor woefully despairing, but reflecting the joys and sorrows of reality as they find it.

Dixieland jazz men were not entirely free from the tendency to attach themselves to an 'authentic' tradition. Especially in the early years of the revival when their youthful fervour was at its peak. the dixielanders claimed that only they played 'real' jazz and dismissed bebop as 'meaningless proficiency' and big band jazz as decadent. Even Graeme Bell came under fire at the seventh convention because he dared to play Ellington pieces from written arrangements. In those days, if a musician did not play like an American jazz star then other jazzers were not interested. Greater maturity has brought with it an encouragement of individual styles. Allied to the idea of 'real' jazz was an insistence on 'purity'. Many played beaten-up instruments that would hardly blow because it matched the image they were trying to cultivate. Saxophones were absolutely forbidden and the ability to read was regarded with faint suspicion. Ade Monsbourgh called the purists the B flat boys and he did a lot to break down the anti-sax barrier.

One leading Melbourne trad player did not want to play any of his instruments too much because he did not want to become too good at them. This was a civilised version of the cargo cult, for no Jew or Christian would have entertained the idea of hiding his light under a bushel and no professional musician would have purposely left his talents undeveloped. This attitude was not howled down by other trad players, and its general, if tacit, acceptance was the result of a romantic, overblown notion of the early days of jazz. This view suggested that the birth of jazz was the result of some immaculate conception by Negroes contemplating their navels in New Orleans and that it would be wrong to develop their skills too far lest they lose their freshness and innocence. Apart from being absurd in itself, that idea ignored how much effort the Australian had already expended to reach the stage of playing dixieland at all, and inhibited him because he was overly conscious of being middle-class and white. The romantic view of jazz emphasised that Bunk Johnson was found working in a cotton field and was given a new set of teeth so that he could blow again, but downplayed the fact that at age seven he began taking cornet lessons from Professor Wallace Cutchey of New Orleans University. The romantic view said that Negro jazz was spontaneous but white jazz was a contrived deliberation; that you had to suffer, you had to be an orphan from the wrong side of the tracks before you could really play jazz. It glossed over how many important musicians had received academic tuition. Jazz has remained vital because it has received people from diverse backgrounds, but the romantic view emphasises only the deprived origins. The point needs to be driven home: the following American jazz musicians born before 1920 (listed in John Chilton, *Who's Who of Jazz* [Philadelphia, 1972]) received conservatory, college or tertiary education, not always in music: Lil Armstrong, Chu Berry, Johnny Best, Jimmy Blanton, Cab Calloway, Bob Crosby, W. C. Handy, Glen Miller, Pee Wee Russell, Fletcher Henderson, Don Redman, Claude Thornhill, Teddy Wilson, Gene Krupa, Jimmie Lunceford and three of his band, Jay McShann, Red Norvo, Stuff Smith and Art Tatum. Half of these were Negroes. Education, if anything, facilitates spontaneity. It would be hard to list all the American jazz musicians who played music while at secondary school. America produces so much good music partly because music is a feature of the education system. By contrast, the status of music in Australian schools has been so low that children are lucky if they learn to blow their noses.

Australian dixielanders were reacting against the commercialism and gooey sentimentality of the swing era, and their inability to understand bop made it easy for them to dismiss it, but their music was no more 'real' than the other, and their fashion for playing dented instruments was simply the reverse side of the coin of the tinsel and satin of a swing band.

The association of traditional jazz with the other intellectual groups in the 1940s had a peculiar long-term result. It is an odd thing that though professional dance and jazz musicians have a longer history than the traditionalists, though they have produced excellent musicians, though they had a trade journal for forty years, though they make more money—the professional dance, studio and modern jazz musician received little recognition from the opinion makers. When Max Harris writes about jazz in the newspaper (e.g. *Australian* 19/2/72, 15/6/74) he refers only to traditional jazz and he implies, by default, that there was no jazz before the Bells nor any apart from the traditional scene. The two most famous names in Australian jazz are Don Burrows and Graeme Bell and many people think that because, historically, modern jazz developed from dixieland, Burrows came out of the traditional scene centred on the Bells. Nothing like that happened. Modern jazz in Australia developed out of the professional dance bands whose origins go back a quarter of a century further than traditional jazz in Australia. The two streams are fairly independent of each other; traditional jazz is the basis of nothing but itself. Both streams deserve to have their history written but, by and large, the opinion makers of today are conscious only of one side of the story because so many of them were amongst the avant-garde of the 1940s who identified with traditional jazz. Being amateurs, they had to develop other skills to earn a living and some became journalists or history lecturers, but professional musicians remained just that, musicians. There are amateurs in modern jazz too, but not as many. Who will tell of the talent of Charlie Munro, or Frank Smith, or the other outstanding modern players unknown to the traditionalists? Not the opinion makers. The first book about an aspect of Australian jazz was written by a traditional jazz pianist, Dick Hughes, who is a journalist, and, naturally, he wrote about the scene he knew best. The jazz community which has more people with literary skills interested in it will have its history better recorded. Such are the unwitting and unintended origins of distortion in history.

That there were two distinct communities was evident in Melbourne. It was more a geographic than a social separation; most of the traditionalists came from the suburbs to the south and east of the city whereas the men who went into the palais bands or became modern jazz players, came from the industrial suburbs to the north. The Bells grew up in Camberwell, all the Frank Johnson band lived in the Brighton–Caulfield area, the Barnard band came from Mentone and Newstead was brought up in Prahran. Amongst the modern jazzmen, Bruce Clarke, Alan Nash and Freddie Thomas came from Brunswick, Brian Brown from the Carlton area, Don Harper from Seddon, Billy Hyde from Moonee Ponds, Graham Morgan from East Brunswick and Wally Norman from Ascot Vale. There was some overlap in the central suburbs whence came Don Banks from South Melbourne, Alan Lee and Tony Gould from Albert Park and Middle Park and Charlie Blott from Elsternwick. There is an idea that life in Australia has been insulated and debilitated by suburbia. Suburbia did not stop jazz. The traditionalists and modernists came from working and middle class back-grounds, but a far greater proportion of musicians from the southeastern suburbs took tertiary qualifications, usually in a field other than music. The palais musician was usually working professionally by the end of his teens and seemed to have neither the time nor the inclination to study. For all their idealism

Charlie Munro in January 1979 at the Sydney Town Hall, with Bruce Cale (bass) and Alan Turnbull (drums).

regarding the proletariat, the Eureka Youth League was blinded by the image of the suppressed Negro and allied itself to a more upwardly mobile group than to those musicians who fitted more closely the classic picture of the working class. There was some animosity on musical grounds between the two groups at first but this has diminished over the years and the communities are more involved within themselves than they are bothered about one another.

The Australian Jazz Convention has remained firmly traditional and makes no claim to represent any other jazz. The ice was broken in 1974 when Clark Terry was brought out for the twenty-ninth convention. The convention has been more tolerant of other styles, but it will not become a Newport-type festival because that is not its aim and because it would not work without the supporters. Alter the aims and format and you alter the type of fan who attends and is willing to work for it. The reunion of friends is almost as important as the music presented. It has the same meaning to the traditional community as the eisteddfod has to the Welsh. Above all, it is fun; where else but at a convention in Cootamundra would the curtain open to reveal thirty naked banjoists playing 'The World is Waiting for the Sunrise'?

The conventions showed the public that jazz was something other than darkie music from the brothels played by degenerates, and they kept jazz going while square dancing and Hawaiian music were more popular. Before the war good jazz was seldom heard on radio, but by 1949 there were five regular jazz programs on the air in Melbourne. Commercial radio played an active part while there was a surge of popular interest, but since then their record has been lamentable. The ABC provided the lion's share of quality jazz broadcasting by securing the services of dedicated and knowledgeable commentators such as Ellis Blain who recorded the first convention, Alan Saunders, Clem Semmler, Eric Child, Arch McKirdy, Ian Neil and Jim McLeod. Their low-key programs were for people who actively listened and between them they covered the whole range of jazz. When they began, the ABC was not sure that it was the proper thing for a cultural station to do with taxpayers' money, but it is ironic that jazz now stands in the same relation to the ABC as classical music. The ABC management does not interfere with the programs compiled by their staff, though once, in April 1975, they tried to remove Eric Child. An unprecedented and at times vitriolic response from listeners quickly convinced them that Child was indispensable. Radio is an important link in the jazz world.

The event which most popularised jazz with the public was the successful overseas tour of the Bell band, renamed Graeme Bell and His Australian Jazz Band, in 1947–48. The Eureka Youth League helped to raise part of their fare because the band was going to appear at the World Youth Festival in Prague, Czechoslovakia, 20 July–17 August 1947. It was organised by the World Federation of Democratic Youth with the aim of bringing together musicians, sportsmen and artists from all over the world. Harry Stein, a drummer and president of the Eureka Hot Jazz Society, accompanied the band as manager and spokesman. After the festival Mel Langdon, an ex-RAN Lieutenant, took over as manager. While the Bells were doing their farewell fund-raising concerts they received the pleasing news that an American jazz critic for *The Jazz Record* (Feb. 1947), George Avakian, rated Roger Bell's 'Alma Street Requiem' ninth in the ten best records of 1946 and classed it as the best foreign record of the year. At one of their Sydney concerts in April, Frank Coughlan performed with them. They recorded six sides for Columbia at Homebush, three of which were original compositions. 'Smokey Mokes' backed with 'South' was a hit. It would have earned them a gold record if that award had existed then. Geoff Kitchen played on the session instead of Pixie Roberts who was nursing a fractured knee-cap after getting drunk and riding a Harley Davidson motor-bike through a wooden door. The Bells' last Australian performance en route to Europe was an impromptu concert at the University of Western Australia at the request of the University Labor Club.

The Bells performed at the Smetana Hall in Prague, a hallowed centre of classical music in Czechoslovakia. With some inward misgivings they launched into 'Creole Belles', but they were received with great applause. The Czechs' uninhibited feeling for jazz was a pleasure to the Australians. An engagement for one month followed at the Fenix Karvarna, a large coffee lounge in Prague. They spent four and a half months in Czechoslovakia playing all over the country often at factories during lunch hours. A UNO film unit made a documentary of the festival which showed the Bells' rendition of 'Ballin' the Jack'. The Bells recorded fourteen sides for Czech Supraphon, including Graeme's 'Czechoslovak Journey' which he had composed before he left. While on tour they recorded eighteen sides for French Pacific, four for English Tempo and eight for English Esquire. Their trip took them to France, Belgium, Holland and England. At the *Gare St Nazaire* in Paris customs officials suspected them of trying to smuggle musical instruments and asked them to prove they were musicians. The Bells obliged with an on-the-spot concert at the station. They were apprehensive about playing for the discerning audience at the Hot Club in Paris but again they were warmly received and had to do an encore. On the strength of that a second trip to France was arranged for two months later. While in Europe the Bells heard some of their heroes in the flesh, including Louis Armstrong, Baby Dodds, Pops Foster and Jack Teagarden.

The Bell band made an enormous impression in Britain which was on the verge of its own traditional jazz revival. They found many young bands making a sincere attempt to play jazz but which were stuck with an overly intellectual approach to it. The Bells were like a breath of fresh air. 'Jazz for dancing' was their philosophy. They opened their own club in the West End one night per week and the police asked them to open twice a week because patrons were clogging up the footpath. Australian traditional jazz made an impact on London's cultural scene long before the artists Nolan, Boyd, Percival and Tucker became expatriates there. The Bells gave impetus to British amateur bands, especially Humphrey Lyttleton's, and formed a public for live jazz. Acker Bilk was influenced by Pixie Roberts's clarinet style. The Australians were a lesson in proper presentation and showmanship, their individual style pointed up the traps of shameless copying from old records, and they were one of the rare bands to feature their own compositions.

Travelling overseas boosted the Bells' confidence. Due to their isolation in Australia and the newness of what they were doing, until they had made their trek they could not be certain that they were good. Their trip proved it beyond doubt. American *Downbeat* magazine carried a full page story on the band which praised them as being better than the bands of Spanier, Watters or Condon.

Graeme Bell and his Australian Jazz Band returned to Australia in August 1948. They were greeted by 1300 fans at Perth. The ABC organised a national tour on which they played to packed houses everywhere. Russ Murphy wanted to resume his studies so Charlie Blott took over the drum seat and Ian Pearce toured with them on trombone. The band was fêted by 'society': it was a prestigious

TONY NEWSTEAD'S SOUTHSIDE GANG

Block Courtesy of "The Age"

Presents a WEEKLY

JAZZ - CABARET

FRIDAY NIGHTS
at the "KATHARINA"

UPPER ESPLANADE . . . ST. KILDA
OPPOSITE ST. KILDA BATHS
LUNA PARK

8.30 to 12-30 — Commencing Sept. 15th

HOT JAZZ!   HOT SUPPERS!

TABLE RESERVATIONS LA 8596 (DAILY AFTER 2 P.M.)

ADMISSION 4/9 (Inc. Tax)

A poster from 1954.
L–R: Tony Newstead (trumpet), Don Reid (drums), Willie 'The Lion' McIntyre (piano), Ray Simpson (guitar), George Tack (clarinet), Keith Cox (bass).

thing to be a member of the Bell band. Their new attire occasioned some comment—Roger had grown a beard, the others moustaches, and they sported berets. One thing slightly marred their return. The Eureka Youth League had expected to sponsor the Bells on their Australian tour but Graeme considered that that would have meant their professional death and signed with the ABC. The secretary of the Eureka Youth League, Mrs A. Blake, denounced the band for their repudiation of their political associations. The Eureka Youth League was disenchanted with the jazz scene and the Uptown Club was eclipsed by other venues as the centre of jazz in Melbourne.

The absence of the Bells in Europe allowed other Melbourne bands to shine. Tony Newstead's band took over the Bells' job at the Uptown Club. They secured big engagements at the Collingwood, Prahran and Melbourne Town Halls. From February 1948 to April 1949 Newstead's Southside Gang had a weekly cabaret at the Maison de Luxe, Elwood. They played at Powerhouse where Toni Lamonde, elder sister of Helen Reddy, was their vocalist. Newstead was regarded as one of the best trumpet leads. He did not employ the rorty 'powerhouse' style so much in favour in Melbourne, but relied on good tone and sure phrasing.

The Bells won a Battle of the Bands against the Port Jackson Jazz Band in the boxing ring at Rushcutters Bay Stadium on 1 October 1948, and confidently expected the same result when they met Frank Johnson's Fabulous Dixielanders on 13 April 1949 at Wirth's Olympia in Melbourne. Johnson's band surprised them and took the honours, and also won the second and third battles held in the following months. The Johnson band had achieved greater prominence than the Newstead band while the Bells were away. Frank Johnson became interested in jazz in 1945 after a friend told him to listen to a band at the Palais de Danse.

Frank Johnson's Fabulous Dixielanders after they won the Battle of the Bands, 13 April 1949, Melbourne Town Hall.
L–R: Geoff Kitchen (clarinet), Jack Connelly (bass), Frank Johnson (trumpet), Geoff Bland (piano), Warwick 'Wocka' Dyer (trombone), Bill Tope (banjo), Wes Brown (drums).

Johnson went along under sufferance because, like many Australians, he could not imagine an Australian band being any good. When he arrived he heard the Bells and changed his mind. Originally he intended to play trombone but could not afford one, so a friend lent him a cornet. With his friends Eric Washington on trombone, Max Marginson on clarinet and Ken Thwaites on drums, Johnson conceived the idea of forming a band—with indifferent results.

The real beginning of the Johnson band came through his friendship with Geoff Kitchen. Kitchen had learned guitar at an Hawaiian academy but Johnson convinced him to change to clarinet. Pixie Roberts most inspired Kitchen's clarinet. Kitchen and Geoff Bland, the band's pianist, attended Melbourne Boys' High School, the best state high school in Victoria. Johnson had been expelled from South Melbourne Technical School after 'a series of heinous misdemeanours'. Music was encouraged at Melbourne Boys' High and there was an orchestra of about thirty pieces to which Kitchen and Bland belonged. Swing was popular but young lads did not go out at night to palais in Melbourne because there was a blackout and many servicemen on the streets. Kitchen, Bland and Don Banks belonged to a jazz appreciation society at the school run by Max and Ray Marginson who had the largest record collection. On V-E Day 1945 Johnson, Kitchen, Thwaites and Washington got together at Bland's home and the band began. Washington left and was replaced by Doc Willis for a short period. Johnson was a good organiser, promoter and leader, and he secured a job for them at the Uptown Club. There they met an extrovert trombonist, Warwick 'Wocka' Dyer, sitting in with the Bells. Dyer was a driving force in the band. He was a good example of the sincere primitive on trombone. While he could play sweetly, he made his impact in public with his outgoing rorty style. All the Melbourne jazz fraternity fondly remember his ebullience and his antics; his secret was that everybody loved him. The band was completed by Wes Brown on drums, Bill Tope on banjo and Jack Connelly on bass and tuba. The major influence on them was the Bell band and through them the Watters sound, at an earlier stage in their development than had been the case with the Bells. The Condon recordings were important, as were the Morton and Armstrong discs, but the band always tried to put their personal stamp on the tunes they played. Johnson preferred to play for dances rather than concerts, and he saw that it was necessary to play the right tempos, which he learned from Victor Sylvester records; the ingredients of the Melbourne bounce come from many sources.

Johnson wanted at least one regular job each week for his band. He approached Bill Freeman, a successful dance promoter who gave them a month's trial in May 1947 at the Collingwood Town Hall. This was the making of the band for they stayed there for nine years. The Johnson band played in a smaller room at the back; the main hall was given to a 50/50 dance. Patrons for the two dances fell into two distinct groups—the 50/50 dancers were mainly locals whereas the jazz buffs followed the Johnson band to Collingwood from all over Melbourne. The band made stage appearances for Hoyts Theatre circuit and accepted country gigs within a hundred mile radius of Melbourne. They often hired Smacka Fitzgibbon's father's Rolls Royce to travel in and big-note themselves.

Johnson was an excellent ensemble trumpet lead but in solo he had limitations. Trumpet solos were taken by Ken Evans who was regarded as a member of the band though he could make it up from Geelong only on Sundays for the gig at the Maison de Luxe. Geelong was close enough to Melbourne so that regular visits were made by leading bands. Bob Gibson was the idol of young jazzers and Claude Carnell's band often played at the palais. The group interested in jazz during the war included Jack Connelly, then on clarinet, George Barby (piano), Vern Dolheguy (trumpet), Ron Grimison (clarinet) and Jack Coster (tuba). Evans began with a boys' swing band on clarinet and sax but switched to trombone and became adept at all brass instruments. He played with the Geelong Symphony Orchestra. The Geelong Jazz Band was formed in 1944 and in 1945 they contacted the Bells and other Melbourne jazz dags. Geelong musicians participated in the first convention. Evans moved to Melbourne in 1951 but left the Johnson band the same year to play with the Steamboat Stompers, led by Smacka Fitzgibbon. A number of changes occurred in the Johnson band in 1951 —Kitchen left and took an interest in modern jazz; Nick Polites took over the clarinet seat; there were several changes in pianist—but the band remained highly popular.

The third band to come to the fore after the Newstead and Johnson bands was the Barnard band, the find of the 1949 convention. Len Barnard, pianist and leader, began with his parents' trio on drums, in Mentone in 1939 when he was nine. His father played banjo, alto and tenor saxes, and his mother the piano. With the trio augmented to six they played swing numbers at the Wattle Palais at Frankston. Len's record collection began with Ellington's 'Exposition Swing' and some Benny Goodman quartets. At the end of the war he developed a consuming interest in early jazz and decided to form a band with his younger brother Bob who had been sitting in on cornet. Bob Barnard (b. 1933) began playing cornet at eleven with the Mordialloc City Band and Chelsea Brass Band which gave him a firm technical grounding on the instrument. Len hated carting drums about and switched to piano. The nucleus of Len Barnard's South City Stompers was complete when they met a clarinettist, Tich Bray, who was working in a timber mill at Mentone. Bray had learned classical flute from Richard Chugg of the Melbourne Symphony Orchestra, but gave it up while serving in the AIF because so many people denigrated him for it. Coming into an established jazz scene, the Barnard band's task to play as a band was easier because in addition to records they had live bands to show them the way. Their banjo player and chirpy, rollicking vocalist, Smacka Fitzgibbon, was taught by Jack Connelly of Frank Johnson's band. The band's home ground was at the Mentone Surf Lifesaving Club. Many livesaving clubs along the bay hired jazz bands for their social functions in those years. The band emulated Louis Armstrong's All-Stars.

Bob Barnard especially was a devotee of Armstrong, and before he was twenty Barnard was rightly being hailed as the best jazz cornetist in Australia. For a few years he was criticised for being too derivative of Armstrong and for playing solo in ensemble passages, but his critics were impatient for him to reach his maturity. It has been worth waiting for. Bob Barnard is one of the best traditional/mainstream trumpeters in the world today. He exhibits a flowing melodic line and a wealth of fresh ideas, and he has an in-built metronome which can swing a band regardless of what they are playing. He ranges widely and masterfully across the chord and the register of his instrument with a tone that varies from a surly half-valve growl to a majestic honeyed brilliance. Barnard has

BACK OF BOURKE (1st theme only)   Dallwitz

(Swaggie Music)

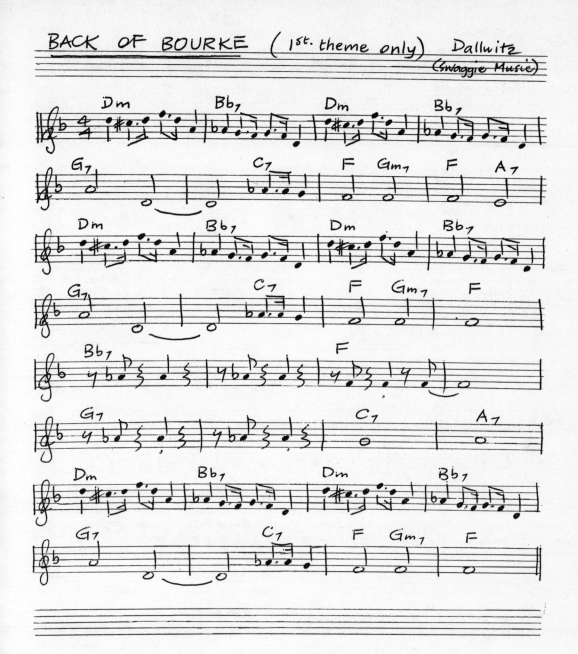

The first theme of Dave Dallwitz's tune Back O'Bourke *and overleaf Bob Barnard's improvisation on it.*

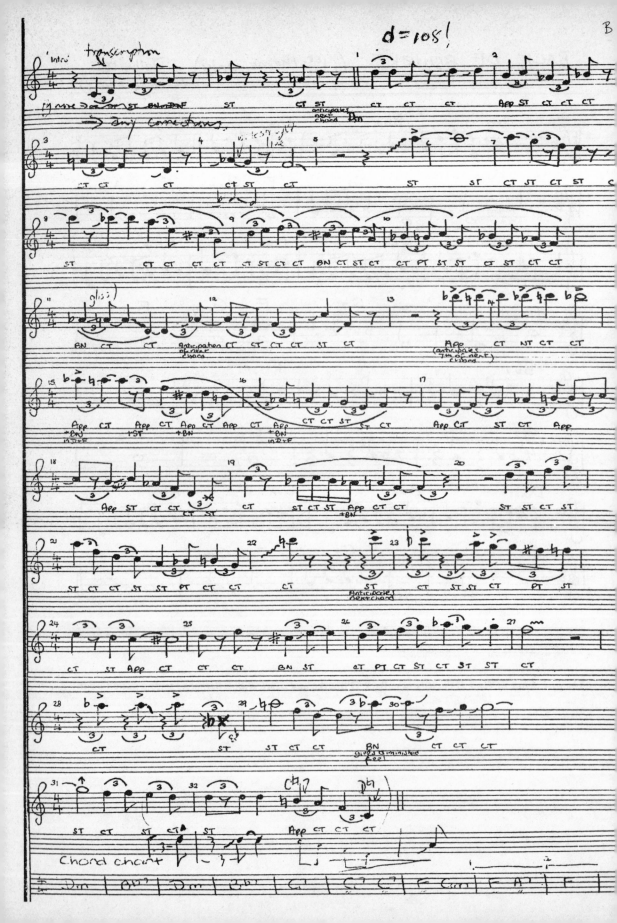

The Bob Barnard Jazz Band, Sydney, 1977.
Back Row L–R: Chris Taperell (piano), Johnny McCarthy (clarinet), John Costello (trombone).
Front Row L–R: Laurie Thompson (drums), Bob Barnard (trumpet).

had opportunities to shine in the 1970s on recordings of Dallwitz's and Sangster's compositions, and with his own band which he formed in Sydney in 1974. This band toured USA in July 1976 through St Louis, Grand Rapids, Toronto, Detroit, at Eddie Condon's club in New York and at the Bix Beiderbecke Festival at Davenport, Iowa. The quiet, solidly built trumpeter and his band were enthusiastically received wherever they played and were invited to return to the Bix festival. Bob Barnard will listen to any type of jazz, but his philosophy is that a player should not have to 'work' at playing but should play simply and from within himself. It does not mean he plays safe. Quite the opposite—he blows out gloriously on what he knows.

VERSATILITY

AUSTRALIAN jazz started to catch up quickly in the early 1960s. Records became more freely available. Their ready availability did not stifle local creativity but inspired it, giving Australians confidence to follow their own inclinations when they had an adequate knowledge of the directions musicians were going in overseas. Sydney began to open up, Lee Gordon opened strip-tease clubs in the Cross and many musicians took small flats there. Established musicians were as accessible to the public as they had ever been. The Australian All-Stars, a quintet comprised of winners of the 1957 *Music Maker* poll, played for seven years at the Sky Lounge, opened in May 1958 by Graeme Bennett, and released two records called 'Jazz for Beachniks' in 1960. The same quintet made appearances on the ABC's 'Six O'Clock Rock' TV show. The Don Burrows Quartet toured New Zealand as the support act for the Oscar Peterson Trio. Burrows and Buddle worked for most of the television orchestras, those of Isador Goodman, Gibson, Limb, Channel 9's 'Bandstand' with Bob Young and Billy Weston, and Burrows formed a septet for the Brian Davies Show on ABC in 1962.

Some of the up and coming players had chairs in studio bands, but they were more often found in nightclubs. Graeme Lyall came to Sydney in 1961, played in Chequers, at Quo Vadis in Martin Place alongside Speers, Weston and Bruce Cale (bass), then to Andre's and back to Chequers before going into TV. Bernie McGann, Bob Bertles and Graham Morgan played in Jimmy Sloggett's band at Sammy Lee's Latin Quarter, performing a lot of rocking soul music. Terry Wilkinson led a band at the Silver Spade Room in the Chevron Hilton at the Cross and often used American arrangements to back visiting artists. They would discovery new things this way, e.g. Billy Eckstine's drummer was Charlie Persip who had an incredible four bar drum introduction to a certain piece which left half the band floundering because it was the first time most of them had heard the Motown beat.

Two saxophonists who had an influence on younger musicians were Keith Barr from England and an American, Bob Gillett. Barr was brought to Australia in 1960 by Lee Gordon for his club. Barr was rated high on tenor in the English jazz polls and had played in the Dankworth band. Gillett had a big hard sound on alto, and, with a healthy self-esteem, had a lot to say about everything on the scene. In particular he brought about the end of Bernie McGann's Paul Desmond phase. Gillett and Barr were in the gutsy but short-lived Basil Kirchin big band, who was also brought from the UK by Lee Gordon. Both saxophonists gave encouragement to musicians and made them think about what they were doing. Barr tried never to compromise. He died in 1971 after falling from a window during a diabetic attack.

The two scenes, the established and the aspiring musicians, were on common ground at the El Rocco. Virtually all jazz musicians who were worth their salt appeared there. The audience, while not always large, was discriminating. Most musicians took a turn to lead a band, and there was a constant grouping and regrouping of trios, quartets and quintets within the same body of musicians, fostering a beneficial interchange of ideas and experience between and within the generations. A fresh influx of New Zealanders made their impact, particularly Judy Bailey (piano) and Lyn Christie (bass), one of the best bassists ever to play there. Christie provided a breakthrough for McGann by hiring him, because the owner did not like McGann's style and rarely let him in. It seemed to McGann that musicians ranked at the bottom of the owner's social scale and doctors at the top. Since Christie was both a doctor and a musician, he was confused enough to let Christie hire whoever he wanted. Christie now lives in America.

Another bassist from the El Rocco to succeed in America is Rick Laird who played with John McLaughlin's Mahavishnu Orchestra and was in Chick Corea's band for their 1978 tour of Australia.

In 1965 an eighteen piece University of Denver Jazz Band visited Australia and naturally went to El Rocco to listen. The band's director was Tasso Harris who had been out twenty-two years before with the Artie Shaw Naval Band. The jazz scene then did not compare with the El Rocco and Harris considered that Australia no longer lagged behind.

The modern jazz scene in Melbourne quietened down until the Fat Black Pussycat coffee lounge was opened in South Yarra in January 1963 by an American, Ali Sugerman. The first band in was Barry McKimm (trumpet), Heinz Mendelsohn (tenor, flute) and New Zealanders Brian Fagan (bass) and Barry Woods (drums). Bertles joined them and they explored free improvisational jazz. McKimm later joined the Victorian Symphony Orchestra. They were replaced by 'The Heads', Bernie McGann, John Pochée and New Zealanders Dave McRae (piano) and Andy Brown (bass). McRae had just returned from eighteen months intensive practice in his homeland and had consolidated a formidable technique. By this time they had discovered who the really important modern jazzmen were, and in the next six months they searched out every nuance of their work. McRae went on to play with the Buddy Rich Big Band in the USA, and made important and successful experiments in the use of electronics in jazz.

Sugerman disappeared and the Fat Black Pussycat was taken over by an eccentric poet, Adrian Rawlins. A rejuvenated Brian Brown Quartet followed The Heads. Their music lept ahead during their time there. Whenever Brown goes through slump or a period of not playing, his band always starts again in a new direction. Usually there is a change in personnel, because there comes a point in every band when its members have said everything musically that they have to say to each other. Brown's quartet had Barry Buckley (bass), Alan Lee (vibes) and

Ted Vining (drums). Lee failed to arrive one evening and Tony Gould (piano) deputised, providing a fresh spark that sent the band forward. Brown assisted Gould to shed his inhibitions regarding the keyboard, stopped him lingering in safe areas and faced him with contemporary aspects of jazz. This period of the quartet lasted until 1971 when Gould left to study at the Conservatorium and Buckley had to concentrate on his work in the dental laboratory. The jazz scene had shifted from the Pussycat to Saturday afternoon sessions at the Prospect Hill Hotel in Kew. Meanwhile, Brown, who has a great capacity for hard work, had taken out his Leaving Certificate and qualified as an architect at Melbourne University.

The upsurge of activity in Sydney and Melbourne had its spin-offs to Adelaide and Perth. After Bertles left the Pussycat, he, Keith Barr, Fagan and Woods played at the Jazz Gallery for four months, then the two saxophonists went to Adelaide to join up with Keith Stirling (trumpet). The modern jazz scene in the mid-1960s had a small following in Adelaide, and musicians were happy if they found somewhere to play, let alone be paid for it. After their evening gigs they gathered at The Cellar to play jazz; pieces by Adderley, Coltrane or Horace Silver. They worked at all sorts of jobs before getting to The Cellar. Adelaide's rock and roll bands provided early experience for some good players. The Penny Rockets, started in 1957, was nearly an institution. Through it passed Ian Drinkwater (reeds), Doug Clarke (sax), Ron Carson (bass) and the most naturally gifted saxophonist of that generation of Adelaide musicians, Bob Jeffery (b. 1941 Port Pirie, SA). The circle of players at The Cellar have been the ones to keep modern jazz alive in Adelaide. The various small groups led by Sylvan Elhay (tenor), known as Schmoe and Co., began in 1964 as 'The Bottom of the Garden Goblins'. Ted Nettelbeck (piano) returned to Adelaide when he became disillusioned with professional music after four years in England. Paradoxically, he has probably played more jazz as an amateur since 1970 than he did before. He formed groups with Elhay and Jeffery and has composed a number of pieces; one series inspired by the Flinders Ranges and his best, 'Not Only in Stone', dedicated to the greatest musical influence in his life, Frank Smith.

Bertles spent about nine months in Adelaide, then three in Canberra before returning to Sydney to join with Johnny O'Keefe at the Latin Quarter. He joined Max Merritt and the Meteors in June 1967, a rhythm and blues band which had Stewie Speers on drums. Merritt let his sidemen take good solos, so Bertles and Speers were able to infuse a lot of jazz into the act. The Meteors went to the United Kingdom in December 1970 and successfully entered the rock scene. Bertles also accepted work with the prominent jazz/rock band Nucleus, led by Ian Carr. A friend of Carr, Neil Ardley, composed a piece based on the five note Balinese pelog scales, which had seven movements, one for each colour of the rainbow. 'Kaleidoscope of Rainbows' won the 1977 European Critics Award. Of the twelve musicians on the recording, one third were from the antipodes—Dave McRae and Brian Smith (tenor) from New Zealand, and Bertles and Roger Sellers (drums) from Australia.

From Adelaide, Keith Stirling went westwards to Perth and started a septet at a casual nightspot, the Melpomene, in November 1964. Stirling provided that spark of incentive to local musicians to extend themselves, which, because of the

The Col Nolan Quartet on the steps of the Sydney Opera House, 1976, before their tour of Japan, Korea, the Philippines and Thailand.
L–R: Laurie Bennett (drums), Bob Bertles (flute, piccolo, recorder, clarinet, saxes), Dieter Vogt (bass), Col Nolan (acoustic and electric piano).

isolation, had been so hard to find. The scene then was quiet. Theo Henderson (reeds, flute) was slowly working his way through most of Perth's nightclubs and being kicked out for playing too much Charlie Parker. Billy Clowes (piano) fared better, tempering his inclination for jazz with popular and cocktail music. The Melpomene was closed by fire and the jazz scene shifted to the Hole-in-the-Wall Club in the old Braille Society Hall. Stirling gathered about him such musicians as Henderson, Tony Ashford (reeds), Jim Cook (tenor, clarinet), Bill Gumbleton (piano), Brian Bursey (bass) and Bill Tattersall (drums), performing pieces by such artists as Silver, Roland Kirk or Theolonius Monk, and some originals by Stirling. The tunes were not announced and no one ever asked, because if you had to ask you were not hip. It was a boring time for audiences around the world because it was fashionable for musicians to play with their backs to the audience. Perth was no different.

Perth's jazz scene picked up considerably after the mining boom brought money to the west. By the mid-1970s there were more outlets for modern jazz in Perth than in Melbourne, though the standard was not as high. Immigrants from the UK and Western Europe brought in new talent. Since 1973, Perth has had the distinction of having the only community-based jazz club in Australia which caters specifically for modern jazz. The repertoire of the group which insured the club's early success, Tony Ashford's Kaleidoscope, reflects the interests of its members—Freddie Hubbard, Bill Evans, Corea, Tom Scott and Herbie Hancock.

From hard bop, jazz experienced a number of changes; the move into atonality and modality, the gradual loosening up of rhythm sections and the breakup of time which led to free jazz. Jazz became aware of non-European influences, incorporating musical structures and instruments from South America, Africa, Arabia, India and Asia. For those Australians who were up with the scene, these changes came as no surprise. They knew well what questions were facing jazz, and while Coltrane and Ornette Coleman answered them best, Australians were making their own explorations in the right areas.

In Melbourne in 1960 and '61, Bruce Clarke led a rehearsal group of musicians who were tired of television work. The group included Billy Hyde and Frank Smith. Prompted by Ornette Coleman, and Lennie Tristano's 1949 record 'Intuition', the group tried sitting in front of a painting and playing what they felt, and blending Indian music with free jazz. The results are on Clarke's album 'Looking Back'.

Mike Nock was exploring modality. Dave Levy learned one scale from him and worked out eleven more which applied to nearly all the chords of which he could conceive. Levy soon moved into free jazz.

Pochée had had thoughts about time while he was in Surfers Paradise for a year in 1962, and when he returned to Sydney and heard the records, the questions and the answers crystallized. He began playing the drums as a total instrument with both melodic and percussive capabilities, broke the time up, chopped it around and became more sensitive to the space and gaps necessary to be left in the music.

When Pochée returned, everyone seemed to be studying George Russell's 'Lydian Chromatic Concept of Tonal Organisation', a theory relevant to the stage jazz was in, which had the merit of presenting the problems in an organised way. The champion of Russell's Lydian concept was Bryce Rohde.

After the Australian Jazz Quintet disbanded, Rohde formed a quartet with George Golla (guitar), Ed Gaston (bass) and Englishman Colin Bailey (drums). Bailey was in Australia accompanying Winifred Atwell, and was an influence on Sydney drummers when he played at the El Rocco. The Rohde quartet took part in the first Australian International Jazz Festival in Melbourne in October 1960, and in the Ninth Festival of Perth in 1961, the first time a jazz group had featured in it. That year the quartet was the supporting act in Australia and New Zealand for the Kingston Trio. The trio's manager, Ed Sarkesian, offered them a five week tour of the USA. Golla pulled out and was replaced by Frank Thornton. Thornton left before the end of the American tour and they used Frank Strozier, one of the important altoists of free jazz. The bassist of the Kingston Trio, David Wheat, had been talking about Russell's concept and had read his book. It opened a new world to Rohde; he no longer felt obligated or restricted by key and time signatures. Rohde's quartet broke up at the end of the tour, Bailey moved to Los Angeles to work with the Victor Feldman Trio, and Gaston and Rohde returned to Australia.

Rohde put together another quartet using Charlie Munro, Bruce Cale (bass) and Mark Bowden (drums). They studied the Lydian concept thoroughly and recorded two albums based on it, 'Straight Ahead' (1962) and 'Corners' (1963). Initially the group were wary of Rohde's direction, playing almost tongue in cheek until they came to see the purposes of it. The records were received with more acclaim fifteen years later when they were re-released than at their first issue. In the early 1960s, the innovative sound which caught the most attention was the searing, jagged, sometimes purposefully ugly solo, whereas Rohde has an abiding love of melodies. In the late 1970s, when many leading American jazzmen retreated from extreme atonality, the beauty of Rohde's work was better appreciated.

Rohde and Cale went to the USA in 1965, Cale to take up his *Downbeat* scholarship to the Berklee School of Music in Boston, and Rohde to make his home in California.

The culmination of Rohde's influence in Australia came through Charlie Munro. Munro felt that he had made good progress with Rohde and wanted to consolidate it. In his first encounters with bop he had been floundering; through Rohde he finalised what he had been trying to do, and with his knowledge of modes, developed linear structures in his playing. Not that anyone else had heard any indecision in his playing. Munro and Frank Smith were the two strongest alto saxophonists to be heard in the 1950s. Bertles was listening the night Lennie Niehaus, sideman with Kenton on his 1957 tour and a respected saxophonist in his own right, sat-in with Munro at his regular club engagement, and Munro carved him completely. Rohde was a catalyst for Munro, catapulting him into avant-garde jazz, freeing his playing and making him receptive to the music of Ornette Coleman, Archie Schepp and particularly John Coltrane. Rohde had had a workshop going with his quartet and Syd Powell (tenor), which Munro continued after Rohde's departure, replacing Cale with Neville Whitehead (bass) and bringing in young New Zealand trombonist Bob McIvor (b. 1942 Wellington, NZ) after Powell died. The results of their weekly workshops were the product of four independent minds. The sessions were democratic, each making a contribution, and as their understanding and empathy deepened, so their playing became freer. Rohde's written pieces were a harmonic sequence based on a scale. Munro wrote from the same viewpoint, not free for the sake of playing free, but free playing developed on the appropriate modal scale. Though Russell said that theoretically, nothing could be wrong, the danger with free playing as Munro saw it, was that anybody could pick up an instrument and play. To Munro that would be selfish. His years of experience in big bands, in the army, with Bob Gibson, the ABC, as a performer, conductor and composer, had instilled in him a desire for discipline and organisation. Any type of music had to have something to appeal and must communicate. The improvising in Munro's piece is free, but within an overall, logical, formal structure.

This growth of jazz from forces within itself was augmented in the 1960s by music from cultures around the world. *Music Maker* printed an article in April

1966 by Don Ellis, the American trumpeter and big band leader, who discussed the merits of complex Indian rhythms and maintained that these and other non-European and non-African rhythms represented one of the greatest challenges to jazz since bop. Munro is a Christian Scientist, and had long had an interest in the culture and music of the Middle East and the Far East. Before leaving on one of four tours of Vietnam with the ABC Dance Band, Munro read a book by Curt Sachs which traced the Islamic influence on Grecian music. This caught Munro's attention because Sachs analysed many Grecian modes, one of which, the Lydian, he had already worked on with Rohde. Sachs's book spurred his interest in Indian and Japanese music—he had worked with an Indian drummer with Rohde and Cale—and made clearer the goals in his own compositions.

Munro and his workshop group, McIvor, Whitehead and Bowden, committed their ideas to a recording in 1967 called 'Eastern Horizons' which is a landmark in modern Australian jazz. It was an authoritative exploration of areas contemporary to the concerns of the jazz world at large; a combination of free jazz with non-European musics achieved entirely on Western instruments, but played with an intensity and flexibility which enhanced and coloured appropriately the different musical forms they used. The 'Islamic Suite' was based on a scale popular in Arabia. Munro began it with the soprano sax played as to give a Bedouin effect. The 'Malahari Raga' was based on the Indian raga of the same name and played with the tenor sax which suggested all the inflections of the cantor. On 'Japanese Love Song', McIvor provided a spare and plaintive accompaniment to Munro's oriental sounding flute, a contrast to his lush trombone on the ballad 'When I Look at You'. And so it was with each musician, bending their instruments to suit perfectly the wide-ranging moods of the album. Munro played six instruments on it—soprano, alto and tenor saxes, bass clarinet, flute and cello.

They had the chance to record only because an astute 'Artists and Repertoire' man from Philips could hear what they were doing. There was little else like it at the time: Sangster recorded a free piece, 'Conjur Man', the same year and Lyall composed Psychadelia III which showed eastern influences in his tenor. Lyall recorded it two years later using McIvor.

Lyn Christie made an attempt at cross fertilization from Aboriginal music in 1965, using the bass to create the drone sound of the didgeridoo, but this has been the extent of such attempts. Apart from a few people blowing didgeridoos, all other jazz attempts have drawn on the poetic aspects of Aboriginal life rather than on the music itself.

Though stereo recording began in Australia in 1958, recording studios were still poorly equipped a decade later. There was no recording booth as such for the Munro sessions and at one stage Bowden had a quiet passage and was forced to play brushes on a record cover to achieve the required balance. Studios improved their equipment greatly in the next decade.

Charlie Munro's remarkable career has direct links with the early days when the dance profession was just begining. A few years after Linn Smith's Royal Jazz Band ended, Smith led the band on the *Niagara*, sailing between Sydney, New Zealand and Vancouver. In 1935 Smith was in Auckland searching for a cellist and a saxophonist when he saw a lad on the street carrying both. After consulting with his parents, Munro signed on, making thirteen trips altogether to

Vancouver on ships. Munro's father was an amateur flautist, organist and choirmaster in Christchurch, and his mother was a competent pianist. Charles, his brother and his sister were taught to play in the Munro family dance band. At seven Charles began on piano, at nine his father taught him the sax, and at eleven he took up the cello. Charlie listened to his father's Red Nichols records and took off Rudy Weidolft solos. At ten he made a tour of New Zealand theatres as a boy saxophonist. Munro joined his high school orchestra and was often called upon to conduct it. He did one year of teachers' college before turning professional. He worked on ships and in clubs in Auckland and Wellington and settled in Sydney in 1938. During the war Munro played in the 50/50 Concert Party in New Guinea, and was given the leadership of the 7th Division Concert Party, then the twenty-eight piece 1st Australian Entertainment Unit and a Liberty Loan Unit. In 1944 he made a record for Prestophone; his pianist was Neville Chynoweth, later assistant Bishop of the Anglican Diocese of Canberra and Goulburn. After the war Munro did more study, with Ray Rixon on clarinet and five years of 'cello at the Conservatorium. The 'cello was a handy double with the ABC, and he refused an offer to join the Sydney Symphony Orchestra.

Munro rarely played at the El Rocco, but two concert series which he and Don Burrows performed in 1966 helped to improve the standing of modern jazz in Australia. Ernest Gibb, orchestra manager of the SSO, approached Munro to form a special twelve piece band to perform with the orchestra in May. The work was a Seiber-Dankworth piece, 'Improvisation for Jazz Band and Orchestra'. A few months later, the Don Burrows Quartet featured in Donald Westlake's series 'Best of Both Worlds', at the Cell Block Theatre with the New Sydney Woodwind Quintet who were the principals of the SSO. Two originals by Sangster were presented, 'Rain on Water', based on a Japanese scale, and 'Kaffir Song'. The intellectual and classical crowd attended both and it was a significant moment for the acceptance of modern jazz on the concert platform. Jazz gained a credibility outside its loyal supporters and no longer had to be a rite confined to downstairs clubs. Why did it take so long for modern jazz to attract an intellectual following when traditional jazz had won over the artists and writers twenty years before? Admittedly, modern jazz of the late 1940s and early 1950s did not compare as well with its mentors overseas as Australian traditional jazz did, and when modern jazz did catch up, the support followed.

While not as innovatory as Munro, Burrows's superb playing won for him wide public and official recognition. In 1967 he went to the Canadian Expo with Bobby Limb's band; in 1970, the government sponsored appearances of the Don Burrows Sextet at the Expo in Japan; a grant from the government and a gift from a Queensland businessman enabled the Don Burrows Quartet to perform at the 1972 Montreux and Newport Jazz Festivals, the first Australian group to play Newport since its inception in 1954. The quartet made tours through Asia and gave countless concerts in Australia under the auspices of Musica Viva Society, and in 1972 he was made an MBE, the first Australian jazz musician to be included in the Queen's Birthday Honours.

Burrows occupies the middle ground of modern Australian jazz; his style is rooted in the technical perfection of the Buddy de Franco school, with a loving debt to Benny Goodman, and so is advanced enough to satisfy the enthusiast without going beyond the understanding of the more numerous casual listeners.

His versatility has won him the admiration of traditional jazz musicians and the open acceptance of young modern players. On clarinet Burrows has a quicksilver fluidity from the top to the bottom of its register. The same effortless clarity shines through on his alto. His baritone has a driving bounce and a grainy, robust tone. The swinging boost that he finds in the lower registers, he reproduces on clarinet with an electronic octave divider. Though he thinks of himself as a clarinettist, Burrows's personality and artistry is best revealed in his flute playing. The flute brings out fully Burrows's sensitivity to time and his awareness of mood, from a hunting speed or fat satisfaction, to a soft delicacy, caressing notes from the instrument without once losing the special tension of the moment. The American Flute Guild, comprised of the principal flautists of American symphony orchestras, invited him to give them a lecture about the instrument. Burrows is musically unselfish, valued by fellow musicians for his open communication and honest encouragement, and with a competent ability to present himself, Burrows has been an ambassador for jazz in Australia and internationally. The influence of Brazilian music on jazz took him to that country, and Brazilian musicians made tours of Australia with him. One of the grand old men of jazz, Stephane Grappelli, toured and recorded with Burrows.

The Don Burrows Quartet from 1963 to 1974 was made up of George Golla (guitar), Ed Gaston (bass), and at different times on drums, John Sangster, Alan

The Don Burrows Quartet of the early 1960s at the Sky Lounge, Sydney.
L–R: John Sangster (drums), Ed Gaston (bass), Don Burrows (clarinet), George Golla (guitar).

Turnbull and Laurie Thompson. From 1970 to 1974 their regular engagement was at the Wentworth Hotel, a gig which almost failed at first because the atmosphere was so different from the El Rocco. Burrows included some straight classical pieces in their repertoire and nowadays plays them at outright jazz gigs too.

Burrows's association with Golla, which continued after the quartet finished, is one of the outstanding partnerships in Australian jazz. Golla tends to play slightly hotter than Burrows, and his harmonic capabilities on his seven string guitar keep Burrows right on his toes. Musically they are a quick and witty pair, and they have been together for so long that the sounds they make are virtually musical ESP. Golla (b. 1935 Chorzow, Poland) came to Bowral, NSW, after the war when his family was displaced. He played sax and clarinet, then guitar. Golla was a studio musician for a long time, then a soloist with the Eric Jupp Orchestra on TV and then joined Burrows.

Jazz in Sydney went through a quiet slump in the late 1960s and early 1970s. Activity did not stop, it was just harder to find somewhere to blow. The El Rocco closed and was turned into a pizza parlour, and the Musicians' Club moved its premises to Chalmers Street, which took musicians a little while to become

The Original Galapagos Duck in The Basement, January 1974, Sydney.
L–R: Willie Qua, Doug Robson, Chris Qua, Bernis Cannon (ABC/GTK producer), Horst Liepolt (manager), Marty Mooney, Tom Hare.

accustomed to. Lyall sensed a slight collapse in Sydney TV and returned to Melbourne to write commercials, play in the Melbourne ABC Show Band, then to become musical director at Channel 9. It seemed that every time Pochée rang up someone, they would be taking their mother to the pictures, so he became musical director for a vocal act, The Four Kinsmen. Dave Levy felt the need for some security and sold real estate. Bernie McGann did not play in public for about three years and became a postman.

The turning point came with the opening of The Basement in 1973, which provided a base for the most popular young jazz group of the decade, The Original Galapagos Duck, and contemporary jazz in general. The Duck began in 1968 at the Kosciusko Ski Chalet. Bruce Viles guessed that the aprés-ski scene could be enlivened by replacing the accordianist with a band led by his friend Marty Mooney. Mooney was a traditional clarinettist and surprised everyone by forming a jazz/rock band with the line-up of Tom Hare, Chris Qua and Des Windsor (piano). Early in 1970 Viles purchased the Rocks Push in George Street, and the band, now a quintet, established itself there and took their present name, an invention from and approved by the British comedian, Spike Milligan. The Rocks Push burned down in mid-72. Viles found a waterlogged basement for rent in a lane at Circular Quay which he pumped out and refurbished. Horst Liepolt became publicity manager for The Basement and personal manager for the band. The Duck were neither aggressively traditional nor self-consciously modern. They appealed to a generation who had grown up with rock and were tired of it, yet who did not want to discard it. The Duck symbolise the merging together of the previously distinct modern and traditional jazz scenes, and the maturity of their audience which could accept such a union. Chris and Willie Qua are the sons of Jack and Pat Qua who are identities in the traditional world. Chris attended Australian Jazz Conventions, was inspired by hearing Louis Armstrong, then Miles Davis, took up trumpet then string bass and played his first job with Alan Lee at the Mocambo where he met Tom Hare. The merger between the two worlds was complete when Len Barnard, the erudite traditional drummer, joined the Duck in 1976. In November 1973, the Duck backed Nina Simone during her tour of Australia. In 1974 they greatly widened their audience through a season with the Australian Ballet, and they composed and performed the music for the film of David Williamson's play, 'The Removalists'. Their pianist at this stage was Dave Levy. Part of the Duck's attraction is the ability of each to play a number of instruments well, enabling them to create a wide range of voicings. Hare specialises in hard, straight ahead tenor and trumpet, but also the other saxes, flute, flugelhorn and drums. Mooney plays clarinet, alto, tenor, flute, bass and percussion. Willie Qua plays drums, flute, soprano and recorder. The personnel of the Duck has varied over the years, but they continued to attract musicians with competence on two or more instruments. In 1978 the Duck played at the Montreux Jazz Festival and made a tour of seven Asian countries, including a visit to Peking.

The world-wide economic recession since 1972 has not affected musicians as badly as the Great Depression, and while pop music is as sweet as ever, modern jazz is in a healthy state in Australia, partly due to the recognition and money awarded to it by the government, and to the efforts of promoters, like Liepolt, who are always coming up with a concert in one guise or another. Two highly

Kerri Biddell, 1978

successful showcases for contemporary jazz which Liepolt organised were the month long series of 'Music is an Open Sky' in 1975 and 1977 at The Basement. When a venue works as well as The Basement does, it stimulates the whole scene.

The seventies saw the emergence of two female singers who are highly regarded by their fellow musicians. Jeannie Lewis and Kerri Biddell resist the tendency to be labelled as jazz singers, or any other type, but for both, jazz has been a strong force in their careers. Lewis (b. 1945, Sydney) had her first professional engagements singing folk songs in the mid-60s. Her parents were interested in politics and she listened to militant singers like Pete Seeger, Paul Robeson and Josh White. Her able interpretation of the idiom led her to sing at the 1966 International Festival of Contemporary Song in Cuba. Classical formal singing lessons were taken at the Conservatorium and she explored blues, rock and jazz. Lewis sings in several languages. In 1970 she sang in the première performance of Peter Sculthorpe's 'Love 200' with the SSO and the rock group Tully; she has sung at the Adelaide and Perth Festivals of Art, played a leading role in 'Hair', and contributed to the soundtrack of the Jim Sharman Jnr film 'Shirley Thompson Versus The Aliens'. The number and variety of her concerts is large. Singing with the traditional jazz bands of Geoff Bull, Nat Oliver and Ray Price taught her the discipline of working in with other musicians. The most experimenting she did with her voice was with Peter Boothman (guitar) and Dave Ellis (bass), two modern Sydney jazz musicians. Alan Lee helped her as he had Judith Durham, opening her ears to all sorts of music.

By this time Lee had calmed down and was no longer destroying his instruments by the physical force of his playing. He started a jazz/rock group, Plant, and during a year in 'Hair' became fascinated by all percussive instruments, mainly Latin American ones. An inspiration was his friendship with Tony Gould, a complementary musical spirit who brought many classically influenced pieces into Lee's quartet from his work at the Melbourne Conservatorium, for example, the band's recording of a Rodriguez guitar piece with a string quartet. Lewis is one of the few singers who excite Lee, by her contribution as a musician, her awareness of what the band is doing and the great intensity with which she does everything.

Softly, in her middle register, Lewis has a shining folk-like clarity; in full flight at the top of her range she favours a marked vibrato. She has a love of theatre and threaded this through the themes which have unified her most memorable concerts—'Free Fall Through Featherless Flight', recorded 1973, which had the theme of flight and freedom through the Icarus myth, and 'Tears of Steel and the Clowning Calaveras', recorded 1976, which was prompted by a film about Allende's Chile and a poem by the Chilean, Pablo Naruda. Both albums were based in the folk and rock idioms.

Kerri Biddell is another who is restoring musicians' faith in singers. Her ideal is to sing the way Don Burrows plays, and she has been content to stay largely in the jazz field. The timbre of her voice is flexible, from a little girl breathlessness which she can subtly alter to a mature melancholy intimacy, to spritely evanescent leaps through her three octave range. She demonstrates that a talented artist can retain her natural accent, breaking away from the mid-Pacific or American accent that is so common and so easy to fall into when singing jazz or popular songs. Both her parents played piano, her grandmother played for the silent movies, and Kerri

The Brian Brown Quartet since 1976.
L–R: Bob Sedergreen (piano), Ted Vining (drums), Brian Brown (flute, tenor), Barry Buckley (bass).

learned classical piano for twelve years. She began singing with a pop group called The Affair, but grew tired of up tempo rhythm and all-stops-out emotion songs. In jazz she found the variety she needed, and has sung with the Don Burrows Quartet and the Daly-Wilson Big Band. She sang with success in Canada and at Las Vegas for a season in 1972, but she returned to her preferred world in Sydney, singing at The Basement and other clubs with the band, Compared To What.

Something new always comes out of Melbourne as the Brian Brown Quartet's first performance at The Basement in May 1974 again proved. They are determined to create a musical expression of their own, and look to themselves for their musical impetus. No one overseas is asking the questions which interest them. Brown's quartet experienced an indecisive period in the early 1970s, engaging in a slight detour through electronics, but which eventually came to fruition with their imaginative and dramatic integration of synthesized sounds into their music in the mid-1970s. Two changes put the band on its latest course —Bob Sedergreen became their pianist and Brown received an Australia Council grant for the year 1974–75 which committed them to rehearsing and

Judy Bailey Quartet, 1974, Sydney.
L–R: Ken James (soprano, tenor, flute), Ron Philpott (electric bass), Judy Bailey (keyboards), John Pochée (drums, percussion).

producing a new set of work. A marked characteristic of their public performances is the almost palpable empathy existing between members of the group, which is particularly apparent in the free sections of their playing. The shape of the piece is determined by the nature of their interaction, not by playing through a set number of solos whether inspiration is there or not. When strict meter and bar lines dissolve, a pulse remains which all four contribute to though it is hard to say exactly where it is. They can contrast that with a relentless, ineluctable momentum and drive in arranged passages, sometimes with a rock or latin tinge. Their satisfaction comes from giving impetus to the others in the band. Few solos are taken, though they do solo in ensemble. Collective improvisation is a hallmark of their work, which relates them in a roundabout way to the first Australian traditional jazz bands of the 1940s, which achieved their identifiable sounds more as a band than as individuals.

The Brown group's first LP, 'Carlton Streets' (1975), contained three descriptive pieces—a tone poem illustrating Katharine Susannah Prichard's story 'Coonardoo', evocations of the streets of Carlton in Melbourne, and a big dipper

The Last Straw, Sydney, since 1975.
L–R: John Pochée (drums), Tony Esterman (piano), Bernie McGann (alto), Ken James (reeds), Jack Thorncraft (bass).

ride at Luna Park in 'The Fair', by their bassist, Dave Tolley. For this record they were a quintet; Dure Dara created textural percussion and read excerpts from 'Coonardoo'. They also used a fiercely blowing brass section to punctuate and boost the band on two tracks. On their second record, 'Upward' (1977), they were a quartet, Brown on tenor and soprano sax, flute, A.K.S. Synthesizer and tam-tam, Sedergreen on acoustic piano, organ and Kong Synthesizer, Vining on percussion and the indefatigable Barry Buckley on bass. Without brass, the mood of the album was quieter, as in the sustained understatement of the track 'Tall Grass', though it had lost nothing in intensity. The first piece was a reflective tribute to Billy Hyde, recorded within a month of his death. The rhythm section, The Ted Vining Trio, made an LP in 1977, 'No. 1'; the trio's music was distinct from that of the quartet's and closer to their roots in Coltrane and other pioneering jazzmen who inspired them. The Brian Brown Quartet made successful appearances at European jazz festivals in 1978.

John Pochée returned to creative playing in 1973 at the invitation of Judy Bailey, whose quartet he joined with Ken James (reeds) and Ron Philpott (bass). Pochée finally decided to make things happen for himself and formed The Last Straw, fiery, hard and straight ahead. He invited McGann to join them instead of regaling the trees in the National Park with his sax. Their playing is complementary. To borrow John Clare's imagery, Pochee sews 'rushing thickets of sound' behind McGann's alto. McGann is no faster than, say, Bertles, but his tone is unique, burred and bristling in all registers.

Of the jazz critics, John Clare is the most conscious of imagery and employs it to effect in his reviews. He performed on the second album of the group Free Kata —Serge Ermoll (piano), Eddie Bronson (tenor) and a fast and expressive young drummer, Lou Burdett—who took an uncompromising stance on free improvisation. Clare improvised his images which the band illustrated and fed back to Clare, sending him on.

The emphasis in the last two decades has been on small groups at small venues, and overseas, the major innovators played in small groups, so it is a little surprising the enthusiasm with which musicians and the public accepted a big band which became one of the musical high points of the 1970s.

The Daly-Wilson Big Band was formed early in 1969 by Warren Daly (drums) and Ed Wilson (trombone). Daly had just returned from a tour of the USA with an American act, The Kirby Stone Four. The tour ended in Las Vegas where Daly joined the Si Zenter Big Band which impressed him because it was a powerhouse band with great dynamics. When the summer lay-off came, Daly played with the Glen Miller Orchestra in Japan and Korea. Daly's Australian background should not be overlooked; without it he would not have got to America. He started with a pop group called The Steeds and made contact with the jazz scene through fortnightly rehearsals with the Dick Bowden Big Band. Daly was also working with the Gus Merzi Quartet and with Bill Barrett's big band when he was invited to join Billy Weston's big band, formed in October 1965, which had a Sunday night show at the Phyllis Bates Ballroom in Liverpool Street, Sydney. Daly was staff drummer at Channel 10 under the direction of Jack Grimsley when he was spotted by the Kirby Stone Four. Ed Wilson began with a pop group called Gus and the Nomads, spent six years with the ABC Dance Band and did casual work

The Daly-Wilson Big Band, 1971.

with the SSO. Daly and Wilson had known each other since they were fourteen. They thought they could make a big band succeed in Australia by founding the horn sections on an electric rhythm section—electric piano, guitar, bass and drums—and by rejecting nostalgia, playing material derived mainly from the better modern pop tunes. During 1969–71 the Daly Wilson Big Band performed more than sixty highly popular concerts. The driving power of the twenty-piece band came from Daly and Col Nolan, a dedicated swinger on piano and Hammond organ. The skills of stage presentation had to be rediscovered by a generation who did not know they were the successors to Frank Coughlan and Jim Davidson, but the dynamic vitality, exuberance and enjoyment of the band shone through. High note specialist, Don Raverty, lit up the trumpet section, and fiery solos from Doug Foskett and Geoff Naughton kicked the saxes along. On the records, Bob McIvor was another strong voice in Wilson's trombone section. Singers with the band included, at various times, Kerri Biddell, Marcia Hines, Jon English and Ricky May.

The band split up in 1971 due to pressure of economics. A tobacco company, Benson and Hedges, was looking for a way to celebrate its centenary and they accepted a suggestion from one of their staff that they sponsor the reformation of the band. The band went on a nationwide tour in 1973, winning audiences at fifty venues. The American drummer, Louis Bellson, sent them some arrangements.

The Daly-Wilson Big Band did not remain in full-time employment but made Australian tours each year thereafter, and made a four week tour of the USSR in September 1976, the first tour of a cultural exchange agreement between Russia and Australia. The band has also toured in S.E. Asia and America.

The Daly-Wilson Big Band was but the peak of a keen interest in big bands by musicians across Australia. Traditional and modern musicians have an abiding enthusiasm for this type of music. The Brisbane Jazz Club has a big band, Alf Harrison formed a swing band in Canberra, high school students in Brisbane and north side Sydney suburbs play in big bands, Johnny Hawker (trombone) led a thirteen piece band at the New Palais de Danse in Melbourne with a repertoire ranging from rock to Glenn Miller, and the Barry Veith Big Band has been on the Melbourne scene since the mid-60s. Neville Dunn formed a sixteen piece band in 1962 in Adelaide for ABC broadcasts and it played at the Festival of Arts. Ten years later, Dunn's drummer, Gary Haines, put together the eighteen piece Our Thing Big Band for the enjoyment of the musicians involved. Almost by accident, Perth found itself with a big band in 1973 led by pianist Will Upson (b. 1945 Middlesex, UK). A television station, Channel 7, had an annual telethon and wanted something different for it. Upson decided to write some arrangements for a larger band, originally a ten or twelve piece, but the word spread rapidly amongst musicians, and a nineteen piece band virtually organised itself. Enlarged to twenty-three by the addition of a guitarist and three singers, they did a three month season at Bob Maher's night club, Pinocchio's, and ABC broadcasts. Upson's formula was to arrange recent pop tunes in a simple fashion which sounded high-powered and allowed room for good solos. The sax section was the strongest of the band. Eventually the band stopped because the club had to be full every night to make it pay.

In February 1977, Horst Liepolt presented at The Basement a small festival of big bands, which were the Adrian Ford Orchestra, a traditionally oriented band; Dick Lowe's 'Iss', rooted in be-bop; George Brodbeck's 'New Ground' with a jazz influenced popular and latin sound; and Craig Benjamin's 'Out Front', an avant-garde band which performed Benjamin's 'Wasteland Suite', 'Heart of Darkness' and 'Symphony No. 1 in F Minor'.

These quixotic excursions underlined the passing of an era. Though big bands retained a thrill for audiences, and though the bands tried to adapt themselves to contemporary music, customs of entertainment had changed and big bands were not economically viable. The Melbourne Trocadero closed in 1959, the Adelaide Palais Royal in 1967 and after a huge auction in 1971, the Sydney Trocadero was given over to the wreckers. They were demolished to make way for, respectively, an arts centre, a car park and a cinema complex. The site of the Brisbane Trocadero is now a railway yard. The natural heirs to the dance bands as training grounds for musicians were the conservatoriums of music, but long after American schools began teaching jazz, Australian conservatoriums were restricted to training classical symphony musicians. It was easier to get avant-garde music accepted than a course on rock bass. Don Burrows had been pressing for a jazz studies course at the Sydney Conservatorium for a long time, and got nowhere until a new director, Rex Hobcroft, took charge in 1972.

Hobcroft was one of a group of talented students who graduated within two years of each other from the Melbourne Conservatorium in the late 1940s. They were Keith Humble, Peter Sculthorpe, Don Banks and Hobcroft. Since Humble and Banks have been appointed to influential positions in, respectively, the La Trobe University School of Humanities and the Canberra School of Music, both institutions have become open to jazz. Humble played piano in the dance bands of Tommy Davidson, Jack Little and Frank Arnold, before he left to further his studies in Europe. He finished his last commercial gig at 5 a.m. in a brothel in Rue Pigalle in 1951.

Banks is a noted composer of third stream music, the meeting of classical and jazz. For his friends John Dankworth and Cleo Laine, he wrote 'Settings from Roget' in 1966. The first two of the three pieces were twelve note in origin and the third was based on Messiaen's second mode of limited transposition. 'Equation III', a continuation of 'Equation I' (1963) and 'Equation II' (1969), was written for a combination of jazz quartet and chamber ensemble with sound synthesizers, and was presented as an audio/visual experience in Canberra and Sydney in 1972 with the Don Burrows quartet and with laser images produced by artist Stan Ostoja-Kotkowski. Banks's longest third stream piece, 'Nexus', was

Howie Smith teaching jazz at the Conservatorium of Music, Sydney, 1973.

for jazz group and symphony orchestra. Originally composed for Dankworth, for its Australian recording in 1971 Banks wrote in extra parts for Golla's electric guitar, Judy Bailey's piano and Keith Stirling's high, filagree trumpet playing.

The Board of Directors and other staff at the Sydney Conservatorium accepted Hobcroft's decision without fuss. Hobcroft was hoping that Burrows might take charge of the course, but Burrows thought that a more experienced educator was needed. American vibraphonist, Gary Burton, then touring Australia, suggested Howie Smith, a superb organiser, teacher, enthusiast and saxophonist from the University of Illinois. Smith was so successful that his stay was extended three times. From his arrival in January 1973, he did not finally return to America until June 1976. He paved the way for a full-time two year Associate Diploma in Jazz Studies, the first tertiary jazz course in Australia. His place was taken by another American, trombonist Bill Motzing.

Smith had a constructive effect on Sydney jazz, not just by his work at the Conservatorium, which included the formation of a big band, but also by his honest playing with the Jazz Co-op, a collective which grew out of the Roger Frampton Trio. The Co-op first performed in May 1974 at The Basement. Frampton has a lyrical and broad scope on piano, with a humorously audacious touch, and is an able composer, as in his 'A La Coltrane' and 'RFO21273'. The rhythm section was Jack Thorncraft (bass) and Phil Treloar, whose muscular and textural drumming contributed much to the density of the group's sound.

Jazz studies are firmly established in conservatoriums and are being taken up by tertiary colleges and other schools. Jazz, and rock and folk, are recognised as important to a changing musical environment, and of interest to those who were traditionally regarded as serious creative artists. The Jazz Action Society was formed in 1974, funded by a government grant through the Australia Council, with the aim of promoting Australian jazz. As an adjunct to the work of jazz clubs it is a unifying force in the fragmented modern scene.

There are few musicians in Australia breaking new ground, but, internationally, there are not many innovators. Most players, in America too, have been and are derivative of the few real originals, which in no way is meant to detract from their ability. What we have are good musicians playing in a variety of styles, and, individually, Australians have gone beyond the copy and have made jazz a real means of expression for themselves. If anyone writes a book about contemporary world jazz that claims to be comprehensive, and fails to mention an Australian or New Zealander, then they will not have done their homework.

AN ONGOING TRADITION

BEFORE the war, except for occasional special public presentations, the palais bands were the peak of jazz and dance music. After the war, while the palais and town hall dances remained necessary for the viability of a band, the most prominent outlet for jazz became the concert hall. The best musicians, modern and traditional, would make themselves available for concerts. The jazz concert era began in Sydney on 2 March 1948 when the Port Jackson Jazz Band put on a concert at the Sydney Conservatorium. It was a resounding success. Three weeks later Ellerston Jones, the director of the Sydney Rhythm Club, presented his first Battle of the Bands at the Sydney Town Hall. Shortly, Bill McColl got into the act with an 'Evolution of Jazz' concert, and occasionally a surf lifesaving club promoted one. These concerts featured a wide variety of styles on the one bill. With a traditional band would be a big progressive band like Ralph Mallen's playing 'Artistry in Boogie', or a bop group like Wally Norman's playing 'Ornithology', each successfully appealing to different sections of the audience. The 1949 coal strike had a depressing effect on dance hall and night club entertainment, but the jazz concerts continued and became an established part of Sydney nightlife.

Jazz concerts began in Melbourne with a 'Jazz Parade' presented by Graeme Bell and Charlie Blott at the Collingwood Town Hall on 30 November 1948. This also successfully combined totally different types of jazz in the one program. The Musicians' Union presented a couple of Rhythm Festivals which featured everything from Frank Johnson's Fabulous Dixielanders to MacDuff Williams and the ABC Dance Band. The longest running series were the Downbeat concerts presented by Don Baker and Bob Clemens at Wirth's Olympia and the Melbourne Town Hall. Clemens kept them going into the 1960s.

A fillip to jazz concerts and the Bell band was given by the five-month tour of Australia by Rex Stewart, from August 1949. Stewart was one of the great jazz trumpeters and the first American jazzman to tour Australia after the war. He made his reputation with Fletcher Henderson's band, McKinney's Cotton Pickers and Ellington. The Bells, when they were overseas, conceived the idea to bring him out and they toured with him. Stewart was customarily presented as a

Rex Stewart being welcomed to Melbourne by Roger Bell (trumpet) and friends, 1949.

celebrity. At his first concert at the Exhibition Building in Melbourne he was heralded by a brass fanfare composed by Ian Pearce, which Stewart topped off with several clear high notes and swung into 'I Got Rhythm'. Stewart could easily straddle both traditional and bop, so, in addition to the Bells and Tony Newstead's Downtown Gang, Splinter Reeves and his Splintette supported Stewart for a modern bracket. In Sydney, the modern contrast was supplied by Jack Allen's band in which Don Andrews (guitar) and Frank Smith (alto) were prominent. Stewart recorded with the Bell band and with modern players in Sydney and Melbourne. As well as the capitals, Stewart visited country districts, showing audiences technically brilliant and assured jazz. His last major engagement was at the fourth jazz convention in Melbourne.

Stewart took under his wing Keith Hounslow who was baggage boy for the tour. He taught Hounslow a lot about the trumpet and helped develop his character. By the end of the tour Graeme Bell and Langdon were persuaded to allow Hounslow on stage to do a trumpet act with Stewart on 'Old Grey Bonnet'.

Through Stewart, Hounslow found himself increasingly interested in contemporary jazz, especially Ellington small groups.

Until 1954 there were no more tours, but then they came with a rush. Lee Gordon, an imaginative promoter from America who had made his money from discount selling, imported Artie Shaw, Ella Fitzgerald, Buddy Rich and comedian Jerry Colona for a concert tour beginning at the Sydney Stadium on 23 July. Fitzgerald missed the first concerts because her party had booked first class seats on the plane and had then been refused them because she was coloured. Professional musicians gained a lot from the tour. Artie Shaw, ever a perfectionist, rehearsed the fifteen piece band of Australian musicians for three hours on just one number, 'Begin The Beguine', until it was played to his satisfaction, and insisted on using them for the whole tour. Rich vastly impressed local drummers, and Fitzgerald's pianist was John Lewis. Within a month a rival promoter brought out Gene Krupa and again, an Australian band, led by Wally Norman, played in support. The cream of American and British talent has since toured Australia at one time or another. Concert tours have the effect of fanning the public's interest in jazz which results in continued support for local musicians and prevents the scene from stagnating. Sometimes a musician's attention will be drawn to an overseas performer who plays better live than on record, or the reverse may be the case. The tours showed many young musicians that their heroes were not gods and that outstanding jazz ability was not achieved by magic. On a less public level, teaching clinics, like those run by the Australian Trumpet Guild, have been of value, because they provide the opportunity for learning in person that might otherwise be unavailable from an artist on a concert tour.

Kym Bonython organised many tours by leading performers. He was the son of a Lord Mayor of Adelaide. Once he sold his school clothes to buy a drum kit and before the war led a band he called Kym Bonython's Pythons. He served as a pilot in the RAAF and took his records and wind-up gramophone with him wherever he went. In Timor the Japanese blew up his plane on the ground. He seconded a pony to carry his records while he and his crew walked seventy miles out of the jungle. Bonython returned to South Australia in peace time to breed cattle, and he became Australian champion of speedway and speedboat racing, and an astute art collector and dealer. His first jazz promotion was to bring Red Norvo west to Adelaide in 1956 from the eastern states where he was touring for Lee Gordon. Many important musicians followed, but from 1967 Bonython began losing money on the shows and no longer takes the risk.

Louis Armstrong made his first tour of Australia in 1954. For traditional jazz musicians it was the emotional high point of the year. Musicians from as far away as Adelaide and Hobart left work for a fortnight to attend every show in Melbourne. Bob Barnard and Tich Bray took a room in the same hotel so they could be as close to him as possible. When Armstrong and the All-Stars came on stage at their first concert some of the Australian jazzmen nearly cried because the moment was so intense. Louis Armstrong, the creator of their dreams, was at last before them. But their adulation was tempered by the subsequent concerts, all of which they attended, because they had been thinking that Louis was big enough to play anything; the chastening realization came that even Armstrong, in public, worked to a formula. Every concert and solo was the same. He had a polished act which captivated the public every time. This lesson about the demands of show business was hard for the jazz enthusiasts to swallow.

The Australian Jazz Convention has brought out a few jazz musicians, including Alton Purnell, Ken Colyer, Clark Terry, Dick Cary and Bud Freeman, and the opportunities to play informally have been stimulating for all concerned.

The recording industry expanded after the war. EMI faced competition from the large overseas companies, CBS and RCA. There were many transient local labels, like Bob Clemens's 'Jazzart' or Ron Wills's 'Wilco', but some, like Festival, White and Gillespie (W&G), Radio Corporation (Astor) and Philips, were successful and secured a place in the market. There was a recording ban in USA in 1942–44 which had the good side-effect that many worthwhile jazz records were re-issued which may not have been otherwise. Ron Wills, who had the collector's interests at heart, was made Record Sales Manager of EMI in Sydney in 1951, and he instigated a program of re-releasing old jazz classics.

The label which has best served the traditional market by recording local artists and by releasing an excellent historical series is Swaggie, begun by five members of the Bell band in January 1950. They were too busy playing to put the required effort into it and in 1954 Swaggie was purchased by one of Graeme Bell's piano students, Neville Sherburn. Sherburn was a woolclasser and livestock buyer who led his own jazz band from 1951 to 1957. Sherburn and Bill Armstrong, who later ran a recording studio, worked out how to transfer the sound directly from metal masters of 78s to the seven inch disc and later the twelve inch LP. By dint of painstaking research, Sherburn found remarkable masters held by US recording companies and persuaded them to let him have them. Swaggie has an esteemed role in the Australian jazz market and has steady export sales to North and South America, Europe, Asia and South Africa.

The Bells made a second tour overseas in 1950–52, based in the UK with short forays into Europe. The two-trumpet lead was tacitly abandoned. Kanga Bentley was added to the line-up on trombone, Bud Baker replaced Jack Varney on banjo, and John Sangster replaced Russ Murphy and learned to play drums on the ship to England. Monsbourgh mostly played his alto on which he was so hot. His tone was husky and mellow, and he spun his phrases of spellbinding simplicity beyond their expected end, always injecting an element of surprise into the band. He could sing well too. For his ability and his position in the scene, Ade Monsbourgh was dubbed the 'Father of Australian traditional jazz'. Again the Bells were a vital element in the British scene. They admired Humphrey Lyttleton's band but the other bands were at a stage Australians had abandoned five years previously— hidebound by the old records, afraid to experiment with other forms of jazz or to compose their own tunes, and staid in their presentation. The Bells were successful everywhere. They appeared at a concert in Festival Hall attended by Princess Elizabeth, and her cousin, the Hon. Gerald Lascelles, invited them to dinner at St James's Palace. On their second trip to Germany, arranged by the German Jazz Federation, they performed with Big Bill Broonzy and recorded with him, though these were never issued. The Bells had problems with teenagers besieging them for autographs. The youthful hysteria which characterised rock and roll was already present in a muted form. Four sides were recorded with Humphrey Lyttleton's band. On their return the Bell band did a tour of the eastern states and were voted Australia's premier jazz band for 1952 in a readers' poll in *Music Maker*.

A feature of their concerts was the number of Australian compositions they included. Out of twenty tunes about eight would be originals, perhaps 'Nullarbor' by Dallwitz, or Roger Bell's 'Cheeky Possum', or others by Monsbourgh, Sangster or another of their friends. As much as any group of musicians outside USA, Australian composers have shown that the traditional form of jazz has not been exhausted and that the New Orleans and Chicago jazzmen laid down the parameters of the style, not its boundaries. The Australian Jazz Convention began an original tunes competition in 1947, but it is in the last decade, when the musicians who began in the late forties have come into their musical maturity and want to put something back into the music which has inspired their lives, that major compositions have been made.

A leading talent is John Sangster (b. 1928), unique in Australian jazz in that he is the only musician who is equally important to both the traditional and modern schools. He has one foot firmly planted in traditional jazz, but the scope of his ability, on vibes and percussion, and his imagination, allow him to range freely through all styles. His father was a sailor who played only 'Swanee River' on mandolin in the bath. His mother played piano a little and his aunts used to gather round and sing Presbyterian hymns. There was no music at Box Hill High School but Sangster bought a trombone after hearing Wingy Manone's 'Corinne Corrina'. Then he bought a cornet and decided that playing with other people would be more rewarding than turning his bicycle upside down and accompanying Benny Goodman's 'Gotta Be This or That' by drumming on the tyres. Then came Bix records which made his father angry so he left home and worked in a bookshop. Since then music has been Sangster's career. He played an earthy, driving cornet which swung any band he played with and he was the find of the 1948 convention. Until Sangster went overseas on the second Bell tour he was a strict traditionalist, but in Britain there were always two bands in the bus doing the concert circuit, and he grew interested in Kenny Graham's Afro Cubists and the Johnny Dankworth 7. Going overseas helped him to realize that he was good enough to play his own compositions and he wrote his first one there. Orchestration interested him, at first the style of Luis Russell because the Bell band could front three saxes plus a trumpeter to do the Red Allen part.

When the Bell band broke up after returning to Australia, Sangster stayed with Graeme Bell when he went to Brisbane. At a hotel where they were playing with two Hungarians, Sangster discovered a vibraphone. The way Sangster tells it, because he is lazy and the trumpet takes daily practice, he became a drummer; drums you have to cart around but vibes have wheels; that trapped him into becoming a percussionist and they have to carry tons of equipment; which is why he composes because all he needs is a pencil and paper, a sponsor and something to drink. A greater attraction than having wheels was that vibes combined the percussive qualities of the drums with the melodic capacity of the trumpet.

After Graeme Bell, Sangster played with the Ray Price Quartet, the ABC Dance Band, 'The Sound of Music' on television, the Don Burrows Quartet, and at the El Rocco nightclub, the centre of modern jazz in Sydney in the 1960s. There he strived for more than Australian style, but Australian content too, asking musicians such as Judy Bailey and Lyn Christie—or Bob Barnard or Johnny McCarthy

—why were they playing American tunes when they were good improvisors and capable of playing their own tunes. It was easier for them to perform the standard repertoire but playing their own material forced them back on their own resources. Sangster experimented with collective improvisation with Charlie Munro, Graham Lyall, Ron Carson and Bobby Gebert, but philosophically he is opposed to total collective improvisation, thinking that free expression does not necessarily equal music, but often instant boredom, though he respects the musicians who attempt it. He is in favour of using established forms. Traditional bands appealed to him because they are hot; he likes jazz to be an emotional experience and he likes it to swing. If he is to compose, Sangster feels he must study all his life, to be open to new experiences. He fell in love with Sun Ra on record and then Albert Ayler and Sunny Murray on an album called 'Spiritual Unity' which American pianist Bob James brought out with him while on tour. Sangster wanted to learn how rock drumming was done, so he took a job playing at the Whisky A Go-Go and in 'Hair'. He described this as a deliberate change of life, 'and by jees, did I have one!' An Indian master drummer, with whom he did a course in Sydney, influenced Sangster to try to relate his music to each day as he lived it. Life cannot be divided into segments the length of a 78.

Sangster composes suites, or groups of pieces linked by an idea if not a musical theme, because he wants to hold his audience's attention for more than three minutes. He hopes to connect their thoughts and create a whole shape from it. Another reason for his aim is that Ellington is the touchstone of his music. Sangster writes for albums, not for performance. Only about a third of his 'Lord of the Rings' music could be reproduced in public. The Beatles' success taught him that he could reach a wider audience through records and he only plays in public to promote his records. He likes to have something to go on while composing and nature films were a good vehicle. The picture tells one story, the narrator a second and the music a third. 'Australia and All That Jazz' Vols. I & II (1971, 1976) was the soundtrack for a film about Australian wildlife by the Australian Museum, half about the parts of Australia with water and half about the dry regions. Sangster chose woodwinds and percussion to depict the abundance of life around waterholes and the tiny life cycles which occur in the open silences of the desert. J. R. R. Tolkien's books, *The Hobbit* and the *Lord of the Rings*, provided the inspiration for a beautiful body of music which has so far filled ten LPs. There is an unmistakable resemblance between Sangster and the stout hobbit who is fond of simple jests, eating, drinking and good company. Sangster combined musicians from different jazz backgrounds on pieces which range from jovially traditional to atmospherically modern. He likes to call it 'cosmic dixieland'. He is always able to play himself on drums or vibes, with a delicate intensity that is not necessarily aggressive. Sangster's most recent project is to acknowledge his debt to the sources of his music, to Bix, Morton and Ellington. This work shows what Australian traditional jazz is all about; the pieces are composed in conscious admiration of the styles of the great jazzmen, but the end result is all Sangster.

Most of Dave Dallwitz's work has been composed in the last decade. In 1952 he grew disheartened with jazz and left it for nearly twenty years. Meanwhile he played in the Burnside Symphony Orchestra and this involvement with classical music made him more adventurous in his treatment of the traditional jazz idiom. He calls himself 'progressively mouldy', which means that while he will never dispense with the banjo and tuba in his own ten piece band, he will try to arrange his music to alter the usual role of the instruments; the band does not do the standard routine of ensemble followed by solos concluding with an ensemble passage. The 'Ern Malley Suite' was Dallwitz's first true suite. His previous compositions were grouped together by a common title, but the Malley suite was composed as a logical succession of contrasting pieces. Dallwitz loved the poetry from his first reading of it, and when he saw Sidney Nolan's Ern Malley paintings he was aroused to produce something inspired by the poem. He wrote it in about a week and in November 1974 the suite was premiered in the Adelaide Art Gallery, the band surrounded by Nolan's paintings. Dallwitz is a firm believer in the importance of Australians playing their own compositions. His music has been sensitively interpreted by others. Limpid laments and chirpy rags came up beautifully on the 'Riverboat Days' album under the sure hand of Sangster, Burrows, Dieter Vogt and the Barnard brothers. Dallwitz was honoured when Earl Hines recorded an album of Dallwitz tunes in his own characteristic style.

Tom Pickering is content to compose in the standard traditional style. He has a nice melodic sense and often Ian Pearce harmonises his tunes for him. Pearce's classical training has a bearing on what he writes. He twists and turns an idea to make it tight within the limits he sets on it.

An experiment in marrying traditional jazz with rock was done by Geoff Kitchen and Ken Evans in 1976. Since leaving Johnson's Fabulous Dixielanders in the early 1950s, both had expanded their jazz experience, particularly Kitchen who became a professional musician in 1957 with Bob Gibson's band in Sydney and he worked in television and in the studios. Evans wrote 'Park Street Suite' which included a fugue, in 1952, but at the time he was told it would be more suitable for a string quartet. Now suites are commonplace. For their experiment they used a traditional front line, playing as it normally would and coupled it with a rock rhythm section. They played original compositions and produced a fairly successful sound.

As with the general standard of singing in Australian traditional jazz, so too with the composition of lyrics, very little can be said in its favour. Rarely do lyrics rise above the banal. Australian traditional jazz is oriented away from the vocal. It has made no attempt to talk about contemporary life. Country and western singers write about troops in Vietnam or Cyclone Tracy blowing Darwin down, but traditional jazzers cannot even come to grips with a love song. Virtually the only band to successfully produce entertaining lyrics was the Captain Matchbox Whoopee Band. The band came from the fringe of the Melbourne jazz scene, and the fringe of nearly every other scene too, being an amalgamation of elements from jug bands, Fats Waller, the Quintet du Hot Club de France and the Temperance Seven brand of dixieland. Mick Conway (b. 1951, Sydney) started it in 1968 as the Jelly Bean Jug Band which performed at folk dens and trad jazz places. It became Captain Matchbox in 1970 and was forced out of the folk/jazz field because they could not make a living there. They were curious to see how far they could go on the rock circuit. Their approach to their songs was vaudevillian, drawing on that tradition in jazz of sending up woeful lyrics. A good example of their boisterous irreverence is their album 'Wangaratta Wahine'. Of all the jazz bands in the 1970s they had the closest association with the theatre, the Pram Factory, and this improved their presentation and made it unique, and was an added spur to maintaining the standard of their lyrics. From 1975 to 1977 Captain Matchbox was overtly political, presenting a show dealing with the leftist issues of the day—nuclear power, Aboriginal oppression, East Timor, inflation, consumerism, sexism, marijuana, the constitutional crisis of 11 November 1975 and an old faithful, the Queen. They made it into a multilingual show and took it to factories which had a high proportion of immigrant labour. No one else did that. But, no matter how serious the issue, they always returned to their forte, the humorous song, the bizarre exaggeration of everyday activity, which distinguishes them from other bands.

Yet original Australian compositions have had no real influence on the development of the Australian style of jazz. If no one had composed a single tune the style would be the same today, because it is the improvisation and the interpretation which determines the style, not the tune itself. Australian compositions exist only on record. Not only do musicians not play tunes by other Australians, they rarely play their own. The acid test is when a pick-up band gets together and plays one of the, say, five hundred tunes which form the jazz literature of the average traditional musician. One of the certainties of life in the southern hemisphere is that seven Australian traditional jazz musicians chosen at random will not know one Australian tune in common. Australian compositions have not penetrated the Australian jazz consciousness and the responsibility for this lies squarely with the musicians themselves. Their homage to everything American and their readiness to fall back on the old war horses blinds them to the large stable of good Australian tunes. However, Australian bands are no different in this respect from British, European or New Zealand traditional bands, and Australians have a commendable willingness to introduce unusual and new tunes on their records.

The musicians who came to the fore in the first five jazz conventions were pillars of the expanding jazz scene. Graeme Bell toured Korea and Japan for the army in 1954 with a six piece band, settled in Sydney in 1957, formed a skiffle group while skiffle was 'in', and in June 1962 formed the first of his All-Stars bands, bringing Bob Barnard up from Melbourne to play at the Chevron Hotel. He had his own nationally televised show on ATN7 for a year, he played with Terry Lightfoot's band in England in 1967 and has kept appearing at concerts and festivals ever since. The Australia Council awarded him a research grant in 1975 to study jazz in USA and he received the Queen's Silver Jubilee Medal in 1977.

Roger Bell did not remain in the public eye to the same extent as his brother, but, leading a band of varying personnel called the Pagan Pipers, which usually included Monsbourgh, he produced some high quality jazz, for example, the album 'The Wombat'.

The Bells' manager, Mel Langdon, promoted concerts with Bill McColl, experimented with night baseball at the Showground, managed an ice show and ran the first concert at the Sydney Opera House while it was still being built.

Tony Newstead gave up leading his own band in the early 1960s because he was too busy with his work. Three of the best jazz years of his life came in 1970–73 when he worked in Washington DC as communications adviser to the World Bank. He was a foundation member of the Potomac River Jazz Club and recorded with Willie 'The Lion' Smith, some of the Condon crowd, and notably Bill Rank who had played with Bix.

In Tasmania, Tom Pickering had to create a new band after the first convention because Ian Pearce and Rex Green remained in Melbourne. Pickering found Keith Stackhouse, a university student who played piano, and convinced some jazz-inclined dance musicians that jazz was the thing. Then, in 1948, he found a place for a dance at a radio station, the 7HT Theatrette. Tom Pickering's Good Time Music, a band of seven with Kay Stavely as vocalist, caught on and became an institution in Hobart during the next twelve years. They have held reunions of the band in the 1970s which have been reunions of the generation which grew up with them. At the Hobart Town Hall in the mid-50s the dance had problems with brawling groups of bodgies and widgies, Australia's home-grown teenage hoods, but it passed. Pickering's band often entered the Professional and Amateur (P&A) Parade radio show in Melbourne with success. Billy Banks, the American Negro singer, recorded with them in 1956 when he was in Tasmania with a show, 'Olympic Follies'. Ian Pearce returned to Hobart in 1955 after five years in the UK. He went there with Don Banks, not intending to play jazz, but after being introduced by the Bells, played trombone and piano with Mick Mulligan's Magnolia Jazz Band and recorded with them. When he came back Pearce formed a modern quintet using the versatile Alan Brinkman on clarinet, which broadcast over Ellis Blain's show, 'After Dark'. Pickering's Good Time Music broke up in 1960 because there was no longer enough work for it, and soon after Cedric Pearce had a mild stroke and had to give up drumming. Pickering and Ian Pearce stuck together in trios and quartets, as well as playing in some of the other jazz bands which had emerged in Hobart. Pickering is one of the best vocalists in traditional jazz, having the same humble genuine approach to his singing as he does to his instruments. Pearce is an empathetic pianist. Years before the American film 'The Sting' appeared, they spotted that no one was doing any ragtime, formed the Pearce-Pickering Ragtime Five in 1967, and aided by a willing sound engineer at the ABC, Jack Smith, recorded an LP in 1970, 'Jazzmania'. They made a short tour of army bases in Vietnam in 1971. Eartha Kitt was so taken with the band in 1975 that she requested a special session with them during her Wrest Point season. The Pearce-Pickering partnership has been a mainstay of jazz in Hobart.

In the north of Tasmania there were jazz musicians in Launceston and along the coast from Devonport to Burnie. The North-West Dixielanders began in mid-1947. The bassist Neil 'Kanga' Yeomans was well-known to mainlanders. Ted Herron began his Jazzmanians in Launceston about the same time. His pianist, Don Gurr, later formed a modern group in Hobart and Herron interested a young clarinettist, Peter Coleman, in jazz, who formed his own dixieland band in the 1950s. Herron's brother Ken became a leading professional trombonist. He is superb in small traditional groups and has a rare ability to create that exquisite tension by understatement in his playing. In Hobart, the Lazy River Five was formed just after the war and were followed by the Wildcats in the 1950s. The main rival to the Pickering band was the Sullivans Cove Jazz Stompers formed in the early 1960s. They appealed to a younger generation and were prepared to accommodate other styles, such as the Tijuana Brass, as they became fashionable.

By 1950 the Southern Jazz Group had made about fifty recordings for Adelaide and Sydney labels. They went to Sydney in May 1950 with Ade Monsbourgh to record with Parlophone and Wilco, and while there recorded hillbilly music with Rodeo Records under the name of Dusty Rhodes and his Jackeroos. But these were the last recording sessions of the band; Bruce Gray wanted a different musical policy and left. During the year Lew Fisher, Bob Wright, Bill Munro and Johnny Malpas went with him to form Bruce Gray's All-Stars. In the late 1950s, as a result of pressure from the pianist, Ted Nettelbeck, and drummer, Billy Ross, and their own interest, Gray and Munro gradually played a more modern sound, moving into early Miles Davis, Chet Baker, Mancini and Brubeck; Munro was never completely satisfied by modern jazz, though it opened up his style and improved him technically. Gray was more at ease with it, but was irked by the opinion that because he played modern he had ceased to be able to appreciate traditional jazz. From 1959, Gray worked in TV studio orchestras. Munro played with the university jazz band in the early 1960s, which became the Campus Six when most of them graduated. It is still going today. Their singer is Penny Eames who has marked influences of Billie Holiday, with her own light phrasing.

Other traditional bands of varying importance were: Richie Gunn's Collegians from which came Ted Nettelbeck and Rod Porter, clarinet, and Gunn himself who was later a federal parliamentarian; the University Jazz 4 started in 1950 with Alex Frame on cornet; Frame later played in the Westside Jazz Band led by Leon Atkinson, clarinet, and the Black Eagle Jazz Band led by John Pickering, trombone. The conductor of the South Australian Police Band, Ernie Alderslade,

The Port Jackson Jazz Band, Sydney, late 1950s.
L–R: Johnny McCarthy (clarinet), Dick Hughes (piano), Ken Flannery (trumpet), Ray Price (guitar), John Sangster (drums), Harry Harman (bass).

is a good, quiet jazz trombonist who came up through Melbourne brass bands, played jazz in Mildura in 1953 with the Sunraisier Stompers and was a member of the Campus Six for many years. Today there are about ten traditional jazz bands in Adelaide.

The success of their Sydney Conservatorium concert in March 1948 put the Port Jackson Jazz Band much in demand and Ray Price organised a country tour for them through northern New South Wales to Brisbane. It was a disaster. Two of the band were members of the Communist Party and Price had several times hired Eureka Youth League premises in which to rehearse, and this connection dogged them wherever they went. A scurrilous pamphlet called 'Things I hear' published by Frank Browne, claimed that all the members of the Bell band and the Port Jackson band were communists, and it was distributed in all country towns ahead of the band. The RSL, the Chamber of Commerce and the Catholic Church in each town made engagements hard for the band. Price was mystified at the poor attendances. Another problem was that one of their two female vocalists, Nellie Small, was a black girl. She was born of West Indian parents in Sydney and wore male attire as part of her stage act. In country pubs they were asked what was the black fellow doing with them. Laborious explanations ensued. Small could not stay in many hotels, and at the Brisbane GPO Farrell had to collect her mail for her. Farrell advised Graeme Bell to check the accommodation before he took Rex Stewart north, and because only one flea-bag hotel would accept him, Stewart did not appear in Brisbane. The Port Jackson entourage also included a blind saxophonist, Dick Jackson, who beat them at poker using braille cards. The single bright spot was a dance organised for them in Ipswich by Sid Bromley, but it was not enough and Price had to wire his father for money to bail them out of the mess. The band split up for a while but reformed within a year and kept going intermittently until the Australia Day weekend of 1965. Marie Harriet, the other vocalist, went overseas and achieved a measure of fame under the name of Marie Benson.

Ray Price tirelessly promoted the Port Jackson Jazz Band, but his publicity also mentioned that he was a double bassist with the Sydney Symphony Orchestra. He was with the SSO while studying for his A.Mus.A. and L.Mus. at the Conservatorium. The ABC regarded the SSO as the Public Service and had the right to determine whether or not their employees could accept outside work. Price received an ultimatum in 1956, took a stand against being told what type of music he could play, and was sacked. He had some belated satisfaction the next year when a newspaper photographed Constantin Silvestri, guest conductor with the SSO, listening attentively to his trio at the Macquarie Arms Hotel, Woolloomooloo. With Dick Hughes and Bob Barnard in the trio, Price was playing some of the best jazz of his career. Hughes has a strong direct style; he was the only Australian pianist to play for the all-black Alvin Ailey American Dance Theatre when they toured. The Macquarie Arms was a mecca for jazz. A woman was raffled every Saturday night in the public bar where brawls often erupted, but in the lounge where the band played there was not one fight in two years. Price formed a quartet and established a niche in the education system, giving entertaining and informative jazz concerts in schools. The prominent musicians to have passed through Price's quartet include Col Nolan, John Sangster, Johnny McCarthy,

King Fisher, Bruce Johnson who was later with Maynard Ferguson, and Dave McRae, later with Buddy Rich.

The Port Jackson band had its spin-offs. Jack Parkes formed the Riverside Jazz Band whose most consistent job was at the North Steyne Surf Club. From it came Johnny McCarthy who soon developed into the leading traditional clarinettist in Sydney. He has been with Bob Barnard's band since 1974; his hot, uninhibited

THE FAMED

Cootumundra
Jazz Band

One of New South Wales' Best Jazz Bands and often heard over the Wireless will be playing   for the

UNGARIE WAR MEMORIAL

HALL BALL

FRIDAY, 22nd JUNE, 1956

EXCELLENT SUPPER & FLOOR

Don't Miss This Night Of Fun.

DANCE TILL 3 O'CLOCK

TICKETS: Ladies 8/-   Gents 12/-   Double £1

THIS NIGHT SHOULD prove to be the BEST OF THE YEAR

Come along & bring your Friends

J. JANSEN, Hon. Sec.   W. E. BREWER, President

"Advocate" Print, West Wyalong.

playing is a perfect counterpart to Barnard's trumpet. Duke Farrell played with the Illawarra Jazz Band. The Sydney Jazz Club began in 1953 in a basement in Martin Place and then moved down to the Ironworkers' hall in George Street. The house band was the Paramount Jazz Band, often with vocalist Kate Dunbar. Jazz in Sydney in the mid-50s was still not as big as in Melbourne but it was picking up.

Jazz is primarily a music of the city, but there have been some notable successes in the country, the most famous being the Cootamundra Jazz Band in southern New South Wales and the Goulburn Valley Jazz Band centred on Shepparton in northern Victoria. The position they held in their home towns, the regard with which they are held in the jazz community, and the quality of their music make them important bands. The Cootamundra Jazz Band was started by John Ansell (b. 1922, Sydney). His musical life began when he was given a drum kit at twelve years of age while he was at Canberra Grammar School, and he first played with Les Pogson (sax) and a pianist at a school social. Pogson was with Eric Pearce in Sydney in the 1920s. Ansell did not know about jazz but he preferred dance music to other types. He had piano lessons for six months from the nuns at Yanco and finished his education at Leeton. Ansell was a wireless operator in the RAAF and at every camp during the war he sought out the musicians amongst the troops and put together small groups. In January 1944 he was shot down over Germany and spent the rest of the conflict in Stalag 3 and Stalag 7. The Swiss Red Cross supplied instruments to the POWs and Ansell joined two session bands in the camps, but jazz did not begin for him until he got home and heard 'Smokey Mokes' by the Bells. He heard Frank Johnson over the radio, wrote to him and made his acquaintance on a summer holiday. These two Australian bands were a major influence on him. Ansell formed a trio in 1947 called The Modernists, with Johnny Costello on drums and his father Eric Costello on trumpet. They played popular tunes by ear. Johnny Costello switched to trombone and Ansell gradually enlarged the band to six pieces and included more jazz in the repertoire.

Work for a country band is different from that of a city band. Many engagements are annual balls, so instead of playing to keep the job from week to week, they have to make sufficient impact to be invited back again next year. An established country band is literally booked up a year in advance. Many balls were held in picture theatres. In Junee, no pictures were shown on Mondays, so the chairs were cleared away and all the balls held on that night. On Tuesdays, it might be Gundagai's turn. All the Catholic balls were held on Wednesdays. Harden-Murrumburrah might see the band on Thursdays, and Fridays and Saturdays were reserved for local dances. At an isolated hall, the band and the guests often arrived by bus. The advent of TV made inroads into the popularity of those dances.

The Cootamundra band had some good and interesting players in it. Costello made the break in the Sydney scene and has made a solid contribution to Bob Barnard's excellent band. On clarinet was Jack Burnett, also known as Jack Mortimer, who had played with Linn Smith's Jazz Band and Danny Hogan's Frisco Six in the 1920s. He was replaced by Greg Gibson, an exciting product of the Melbourne jazz scene who is of the top echelon of Australian traditional clarinettists.

The Cootamundra band finished when Ansell moved to Wagga Wagga in 1960, but he established himself there by forming the Riverina Jazz Band. Previously he had played piano only, but he brought his wife Shirley in on piano and turned his hand to any instrument that might be lacking from the line-up. The band achieved the same busy success of its predecessor and has heightened the jazz content and professionalism of other bands and musicians in the district. John Ansell has worked by day to play good jazz at night for the region for over thirty years. He thinks about jazz between jobs, goes to the jazz club wherever he is and the trip to the jazz convention is an annual feature of his life.

Wagga Wagga and Shepparton, like many prosperous country towns, had amateur dance orchestras long before traditional jazz became popular. Wagga Wagga had an open air dance floor in the 1920s called Dixieland which hung over the river before the levee was built, but it was washed away by a flood in the early thirties. The leading band was the Melody Masters, a nine-piece band (2 trumpets, 3 sax, 4 rhythm) which was runner-up to the Don Rankin band in the 1936 P&A Parade in Melbourne. Their rivals were the Riverina Revellers. The Melody Masters continued until the war. An amateur dance orchestra of violin,

The Goulburn Valley Jazz Band jamming with the Dutch Swing College Jazz Band in the parking lot of a hotel, Shepparton, Victoria, 13 June 1974.
L–R: Dick Kaart (trombone), Bruce Eddy (bass), Alf Hurst (trombone), Neville Stribling (soprano, alto, tenor, baritone, clarinet), Dudley Griffiths (guitar, banjo), Peter Schilperoort (clarinet), Ken Parsons (drums), Huub Janssen (drums, washboard).

cornet, flute, piano and bass was begun in Shepparton shortly before World War I by Frank Young. A trumpeter, Charlie Fennell, began the first of Shepparton's Blue Moon Orchestras in 1934. It began as a five-piece and grew to nine after the war while the Glenn Miller sound was still popular. It was the resident band at the Star Palais until 1962. Jim Beale, drummer at Smacka's restaurant in Melbourne in the 1970s, came out of it, and Dick Tattum, well-known Melbourne trumpeter and Ken Parsons, drummer with the Goulburn Valley Jazz Band played with the Blue Moon Orchestra at various times.

The mainstay of the Goulburn Valley Jazz Band is Neville Stribling (b. 1936) who is a measure of how well an Australian can play if he models his playing on another Australian's style, and the extent to which Australian jazz is moving under its own impetus. Musicians like Stribling are proof that if Australian jazz were to be cut off from all contact with American jazz, if all the old 78s disappeared and young musicians had only older Australians to learn from, Australian jazz would continue in strength. Stribling was sensitive to the musicians he played with in his early development; three factors which influenced him were the Frank Johnson band which gave him confidence, Nick Polites who taught him theory, and the alto of Ade Monsbourgh which Stribling esteemed to be the epitome of hotness. Stribling's alto reflects his high regard for Monsbourgh. Stribling is a thorough musician who burrows into a chord. The Goulburn Valley Jazz Band has been active since 1957, based in Shepparton but doing gigs in the snowfields in the Great Divide, in border towns along the River Murray, as far west as Horsham and as far north as Deniliquin. The personnel of the band has varied, sometimes incorporating Melbourne musicians Dick Tattum, Rex Green and Graham Coyle while they were resident in Shepparton, and Monsbourgh often played with them. The band was formed into the present quintet with trombone and alto in the front line in October 1973, and now all its members live in the district. The band is proving an all-jazz policy is very popular.

In just about every town of 5000 or more in the regions covered by the Goulburn Valley and Riverina jazz bands there is one musician interested in jazz, and since the early 1960s they have congregated at different towns for informal blows. The first was a meeting of Cobram and Wangaratta musicians in the corrugated iron shed next to the hall at Tarrawingie. Gradually more jazzers attended the gatherings, and as they were held in different towns it became a competition as to who could out-cater who. This was resolved when they decided to hold their country jazz festivals each Easter at Deniliquin, because Deniliquin is the town most equidistant from Sydney, Melbourne and Adelaide. By virtue of its small, informal organisation, the Deniliquin festival is reminiscent of the early Australian Jazz Conventions, and has the same stimulatory effect on jazz in the district.

Peculiar things happen to country jazz bands which do not happen to anyone else. The Great Northern Jazz Band of Darwin had a change of instrumentation at Christmas 1974 when Cyclone Tracy blew away the piano.

Canberra is a stronghold of traditional jazz, not being large enough yet to support much mainstream or modern jazz. The overwhelming majority of musicians old enough to play jazz were not born there; most came from Sydney or Melbourne in the influx which has tripled Canberra's population since the mid-1960s. The two leading bands in that period were The Fortified Few, and Clean Living Clive's Goodtime Palace Orchestra led by Neil Steeper who plays trumpet and sings with the galvanic subtlety of a scrum on corrugated iron. The leading mainstream bands were the Sterling Primmer Trio and Mood Indigo, a fruitful partnership of Greg Gibson and Graham Coyle, piano. The Australian Public Service has employed Gibson in the Department of Foreign Affairs since 1959 and wherever he has been posted, in Asia or Europe, Gibson has joined the local jazz community, as well as carrying out his departmental duties. By sending jazzers like Gibson, or Lachie Thompson of the Army, overseas, the Public Service is inadvertently aiding the continuation of that long tradition, which goes back to vaudeville days, of Australian musicians performing in Asia.

The first flush of the dixieland revival lasted not quite a decade then paled markedly in the mid-50s, which was a disaster for Melbourne's Len Barnard's Famous Jazz Band. They turned professional in March 1955 and embarked on a fund raising tour prior to a proposed overseas trip at the very time the public lost interest. The first part of the tour, through Gippsland, was a success, but attendances gradually fell. Broken Hill at Easter was like a ghost town and the band paid itself less and less until it got down to 10/- each a day. They slept in in the mornings so they would only have to eat twice—two hamburgers, one packet of cigarettes and a bottle of beer a day. Floods in central New South Wales made the tour more difficult. Most country roads were unsealed and inches deep in mud. Many shows on the road went broke that year. Barnard's band might have done better if they had had a floor show with them, a hypnotist, a female singer or someone to catch bullets in his teeth. The band had some respite in Sydney, working the Paradance circuit and on some half-hour shows for the ABC, but by the time they reached Brisbane they were penniless. They needed to make £700 on the last concert and made only £150. Disgruntled and disenchanted they broke up; two stayed in Brisbane, one in Sydney and the rest struggled back to Melbourne.

Compounding their gloom was the tragic news of Wocka Dyer's death in a car accident while returning along the Goulburn Valley Highway from a footballers' ball at Nagambie on 21 September 1955. It cut the ground from under the feet of the traditional jazz community and Frank Johnson's band folded soon afterwards. The Johnson band had survived many changes of personnel but could not sustain the loss of Dyer. By the end of 1955 Melbourne had lost three of its best bands—the Graeme Bell, Frank Johnson and Len Barnard bands.

Other factors were causing a temporary decline of the jazz scene in the mid-50s. Television began in 1956 in Sydney and Melbourne and in the other capitals within a few years. Rock and roll captured the rising generation of dancers from 1955 and though some jazzers conceded that the beat was exciting, it seemed so moronicly simple that they were uninterested in it. Young dancers went elsewhere for their entertainment. The third factor affecting the jazz scene was the introduction of ten o'clock closing in pubs in Sydney. There already was more money for music in Sydney but this sealed it, though rock and roll bands were often hired because they operated with four musicians where most jazz bands preferred six. Melbourne did not allow late closing until 1966. It lost many musicians to Sydney as a result. Also, NSW had poker machines which meant

Judith Durham.

that clubs could afford professional musicians. These factors ushered in a new period for jazz.

Dedicated jazzmen keep blowing whether jazz is in decline or booming; if a paid job disappears then they play at private parties. The dedicated buff is happiest when jazz is in decline because his heart is fired with a proselytizing zeal, but when it has a surge of popularity he feels a contradictory antagonism to these Johnny-come-latelies who he is certain are ignorant of the history of jazz and have no emotional investment in its future.

From the trough of the mid-50s, jazz experienced a resurgence of popularity that exceeded the peak of the revival ten years previously. Around Australia new, young bands sprang up, and the boom was centred again in Melbourne. Young Melbourne musicians seemed to be more sensitive to the traditional jazz boom happening in England than their contemporaries in Sydney, more of whom were the early stars of Australia's pubescent rock and roll craze. The success of English musicians like Acker Bilk, Chris Barber, Kenny Ball and Ken Colyer had a great influence on the styles adopted by the new bands, and, like any healthy art form, Australian traditional jazz experienced a split in its ranks due to factional differences over style.

The era of Melbourne's casual dances was well under way by 1960. Teenagers wore duffle coats, sloppy joes, corduroy trousers and desert boots. The dances had names such as Opus, Powerhouse, Esquire, Dante's Inferno, Penthouse, Black and Blue or the Keyboard Club. After the visits of the Bell band, English jazz had taken off and, in turn, influenced Australian jazz. The records of George Lewis and Bunk Johnson were in favour in England. The specious idea was that because Lewis and Johnson had stayed in the south their jazz was more pure than the Oliver/Morton jazz favoured by most previous revival bands. Whether or not there was any substance to that argument, there was no doubt about the reality of the division between those who espoused New Orleans jazz and the others who disparaged it as 'underwater music'. Amongst the new crop of musicians were a number who were unimpressed by 'Australian' jazz as epitomised by the Bell and Johnson bands. The first New Orleans band was formed by Llew Hird, Frank Turville and Nick Polites in June 1957, which became the Melbourne New Orleans Jazz Band. They came to prominence through Horst Liepolt's Jazz Centre 44 at the Katherina Coffee Lounge in St Kilda and were favourably received at the 1957 convention in Adelaide. They increased their following when a good folk/jazz singer from England, Paul Marks, joined the band. His total absorption in his singing was exciting for their audiences. The folk and jazz scenes were close then; Marion Henderson and Margaret Roadknight were folk singers who sang with jazz bands in their early days. Roadknight has retained firm links with the jazz world. She strives for a negroid timbre in her singing voice and presents spirituals and gospels. Political songs have increasingly concerned her.

The Melbourne New Orleans Jazz Band left on a successful overseas tour in August 1961. Many traditional jazz bands have gone overseas since then and it is no longer remarkable, though it is exciting for the band involved and often educational. An important lesson that alert Australian musicians have learned in the USA is that American musicians play both softer, and louder, than Australians. Australians have to expend a lot of effort to get hot, but Americans seem to play at only half pace yet they are still as hot as stoves. The average volume of American playing, whether it be by a traditional or a modern band, is quiet by Australian standards, but the climax of an American band is astonishing. The reasons why Australians tend to play at full-bore and neglect dynamics can perhaps be related to the difficulties which they have in singing. Because Australians are diffident about expressing their emotions, they aim at an emotional plateau that is comfortable and stick to it. The past decade has been so fruitful of good jazz in Australia because the musicians of the first revival have reached the maturity of their interpretative powers, and have the courage and self-awareness to leave the plateau behind.

The Melbourne New Orleans Jazz Band left their regular engagements to another New Orleans band, the Yarra Yarra Jazz Band, formed in 1958 by Maurie Garbutt, trumpet. It is still a presence in the Melbourne jazz scene. Like the Melbourne New Orleans Jazz Band, they featured a vocalist; Judy Jacques was the best known of their singers. A number of female singers came up at the time—Helen Violaris, Pat Purchase, and Kerri Male were some, but the singer who achieved international fame was Judith Durham. As a little girl she loved to sit at the piano and sing with her sister Beverley. She qualified for her A.Mus.A. on piano and had singing lessons at the Melbourne Conservatorium. Anyone who sang in a full-blooded way interested her, from Ethel Merman and Sophie Tucker to Bessie Smith, Nina Simone and Mahalia Jackson. Piano rags attracted her. In her teens she went to casual dances and caught the desire to sing in public. She had asked three bands to let her sing with them when the Melbourne University Jazz Band at the Memphis dance at the St Silas church hall in Malvern accepted her. The organiser offered her £5 to come back each week and sing. John Tucker helped her put a chord book together. After the summer break Memphis started again with Frank Traynor's Jazz Preachers, and Traynor presented Durham professionally for two or three sets a night. Her confidence grew with her experience; she appeared on television, at Downbeat concerts with John Hawes's and Sny Chambers's bands, and her break came when she was given a standing ovation at the Myer Music Bowl for her performance of 'The Lord's Prayer'. At the same time she was singing with a vocal group called The Seekers, gradually getting more sophisticated jobs and feeling a little embarrassed at what the jazzers might think until they won a free trip on a ship to the United Kingdom—jazzers approve of anything free. What was intended to be a short trip became five years of chart-topping success, but Durham never thought of herself as a folk singer and regretted that she was unable to sing all the music she felt, not only jazz, but musical comedy and opera too. After The Seekers finished in 1968 she returned to jazz, but English and Australian audiences could not see her without thinking of The Seekers, so she went to America in 1972 to discover if she could be appreciated without that aura. She was totally accepted by American audiences, particularly at Turk Murphy's Club in San Francisco, Earthquake McGoon's. It was a musical turning point, giving her courage to return to her home with a broad repertoire that embraced everything she liked.

Jazz is a man's world, both in Australia and internationally. Few women have made a contribution to it. The reasons for this absence are complex and can only be hinted at. Certainly there are social restraints; girls are not encouraged to take up instruments which make a loud noise and cause the player to go red in the face and sweat. It is probably not physical; though it requires effort to blow an instrument, correct technical production minimises that, and Pam Hird, and Barbara Kidman (daughter of the South Australian cattle baron) had no trouble holding their own on trumpet. Breaking into a man's world is hard, but Pam Hird found she was accepted once the men understood that she knew what she was doing. As a general rule the only female musicians in jazz are the exceptions.

Women's liberation has not helped much yet. Too many women imbued with the tenets of radical feminism are making the same error the Eureka Youth League made—mistaking the image of the performer for the sound they make. For example, in 1977 a clean Swedish pop group, Abba, toured Australia and no young intelligent girl who thought she was radical and fancied her own taste in music would admit to liking them and dismissed Abba as pre-packaged, pre-programmed and sexless. But these same girls were prepared to put down Tina Turner, the hardest-working woman in show business who sings and dances magnificently, because she was too sexy. Plenty of these girls have acclaimed Mick Jagger, who has composed sexist songs, performs in revealing costumes and deliberately plays up sex on stage, because his leftist credentials seemed impeccable. Both Jagger's and Turner's shows are exciting and for many of the same reasons, but many women will not let another woman win, and in this way women's liberation is perverted into old-fashioned bitchiness. Any woman who can perform without taking her clothes off should be supported, but in judging her music, whether she chooses to dress cleanly, fashionably, ethnically or scruffily, her appearance and politics should take second place to the sound she produces. Too zealous to accept the joyous difference between sexy and sexist, radical women have more trouble hearing past a shapely figure than men do.

The Red Onions in Melbourne were initially a New Orleans style band but, under the guidance of Ade Monsbourgh, they veered towards the Oliver/Morton school. 'Trad' jazz was so popular by the time they started in 1960 they took engagements before they could play properly. The drummer, Allan Browne, engineered his way into the position of secretary of the local Presbyterian Fellowship of Sandringham and engaged the band for a dance—they were paid on their first gig! Such enterprise had to pay off. They worked at dances in the area and made a big impression at the Sydney convention in 1962, the beginning of their national reputation. The casual dance era ended when ten o'clock closing came in, but the Red Onions took it in their stride at a two year engagement at the Royal Terminus Hotel, Brighton, the best period of the band. They made two overseas trips, in 1968 and 1970, and faded from the scene in the early 1970s.

Trad jazz waned for a couple of years after ten o'clock closing was introduced, until the Victorian Jazz Club was formed in September 1968, providing a focal point which had been lacking since the demise of the Melbourne Jazz Club four years earlier. Older musicians are often anxious lest there be no young players to continue in jazz, but Melbourne seems to produce at least one good traditional band for every new generation, and the New Harlem band, formed by trumpeter Ian Smith in 1968, is a case in point. Another interesting band to emerge since the foundation of the Victorian Jazz Club is the Storyville Jazz Band, different from the bands mentioned above in that it brought together musicians from a strong undercurrent in Melbourne who are interested in mainstream. It has included Graham Coyle, Dick Tattum and Ken Jones (reeds). The drummer and leader, Alan Leake, preferred the band to have arrangements, if only because arrangements would set it apart from pick-up bands. With two brass and two reeds there was scope for good backing for soloists and he could work brass against reed like a swing band.

A few musicians prominent in the casual dance era broadened their outlook and got involved in modern styles. Dave Rankin, a Rabelaisian trombonist with the Melbourne New Orleans Jazz Band, formed a jazz-rock band in 1972, and some of the Red Onions explored bop and post-bop jazz. The widening scope of younger musicians is similar to the growth of interest in mainstream which an older generation experienced. Others stayed with traditional jazz. Max Collie, who led his Jazz Kings in the 1956 3KZ Swallow's Parade, in 1975 led his English band, the Rhythm Aces, to take out the World Championship of Jazz held in Indianapolis. Traditional jazz continues strongly in Melbourne, central to a community which boasts exponents of many styles.

New Orleans jazz did not have as many followers in Sydney as in Melbourne, and the Sydney musician most closely identified with it, Geoff Bull (trumpet), spent a year with the Melbourne New Orleans Jazz Band before forming his own New Orleans style band in 1962, the Olympia Jazz Band. By 1977 Bull had made five journeys to New Orleans, playing and talking with the local musicians with the aim of assimilating their approach to jazz so that he could express himself the same way. The Olympia Jazz Band played for eight years at the Orient Hotel in Sydney. Bull's band was a proving ground for a number of talented musicians, including Paul Furniss, an electrical engineer turned professional musician, who is the most exciting prospect on reeds from the Sydney trad scene since Johnny McCarthy, and Adrian Ford, trombone and piano. Ford toured Europe and the USA with the Yarra Yarras in 1969, wrote the music for a dance sequence in the 1974 Australian film 'Between Wars', and formed a big band with the same line-up as Luis Russell's orchestra of 1930. Its repertoire ranged from King Oliver to late Ellington and pieces written and arranged by Ford with the assistance of Furniss. It was a fresh and successful excursion into an area musicians would love to visit more frequently if the economics of a large band would allow it. Since the late 1960s, aided by the migration of Melbourne musicians, traditional jazz in Sydney has flourished more than in Melbourne. From solo pianists to big bands, from ragtime to mainstream, it has depth and variety. The jazz scene turned full circle in 1976 when a young Californian, Tom Baker (b. 1952) formed his San Francisco Jazz Band in Sydney which had a bright sound with its two trumpet lead, which brought many memories back to the veterans from the days of the Bell band.

A top band in Sydney, 1962–65, was from Perth, the Riverside Jazz Group. After Hounslow went east in 1947 the Westside Jazz Group dissolved and a new band came up, called the Alvan Street Stompers. For the next two decades traditional jazz in Perth was played by various combinations of these two bands, with other musicians joining in along the way. They formed the band at the 6PR Symphony and Swing Club. An inspiration to all jazzmen in the 1950s was Jack Harrison's quartet at the King's Park Tennis Club. He favoured Buddy de Franco's style of clarinet. Harrison became principal clarinet with the Perth Symphony Orchestra. The Riverside Jazz Group began in 1955 and established themselves at a dance at the Claremont Football Pavilion. Upon the arrival of King Fisher, the son of the American bandleader Freddie 'Schnickelfritz' Fisher, the band split in two, the Riverside band becoming a Chicago style band and the other forming the earlier styled Westport Jazz Band. When the Riverside band left, a utility band, J.T. and the Jazzmen, whose styles ranged from New Orleans to the Bobcats, Tijuana and rock, took over the best engagements. Perth has had a large proportion of English migrants, and their involvement with jazz, and that of the Germans and Dutch, has contributed strongly to the jazz scene. Traditional jazz musicians in Perth face all the problems of small town musicians, particularly feeling the absence of enough like-minded musicians to create their own momentum. Whenever a Perth musician goes east for a jazz convention, on his return his playing is lifted for about three weeks, but it slowly subsides to its previous level. As yet there is no distinctive sound to Perth jazz.

Jazz was given a lift in Brisbane in 1955 by Len Barnard and Tich Bray; they formed a quartet at the Storey Bridge Hotel with Billy Townsend and Ray

'Skippy' Humphries, and Bray got the seventeen-piece Cloudland band to swing when he led it for a couple of years in the early 1960s. But until the trad boom began there in 1959 the jazz scene was quiet, partly because a Queensland law forbidding the consumption of liquor within one mile of premises in which dancing was taking place was still being enforced. The trad boom started with the formation of the Varsity 5 by a group of university students which quickly became the band for all balls and social functions for young people in Brisbane. The banjo player, Mileham Hayes, felt there was an Australian tradition which they could be part of, and listened to a high proportion of Australian records as an aid to evolving their own sound. King Fisher played with them before moving to Perth. The drummer, Ian Bloxsom, later worked on Sangster's recording sessions, with a jazz-rock group called Crossfire, and with the SSO. The Varsity 5, 1959–64, inspired a few other traditional bands but jazz slipped into the doldrums again until the Australian Jazz Convention was held there for the first time in 1976. Whenever there is a surge of interest in jazz in Melbourne or Sydney it is usually accompanied by more jazz activity in the smaller capitals.

Jazz in Australia is here to stay. Its popularity may wax and wane but it will always have a hard core of adherents. Developments in music in the USA will continue to be its major influence, but more and more Australian musicians are thinking and composing for themselves (and finding a public who will let them do so) which gives Australian jazz a certain independent momentum of its own. This momentum can be traced, growing in strength, from the early vaudeville days, through big bands, to the present. Australia probably has as many jazz musicians per head of population as any other country, but their interests are not enslaved to current fashions overseas. Traditional jazz is proportionately stronger in Australia than in America, and has, in turn, influenced the traditional jazz of other countries. Modern and traditional Australian jazzmen are being recognised for their artistry at home and abroad. They have made the music their own, infusing it with a distinctive flavour, best described as 'Australian'.

AFTERWORD
Jazz through to the 1980s

BRUCE JOHNSON

Reading Andrew Bisset's concluding comments to *Black Roots White Flowers* nearly ten years later I am struck by two things: on the one hand, how apposite certain of those comments were in the late seventies; and on the other, how the general picture he describes has altered during the intervening period. He refers to the momentum of Australian jazz, and in retrospect it seems clear that from the mid seventies the music enjoyed what Ron Morey in Perth in 1977 had already called a 'renaissance', the biggest resurgence in activity for more than a decade. It is also true, however, that the general effect of this resurgence was progressively to modify the stylistic mixture of jazz in Australia. In 1979 Andrew noted the conspicuous vigour of traditional styles of jazz in this country. With due allowance for the flexibility of the notion of 'traditional' jazz, I think it has to be said that the 'renaissance' of the last decade has generally tended to alter the balance of things in favour of more progressive styles.

It is very difficult to pick up the threads of another historian's account and attempt to tie them to one's own view of the matter, but these two points — the jazz 'renaissance' and its stylistic effects — make a useful way of reviewing the significant developments since the first edition of this book. To establish a sense of continuity, of historical perspective, however, it is important to see recent developments as growing out of earlier movements. Because Andrew and I inevitably perceive those movements in our own individual ways, I have briefly to go back to an earlier jazz vogue to explain why the events of the last decade unfolded in the way they have. I do this without necessarily subscribing to or challenging my predecessor's version of Australian jazz history up to 1978, but simply in order to create a context for my own version of that history since then.

The essential element in that context is the movement which attained its peak in the early sixties, and which even at the time was being referred to as the 'trad boom'. The word 'trad' was a contraction of 'traditional', and although generally resented by musicians who had come to the music earlier, the diminutive signalled both the main source and the predominant stylistic thrust of the vogue. 'Trad' was an English importation, and referred to an English jazz style ultimately based on the pre-swing jazz of the twenties. Ironically, the ascendancy of that style in

Graeme Bell and his band, returning from a tour in the 1950s

England throughout the fifties had been stimulated to a significant degree by the activities of Graeme Bell and his band during tours of Europe during 1947–48 and 1950–52. By presenting jazz for dancing, Bell had helped change the audience for jazz from a rather donnish coterie to young people who simply responded to its energy and unrestrained high spirits. It is reported that within weeks of opening their Leicester Square jazz club in 1948, the Bell band were prevailed upon by the authorities to increase the number of nights so that the waiting crowds congesting the pavements would be thinned out.

The pigeons came home to roost in Australia about a decade later through the music of Kenny Ball and Acker Bilk, and through the film 'It's Trad Dad' which opened in 1962. But 'trad', although the most prominent of the newly popular jazz styles, raised public consciousness of the music in general as something separate from other forms of pop. In the same year that Kenny Ball's 'Midnight in Moscow' was occupying the hit parades, so was Dave Brubeck's 'Take Five'. If a lot of traditional clarinet players began sounding like Acker Bilk, a lot of progressive saxophonists also absorbed the influence of Brubeck's limpid altoist, Paul Desmond. The emergence of jazz into such prominence had a curiously ambiguous effect on the subsequent history of the music. In the short term it actually worked to its detriment. The saturation of the market with scores of barely competent young bands, all sounding much the same in style and repertoire, had the same effect as a similar Australian jazz vogue in the twenties: the music ossified. Furthermore, the very distinctiveness of the various jazz forms as opposed to other forms of pop deprived them of common ground which they might have shared with the fully electrified sound of the Beatles which infiltrated Australian youth throughout 1963–64.

For the first time, jazz bore no resemblance at all to rock 'n' roll, and the ascendancy of the latter thoroughly eclipsed the former. From the mid sixties the boom fell silent, and jazz entered its worst slump since the onset of the Depression in 1929. In every city, venues either closed or changed to a non-jazz policy, and the late sixties saw the end of some of the most important centres of activity in the history of Australian jazz. The music did not stop, but it ceased to occupy centre stage and was almost wholly drowned out by the sounds of sixties psychedelia.

Yet even this slump was preparing the music for its return to public audibility from the mid seventies. The boom, and the subsequent slump, had one effect in common: they identified and isolated jazz from other forms of popular music. Even into the late fifties, the general public had continued to think of jazz as almost any music emanating from America, having high energy level, and using horns. One could describe thus the rock 'n' roll (or 'rockabilly') of Bill Haley. Indeed, a number of early Australian rockers, including Johnny O'Keefe, performed under the billing of jazz concerts. Discriminating definitions of jazz were generally confined to the group of traditional followers known as 'mouldy fygges', and the flaming youth of the mid-fifties were just as happy to jive in the aisles to 'Boogie Blues' as to rhythm and blues. The boom of the early sixties saw a widening of the radius of jazz circles, until the relatively uninformed public gradually became aware that jazz was a distinct component in the array of modern popular music. It was a distinction emphasised by the passing of one era, and the onset of another. Since the war, jazz had often been bracketed with the kind of popular modern music which had been played in ballrooms, cabarets, night-clubs, and indeed a certain amount of jazz *was* performed in these settings. But while the new youth music of the sixties was attracting publicity, these tokens of an earlier entertainment era were quietly receding into history. Ballrooms closed, nightclubs and cabaret-restaurants were changing policies and basic functions. The old clientele for these venues was now raising families, consolidating careers, and settling down to an evening in front of the newest entertainment revolution: television. The musicians disappeared into studios, clubs, switched to rock groups, or withdrew into entrepreneurial activities. A major tradition of popular entertainment was fading, and its disappearance left jazz defined in bolder relief.

At the same time, the advent of guitar/drums/vocal groups like the Beatles sharpened that relief even further. A member of the public could fairly easily bracket together a jazz band with a rockabilly group which included saxophones, piano, acoustic bass, and playing a shuffle blues with a boogie line. In Hobart, Tom Pickering accommodated the first wave of rock 'n' roll simply by doubling on guitar. It required however an improbable degree of hebetude to confuse the

Beatles singing 'A Hard Day's Night' with 'Midnight in Moscow' or 'Take Five'. The point here is that since the mid-sixties, jazz has been recognised as something other than the youth music known as pop — by its ambience, its performers, its venues and, above all, by its instrumentation. Until the mid-sixties most Australian children were able to identify wind instruments, through the brass and dance band traditions. During the subsequent decade or so, several generations passed through the school system being able to recognise only guitars and drums. Ray Price's school jazz concerts during this era attracted as much interest in the physical operation of the horns as for the sound of the music and the commentary of the leader. Trombonist John Colborne-Veel was regarded with special fascination, one child asking him how, like a nimble sword swallower, he was able to ingest and regurgitate part of the instrument so quickly.

When Bryce Rohde announced an ABC television programme in 1970 with the title 'Jazz is Something Else', there was an important affirmation inscribed in the hip cliché. The music had new clarity and a new image, and these would determine its development through to the mid-eighties. The image was one of artistic respectability, intellectual seriousness. Since its arrival in Australia, jazz had been tinged with moral impropriety and artistic triviality in the eyes of the general public and the cultural establishment. At various times radical or 'underground' artistic causes had rallied around jazz as an authentic music in a philistine wasteland — the Contemporary Art Society, the Angry Penguin group, and various individuals with experimental inclinations. For the most part, however, jazz had been regarded as a threat to moral and artistic decorum. This image had been relentlessly cultivated by the media, particularly in films, from the 1919 Australian production 'Does the Jazz Lead to Destruction?' to 'The Crimson Canary' ('Rhythm Cults Exposed!' proclaimed the posters) of 1945, and others. The persistence of this attitude is stridently advertised in the following letter from as late as 1963 in *Music Maker*:

> *I cannot but boggle at all the twaddle I have been reading lately about this rubbish — jazz. Could not your fine magazine do something towards promoting really good music, such as is played by Lester Laiun's [sic] orchestra or probably more timely as he was recently here, Carmen Cavallaro? These people play music not noisy, untuneful garbage that is churned out of negroes and drug addicts. We do not want our children to idolize such maniacs who are only playing for idolation [sic] and financial gain (unlike Lester and Carmen, who are devoted to their art) so PLEASE 'Music Maker', do something about it, as I want my children to tread the right path in life — the cultural path.*
> *S.W.*
> *Marrickville*

This letter is an interesting disclosure of the tenacity of the presumed association between jazz and irresponsible triviality. Although an identifiable residue of this persists, particularly at a conservative academic level, 'S.W.' of Marrickville was trying to stem a rising tide. As the new wave of pop moved away from jazz, it also took with it much of the odium which had tainted the latter. Although jazz was a major form of pop music during the early sixties, it was primarily for an upper middle-class, undergraduate audience who wished for something that had the slightly rebellious energy of rock, but with some intellectual gravity to offset what was fastidiously felt to be the brute mindlessness of the latter.

Jazz developed an intellectual image, and associated itself with a university atmosphere through band names like the Campus Six, university concerts, and the short-lived Inter-varsity Jazz Festival, inaugurated in Adelaide in 1963. At the same time, to increase its distance from what its audiences felt was the plebeianism of rock, it established alliances with other more 'legitimate' art forms and musical traditions. Don Burrows was a crucial figure in this process, with his high public visibility in enterprises like 'The Best of Both Worlds' concerts with symphonic musicians. The Sydney Symphony Orchestra performed with jazz musicians on ABC television in 1962, jazz groups played in conjunction with experimental activities in other arts — galleries, poetry and jazz performances, sound tracks for documentary film. There had of course been attempts to increase the respectability of jazz going back to the twenties (Paul Whiteman, Ravel, Stravinsky, et al.) and in Sydney the Port Jackson Jazz Band had given an important Conservatorium concert as early as 1948 with the blessing of Eugene Goossens.

The legitimising process of the sixties, however, had a decisive effect on the subsequent development of the music: it touched a significant section of that generation of undergraduates who would over the next two decades gradually enter important administrative positions. It is precisely the effect of this, I would argue, that has led to the unprecedented cultural enfranchisement of jazz over the last decade, and which in turn has created the climate in which the newest generation of jazz musicians have enjoyed a degree of material and pedagogical support to which none of their predecessors had access. When we seek to define and to understand what has happened in Australian jazz since the mid-seventies, these two effects of the 'trad boom' of the early sixties cast a long shadow: the emergence of jazz and jazz musicians as fully differentiated items in the landscape of popular music; and the hospitality with which they were received by what would become the teachers, administrators and other 'trustees of consciousness' of the coming decades.

Seen against this background, the beginnings of the resurgence of jazz, as noted by Andrew Bisset is the first edition of this volume, take on increasing significance. Now, in 1987, with a deeper perspective, we can form a fuller appreciation of what was happening and why.

The time scale begins to make sense, for example. The undergraduate population which had done so much to sustain the boom of the early sixties, disappeared from view for the same reasons that earlier generations of jazz supporters had. They ended their youth, they began establishing families, they redirected their energies to laying career foundations. And these careers were in the areas of influence dominated by more or less intellectual upper middle-class sensibilities in Australia: teaching, arts administration, middle level government, journalism, publishing, radio, television, film. To put it simply, through the seventies the cultural establishment of Australia received an unprecedented influx of people who, from their adolescence, had a sympathetic attitude to jazz. Throughout the post-war period, members of earlier generations had been spokesmen for jazz in the establishment. Clem Semmler had been associated with jazz in the forties, and through the fifties and sixties was fighting a rather isolated

Barry Conyngham, 1973

battle for jazz in the corridors of the ABC. Ron Gates had written reports on the Bell band's first tour, 1947–48, and was now influential in tertiary education. Max Harris, editor of *Angry Penguins* in the forties, had become a voice with influence in the establishment. Jazz musician Greg Gibson was with the Department of Foreign Affairs. Keith Humble, Gordon Jackson, Peter Burgis, Don Banks, Rex Hobcroft were moving into positions of administrative influence, and all had been sympathetic to jazz in their youth. Until the early seventies, however, such individuals were isolated instances. With the arrival of the baby-boomers who graduated through the sixties, the general climate altered, the context for administrative initiatives changed. Individuals like Barry Conyngham and Martin Wesley-Smith, who have influential teaching positions at Melbourne University and the NSW State Conservatorium respectively, are representative of the rising tide of academically accredited and influential composers/musicians/teachers, who came through the boom of the early sixties and brought with them a respect for jazz.

The period of jazz quiescence from about 1965 also generated unforeseen benefits for jazz. The pop culture of the sixties was a time of radical revaluation of received notions, but at a level which was accessible to a non-academic mind. In the 1960s there was a persistent compulsion to reassess the conditions of life. Part of this naturally expressed itself in the form of iconoclasm and de-categorisation. The established authorities were questioned, down to their most fundamental and cherished assumptions, and the conceptual components of the culture — political, religious, artistic, historical — were rearranged in new hierarchies. Artists were discouraged from sealing off their thinking, notions of artistic seriousness were challenged, and all this became a pervasive habit of consciousness, not simply a sectional doctrine. Whatever you were engaged in, if you had any general receptiveness to the mental climate of the sixties, it affected that activity. Bearing a new sense of the intellectual or artistic moment of the music, jazz musicians carved out new channels during this subterranean period of its history. Commentators lamented the conservatism of some areas of the jazz fraternity, but the fact that such comments were made in itself signals the emergence of radical perspectives. Extensive experimentation was going on in order to force a revision of attitudes. If much of this was pretentious, that was the price to be paid for an essential prising open of the categories sealed shut during the boom. Roger Frampton was an important force in this process, with presentations like the performance experiment 'Telejazz', sponsored by the avant-garde 'AZ' agency in 1972. Even during the slump in visible jazz activity, the music in its underground channels was being redefined, infused with a new creative energy in readiness for its imminent resurfacing. If the psychedelic sixties occluded jazz, they also established an ambience from which it profited.

The foregoing isolate the more distant roots of the recent resurgence of jazz activity; there are several more immediate causes which are difficult to quantify statistically, but which have progressively manifested themselves during the eighties. These have been particularly apparent to musicians who have been closely and continuously involved in the jazz scene since the sixties. They are to do with the glacial movement of different generations of musicians into new stages of their creative lives.

In the seventies, pop culture entered its own period of exhaustion. Youth style in general and youth music in particular lost momentum, and has been faltering between the increasingly vapid recycling of the energy of the sixties, a shrill cynicism in search of form, and occasional attempts at originality which conclude in illogicality. The revolution of the sixties has cast as much of a shadow over the future as over the past. Jazz has profited from this enervation of pop music in the same way that it did in the decade following the war. The young musicians who have been coming to technical maturity during the last ten years include a large number who have moved into jazz simply because pop was no longer able to challenge them. The relative proximity of jazz (as an adjacent and indeed overlapping 'folk' form) has inevitably attracted their interest, a circumstance catalysed by the increasing accessibility of jazz skills through formal educational programmes, as discussed below.

At the other end of the spectrum of generations, the last decade has seen a substantial number of older musicians returning to the jazz scene. I mentioned earlier that many of the nightclub musicians from an earlier era retreated to the licensed clubs and the television studios when the post-war jazz scene contracted. In New South Wales in particular, the licensing of poker machines in 1956 ensured revenue which would make the sporting clubs the biggest employers of non-symphonic musicians, musicians who were in most cases able to improvise in the jazz idiom. From the early eighties, two developments in Australian leisure caused a contraction in club music opportunities: the introduction of random breath testing began to discourage people from alcoholic entertainment outside their homes, and the arrival of home video gave them a safe alternative. In addition, musicians who had spent much of their professional lives in the well-paid, but musically constricting atmosphere of the clubs, were often reaching an age at which, with children having grown up and left home, and mortgage commitments diminishing to zero, economics were no longer such a powerful determinant of where they worked. Bass player Cliff Barnet's experience typified that of many other musicians. He had dropped out of the casual jazz scene years before, but by the 1980s was beginning to notice that club and session work was thinning out. The situation had not been helped by a strike by television studio musicians over the award rate, leaving employment in that area stagnant at best, contracting at worst. On 31 December 1982 he had a gig at a suburban sporting club. Whatever else was happening in the music industry, the New Year's Eve gig was traditionally a well paid and exuberantly cheerful event. Random Breath Testing had recently been introduced amidst much cautionary publicity, however; the evening began on a subdued, almost furtive note, and declined from there. It finished up being the first time Cliff, and many other musicians, had ever played New Year's Eve only to see all the merrymakers leave before midnight. The band played Auld Lang Syne for the bar staff and the janitors.

The most visible effects of all the foregoing developments have been various forms of institutionalisation of jazz, with an increasing corps of young musicians available to take advantage of the fact. The most important pioneering development in this area took place in time for inclusion in the first edition of this volume: that is, the establishment in 1973 of the jazz studies courses at the NSW State Conservatorium as a result of discussions between its new director, Rex Hobcroft, and Don Burrows. The ripples of this initiative have spread across Australia, and while there exists considered controversy over the effect of these

Don Burrows advising members of a newly-formed jazz band at St Joseph's College, 1975

Judy Bailey   *John Sangster*

courses on the music which is actually played from week to week in the country's jazz venues, there is no doubt that some of the most publicised young musicians and groups to emerge since the late seventies have come through some version of a tertiary jazz studies programme. By the end of 1986 there were at least sixteen conservatoria, universities, colleges of advanced education or similar government-funded tertiary institutions, in which jazz studies could be taken as part or all of a diploma programme, covering every state except the Northern Territory. Jazz education is gradually percolating into the secondary school system also, and the movement has expanded so rapidly in the eighties that, following a series of exploratory meetings, in March 1987 an executive committee of Australia's first Jazz Educators' Association was established in Sydney.

In the new bureaucratic and administrative energies which developed out of the sixties and which broke through the political surface with the election of Gough Whitlam's Labor government in 1972, jazz has gained formal recognition from numerous government and other institutional sources which once regarded the music with condescension. As long ago as 1967, the Australasian Performing Right Association commissioned compositions from Judy Bailey, Bernie McGann and John Sangster. That rather bold move is today more commonplace, and jazz receives a certain amount of funding from the Australia Council, from Arts Councils, and other state and municipal authorities in forms including funded workshops and concerts.

It is the Music Board of the Australia Council which has played the most conspicuous role in this institutional support for jazz. Two prominent jazz musicians, Judy Bailey and Sylvan 'Schmoe' Elhay have served on the Board. In addition, the Board established in 1983 the national Jazz Co-ordination programme. Under this scheme, six salaried Jazz Co-ordinators were appointed, each with an advisory committee, to fill the posts in the state capitals. The Co-ordinators have acted as lobbyists, as clearing houses for the dissemination of jazz information, as publicists, and have generated numerous important initiatives in education, performance, patronage and sponsorship, from the establishment of the West Australian Youth Jazz Orchestra in Perth to the setting up of the Sydney Improvised Music Association. Each Co-ordinator has had to form an individual appraisal of local conditions and needs, and the path has not always been an easy one. Jazz followers frequently have only the haziest notion of the labyrinthine operation of institutional administration, and they often find polemical fictions more comfortable than carefully researched conclusions. The Co-ordinators have had to tread a difficult line between their governmental creators who are practised in the Byzantine world of policy administration, and the jazz fraternity who are likely to find consolation in a more simplistic and anecdotal version of things. Factionalism in Brisbane terminated the post of Queensland Jazz Co-ordinator at the end of 1985. In the meantime, the Music Board continues to take jazz into its considerations, even if comparatively marginally. Its Medium Range Plan released in October 1985 included proposals for the development of jazz enterprises with reference to such matters as concerts, venues and the encouragement of composition as well as performance.

Other important entrepreneurial bodies which have taken jazz more seriously from and through the seventies, include the state Arts Councils. These are private bodies operating with the assistance of government funding. They have helped to organise tours for jazz groups, but since these are usually in response to specific requests from rural areas, these activities tend to favour the groups and musicians who are best known. Consequently, while they are bringing live jazz to the attention of more geographically remote audiences, they tend also to perpetuate the existing jazz establishment, and have little direct effect on the development of new or relatively unknown musicians. Musica Viva is another private group operating with government assistance. Established in 1945, it is now the world's largest chamber music organisation. Since the early seventies it has increasingly given attention to the administration of jazz tours ranging from those by Bob Barnard to more contemporary groups, in conjunction with the Department of Foreign Affairs and the Music Board.

The increased receptiveness of government funding bodies to jazz activities has arisen partly out of the lobbying energy of other private organisations, above all, the new style of jazz club which has evolved since the establishment of the first Jazz Action Society (JAS). Since the advent of Swing in 1935–36, there have been clubs devoted to various aspects of modern popular music in Australia. Many of these presented recitals (live and on record) of a wide range of styles, from Latin American to novelty material, with jazz or swing also given some prominence.

Other activities of these clubs included simply providing a focus for socialising and courting for young people of the day.

Within the general category of modern music societies, however, there emerged a series of clubs with an almost evangelical fixation on jazz in particular, and in the early phase of their history, the emphasis was most frequently on traditional jazz. The longest surviving of these is the Sydney Jazz Club which, with changes in its legal status, has operated since 1953. The launching of the JAS of New South Wales in 1973 represented several important variations on this tradition, however, resulting in the JAS movement eclipsing the earlier jazz clubs as a national phenomenon. The JAS differed in, first, seeking consciously to promote later styles of jazz and, second, in developing itself as a political lobby, with the result that it was able from the outset to attract government support for its music. Although they are not affiliated in any way but their name, there are about a dozen Jazz Action Societies throughout the country, including in Darwin and northern Tasmania. They have not always found the local soil hospitable, however, and the Melbourne JAS in fact has withered. They have nonetheless established a sense of national solidarity which had earlier been the property of the traditional styles. This has particularly benefited post-traditional jazz.

At the same time, a parallel development in the jazz club tradition has become evident: that is, the sudden and vigorous regionalisation of the phenomenon. Never before has there been such a proliferation of jazz clubs in areas outside our capital cities as over the last decade. Of the three dozen or so jazz clubs throughout Australia which I have on file, about one third are outside capital cities, including in a centre as remote as Kalgoorlie (bearing the appropriate name 'the Goldfields Jazz Society'). A surprising number of these, like the Deniliquin Jazz Group, the Central West Jazz Club and the Down South Jazz Club, have established highly successful annual jazz festivals and have stimulated regular local jazz activity where before it had been so unfocussed as to be invisible.

The case of the Jazz Action Societies indicates how the cause of jazz has been advanced by the development of energetic pressure groups outside the traditional channels of influence. Nowhere has this been more evident than in broadcasting. To whatever extent jazz has enjoyed exposure on air in the post-war period, the ABC, or more correctly a few dedicated individuals within the Corporation, are primarily responsible. Since the sixties, jazz on ABC radio has become increasingly marginal in terms of quantity, slotting times and quality (invaded as it is by the category of music often known as 'easy listening'). The advent of the series 'The Burrows Collection' on ABC television should be noted and applauded, even though it is pushed into a late night slot. In terms of jazz broadcasting, however, the ABC now has very powerful competition in the form of the community FM radio stations. Since the establishment of the first of these, Sydney's 2MBS-FM, in 1974, these stations have proliferated in much the same way as jazz clubs, although not with the same exclusivity of function. The community FM stations serve a variety of needs — religious, ethnic, educative — and are unquestionably the most important media development towards providing a genuine community service rather than a covert ideological forum for large corporations through programming and advertising. Many of them carry regular jazz programming and the most fully developed, like 2MBS-FM, record gigs, promote and broadcast concerts, commission and record original works, and issue their own recordings, frequently with the assistance of government funds. Along with Jazz Action Societies and other clubs, with whom they often co-ordinate their activities, these stations have been particularly important in fostering lesser known musicians, and to that extent they have opened up the jazz scene in ways that even the more mainstream media are having to recognise and to some extent follow. Dedicated jazz followers frequently note that these media — newspapers, radio, television — concentrate on fully established names and ignore the 'street' scene, the less glamorous venues where the music is sustained from year to year. Throughout the last decade JAS concerts and FM community radio have done much to clear this log-jam in the public perceptions of jazz.

In print, jazz has found its situation marginally improved over the last decade, above all through the national magazine *Jazz*, which began life under the editorship of journalist Dick Scott before passing into the hands of Eric Myers. The magazine has tried to maintain a bipartisan, national coverage and, unlike much mainstream jazz journalism, has maintained a well-informed and critically rigorous standard. That it has had to contend, not always successfully, with the apathy of its own audiences, causes one to wonder if, finally, jazz followers get what they deserve. It is hard to imagine, however, what they have done to deserve some of the hopelessly ill-informed and stereotypical coverage provided by the daily newspapers. Occasionally acute pieces appear in these journals, but often the idea of jazz criticism is an afterthought and the job farmed out to someone almost wholly ignorant of the subject. One writer for the *Sydney Morning Herald* in the early eighties, signing himself David Lin, had what could be safely described as a curious view of the English language, which led to some extremely opaque discussions of the local jazz scene: it is difficult to know what to make of the following extracts from a review of Graeme Bell's band:

> *While trad-ragtime may not have a popular multitude of adherents, we can safely say it's the way a jazz song was intended to be played, no ifs or buts... The trick to the Allstars must be in each band master's maturity despite their belief that the Saints will come marching in over South Sydney. Everyone has paid their dues over the years, without having to labour over their own personal satisfaction in playing their music.*

Lin had been appointed some months after the newspaper terminated the services of Eric Myers, who had been their first regular jazz critic. The reasons given for this termination were that the paper wanted someone 'more independent of the jazz world', and the position was offered to a number of journalists including the industrial editor. Only the most bloodthirsty mind would care to imagine what would happen if the same policy (with equivalent results) were applied to sports writing. Even putatively specialist journals of the arts tend still to treat jazz as an inconsequential afterthought — the glossy magazine *Performing Arts* carried an article by Ginette Lenham (No. 3, Dec/Jan 1985–6) on Bernie McGann, in which Ms Lenham spoke of McGann's apprenticeship during the fifties as being the time of the swing era. It is difficult to imagine how someone could become acquainted with the term 'Swing', and yet situate it historically so inaccurately, rather like calling Robert Browning a Renaissance poet. When the press carries such blithely unconcerned nonsense, it is little wonder that the jazz community, and musicians in particular, retain a strong contempt for jazz commentary.

Jazz has become increasingly 'administered' since the first edition of this book. It is this process which more than any other has wrought change in the national jazz movement since the mid-seventies, and in general represents jazz's entry into the official notion of culture. But how in practical terms has this affected the actual music played and heard throughout the country? For historical reasons, reaching back beyond the scope of this chapter, one of the distinguishing features in the post-war jazz landscape has been the chasm which has divided the traditional styles from what have been loosely been termed the modernists. The term 'modern', as applied to jazz, is problematic. Scholarly definitions of the term differ from each other, and also from the lay understanding. In any event, it has evolved a sense not consistent with its literal meaning, and it is probably time that this, and other stylistic terminology, was re-evaluated. However irrationally, the terms 'modern' and 'traditional' are generally used to refer to a perceived bifurcation of the jazz tradition between pre and post-bop styles. Naturally, scholars will introduce more subtly discriminated stylistic shades, but when reviewing the impact of jazz developments on the general public perception, it would be precious to pretend that those discriminations are common currency. For purposes of this discussion, 'modern' jazz is to be regarded as jazz inflected by developments leading immediately up to, and since, the bop movement of the forties. If we attend to the balance between these two categories of the music, then it is difficult to avoid the conclusion that the institutionalising process has more frequently favoured the later (through not necessarily the latest) styles.

The reasons for this lie partly with the changing cultural ambience of the period, and partly with certain attitudes which have often characterised the traditional movement. Regarding the former: as I have described above, the developments in the popular (and academic) consciousness of the sixties and seventies were broadly in the direction of revaluation, rather than re-affirmation, of traditions. The example of feminism is the most visible and potentially far-reaching example of the tendency. It is also apt because its effects have trickled into the jazz movement, particularly at its 'administered' level. There have always been women who have played jazz in Australia, and indeed in the twenties they were probably more numerous than in subsequent periods. It seemed not to be considered even a novelty for a woman to lead a jazz group. It is only in the eighties, however, that the relation of women to jazz has become a specific issue. Julie McErlain organised the first 'Woman and Jazz Workshop' at the Victorian College of the Arts in October 1983, and in March 1984, following an initiative by the NSW Jazz Co-ordinator Eric Myers, the establishment of Sydney Women in Music (SWIM) led to the first of several workshops for female jazz musicians, assisted by Music Board funding. Other related enterprises have included a National Womens [sic] Music Festival organised by the Lismore Womens [sic] Music Collective in October 1985. The bands led by the gifted composer/saxophonist, Sandy Evans, have presented audiences with the image of women playing jazz which is fully authentic on its own terms, as opposed to the sexist novelty of some of the all-women bands of the forties.

Apart from the inherent interest of such developments, they are also significant symptoms of the kind of revisionary consciousness which is exercising influence in the arts. When that influence extends to jazz, it is not surprising that it should encounter less resistance in more contemporary styles: after all, contemporary jazz is itself the expression of a willingness to reassess conventions. And across the full spectrum of styles, it is equally unsurprising that the slowest to register such changes would be styles rooted most tenaciously in tradition. Traditional jazz has frequently projected an image in which a locker-room beer-drinking sexism is latent (if not overt), and we are now living in a climate of awareness in which the authority of this image is very much under question.

More superficial, but palpable, gusts across this new climate of consciousness include a degree of nostalgia for the fifties. Youth fashion has recently displayed this revival, particularly in Melbourne, where Vince Jones and more recently Kate Ceberano have projected something of this image. The release of the cultishly successful film *Round Midnight* has given impetus to this revival. It is sometimes a mild shock to remind oneself that the interval separating the revivalists of the late fifties from the classic jazz of the late twenties is the same as that which now separates emerging young musicians from the fifties. That is, what to traditional players of thirty years ago was (and is still residually) regarded as 'modern' jazz is now itself the subject of a kind of antiquarian revivalism. On a recent gig with two musicians in their early twenties, they and I were finding it difficult to establish that margin of common ground necessary to make the music work. During the break, a tape was playing of a Charlie Parker recording of '52nd St. Theme'. The young players stood listening intently, staring at the floor and, I assumed, sharing my awe at this reminder of how audaciously the Bird had pushed the music of his day forward. Thinking that this might be the common ground, I approached them as the track finished. The comment one made to the other, however, opened up the gulf even wider: 'Gee, they played fast in the old days, didn't they.' The fact is that bop itself is now so thoroughly accommodated in the succeeding conventions of the last forty years, that it has become 'revivalist' music, and is riding on the crest of fifties nostalgia.

The enormous spread of jazz education has also favoured post-traditional styles. The central thrust of jazz studies courses in Australia is towards the performable aspects of the music — harmony, ensemble work, improvisation and basic instrumental tuition. The way in which these characteristics of jazz relate to the cultures which have produced them is something of a blind spot. The history of the music and its socio-political matrix are touched on in some courses (La Trobe University in Victoria is exceptional in prescribing a mandatory unit in Jazz History), but the general tendency of jazz education has been not only to neglect these areas (particularly Australian jazz history), but by doing so to imply that a knowledge of it is of negligible significance to a musician: in other words, to legitimise historical ignorance. The Australian suspicion of any knowledge which cannot immediately be translated into visible (or in this case audible) effects, has thus engendered serious blind spots — call them prejudices — in most of the students who have passed through its jazz studies programmes. Post-traditional styles are favoured, partly because they are not embedded so deeply in the past, and partly because mastery of their conventions more easily enables the student to do the only thing which our society believes confirms the validity of learning: to get a job. It is also true that the overt intellectual challenge of post-bop conventions gives more obvious validity to its study; it is far more difficult to present history in a way that discloses the vital importance of the subject.

For all these reasons, formal education courses have tended to emphasise more modern jazz movements, and in one or two regrettable cases, its spokesman have positively devalued Australia's highly influential pre-bop tradition. At one of Judy Bailey's concerts during an interstate tour in 1985, among those present were the director of one of the local jazz studies programmes and a number of his students whom he had encouraged to attend in order to hear the featured group. At the end of the concert, the teacher thanked her and then noted that among the musicians scheduled for future performance was Bob Barnard (who is internationally regarded as one of the most gifted creative exponents of his style in the world). But that style is pre-bop, a compound of traditional and mainstream. Characterising Barnard's music as 'just dixieland', the teacher suggested that his students not waste their time attending, a recommendation not only to miss a musician without peer, but also to carry into their careers a conviction that this essential stylistic link in the history of the music was of negligible significance. Fortunately, on this occasion, Judy Bailey delivered a passionate reply that disabused the young tyros of this misapprehension.

The manifestation of such myopia makes it difficult, even after nearly fifteen years, to assess the possible long term effects of these education courses on the development of the music as an organic component in our culture. In jazz as in the other arts, it is almost invariably true that the most creative innovations appear from outside the institutional framework. One can teach students how to play licks developed by Armstrong, Parker, Coltrane, but what 'institution' taught Armstrong, Parker and Coltrane? They produced what they did because they were fully immersed in a local culture which spontaneously expressed itself through jazz. Lift a learner out of such an environment, place him in an institutionalised context, and all one can guarantee is that competent students can be taught competent musicianship. The 'hothouse' conditions under which young talent blooms in the insulated context of formal institutions certainly shortens the period of technical apprenticeship to a degree which earlier generations of jazz musicians can only wish they had had available. The theoretical foundations of current jazz improvisation have now been codified, freeing younger players from a slow and extended period of exploration by trial and error, and permitting the most gifted to enter sooner into that creative phase of their careers which actually advances the music.

At best, in the larger centres, there exist parallel opportunities for the formally tutored musicians to exercise themselves in the stress of field conditions. There is for the student an unforeseeable difference between learning and playing jazz in an environment structured for that purpose, as opposed to performing amid the distractions of a public jazz venue. The co-ordination between the jazz studies programmes at the NSW Conservatorium and seasons at The Basement in the mid seventies provided an exciting stimulus to the music, a point of incandescent contact between engineered development from above and spontaneous development from below. It is true also that the most visible exponent of the bop tradition to emerge in the last decade, James Morrison, was in part a product of the jazz education system. As an emissary of the music, Morrison's flamboyance is making the kind of impact that points to his becoming a successor to Don Burrows as the individual most closely associated with jazz in the public eye.

There are other, and highly creative, musicians like saxophonist Dale Barlow, who are making major contributions to jazz, but in a way that is less publicly visible. While Barlow himself also came through the jazz studies programme, some have found that programme less congenial. There have been, indeed, important creative initiatives which have emerged outside the institutional frameworks. These have involved individual musicians, bands, informal co-operatives, and venues. The Keys Music Association and the Paradise Jazz Cellar in Sydney were crucial incubators from the late seventies, particularly in nurturing musicans like Mark Simmonds and members of the group which became The Benders. In Melbourne, similar energies issued from such groups as Pyramid, Odwala, and in the group Onaje an earlier generation of musicans advanced convincingly into more contemporary areas. There is debate regarding the causal connection between formal jazz studies and public jazz performance. Nonetheless, there is no doubt that the institutionalising process of the last decade has coincided with the biggest influx of youthful musicians, fully versed in relatively contemporary jazz canons, to appear since the sixties.

The same cannot be said of the traditional movement. In the history of our musical culture, the traditionalists have been much more significant than is now widely appreciated. The existence of an Australian jazz style, while a matter of contention locally, is an accepted fact for many overseas writers and musicians. It is a style based on the traditional idiom transmuted into Australian terms during the forties and fifties, particularly by the bands of Graeme Bell and Frank Johnson. In the history of Australian jazz, it is the traditional style which has had the greatest international impact, in terms of modifying the development of the music in other countries. The authority of the traditional school in Australia during the immediate post-war period was such that the public generally made a simple equation between 'jazz' and 'traditional jazz', and even many musicians playing in more progressive styles in the late forties hesitated to think of themselves as jazz musicians.

The developments of the last ten years have seen a significant reversal in the balance of that authority, and for many reasons. The emphasis of the jazz studies courses obviously points to clear advantages for the state of post-traditional forms. At the same time, traditional jazz, in suffering something of an eclipse, is experiencing the consequence of one of its own initiatives back in the fifties. At that time there developed a strong purist consciousness within the young traditional jazz fraternity, by which its members sealed themselves protectively within a relatively narrow definition of their music. At at least one Australian Jazz Convention, for example, musicans playing ideologically unsound styles were ordered from the stage, and even Graeme Bell was criticised for using arrangements. Through the seventies and eighties some of this exclusivism persists, effectively disenfranchising traditional jazz from the benefits being accorded to other forms. If this style is being neglected in the institutionalising process, it is also itself putting less into that process. In 1978, Ray Price stopped leading his band for school recitals, and while they were continued throughout the next year by his clarinettist Jack Wiard, then his trombonist John Colborne-Veel, from 1980 they ceased altogether. From that time, until 1987, traditional jazz had virtually no sustained national visibility to the new generation of students. When the Sydney Jazz Quintet began presenting school concerts it provided an admirable service in bringing jazz to the attention of children, but its emphasis was on mainstream to bop. Not until the advent of the 'Jazzin' Around' lecture/recitals in 1987 has traditional jazz returned to a wide range of school children.

This lack of visibility is aggravated by the advancing age of traditional jazz musicians and their followers. Not since the trad boom of the early sixties has there been a significant wave of young traditionalists, and there is not even any individual musician in the style who has entered the scene since the seventies who has achieved the national prominence of veterans like Graeme Bell and Bob Barnard, or of post-traditional players like James Morrison. Nearly all the traditional groups in Australia include veterans from the early sixties. Traditional jazz has developed a late middle-aged image, in a society in which narcissistic youth dominates popular entertainment. The twenty and thirty-year-old techniques of presentation, the jokes, the rhetoric, simply have no meaning to young audiences, let alone glamour. A Melbourne musician tells the amusing story against himself of taking a break during a gig in the late seventies. Approached by an attractive young woman at the bar, he recalled the halcyon days of the sixties and 'thought his luck had changed'. While she enthused about the atmosphere, his ego and his expectations became tumescent, to be deflated by a comment which she intended as a compliment — '... and I love watching you play. It's just like one of those old documentaries.'

There are always exceptions to any tendency and, particularly in Melbourne, there are younger musicians enlisting in the traditional movement. To maintain a 'movement' as such requires more than a trickle, however. In the absence of a major influx, the core of the traditional scene continues to be the trad boom veterans. That core is contracting as its musicians retire or, in many cases, develop stylistically into other areas, leaving behind those followers whose preferences have not broadened. In the last few years the Sydney Jazz Club has reassessed its own function in relation to this problem but, again, there is a limit to how far entrenched public attitudes can be changed through policy decisions. During a private party in Sydney in 1977 a jam session developed, involving a number of musicians who had been associated for years with the traditional scene. As developing players they had inevitably absorbed aspects of later styles and increased their fluency, but were still playing an accessible mainstream approach. They were loudly berated by one of the listeners, who indignantly demanded, 'Why don't you play something we can understand?' If audiences refuse to 'understand' anything more recent than sixty years old in a music still well short of its centenary, then they must expect to become bewildered. Many modernists show little grasp of what went before, but it is equally stultifying that many traditionalists have no grasp of what came later.

The strengths and the weaknesses in Australian traditional jazz are summarised by the condition of its major annual event, the Australian Jazz Convention, which is still held after forty-one years. The history of this Convention is a seismographic record of the history of traditional jazz in Australia since 1946. Wherever it is held, it produces a surge of local interest in the music which gives impetus to the movement. Conventions held in Brisbane (1976), Hobart (1977) and Fremantle (1979) have provided local momentum which has sustained the music for years afterward. More recently, the Convention has reflected the tendency of jazz to regionalisation, with seven out of the last ten being held outside of capital cities. There has been some extension of its stylistic tolerance over the last ten years, but the event is still primarily a traditional affair. Attendances have generally continued to increase, running over the thousand mark, and consisting mainly of people of middle age and middle class, a relatively affluent group who inject considerable funds into the area where the Convention is held. At its best, it still generates unexpected sparks of brilliance, but the advancing age of the delegates and musicians is increasingly evident in the predictability of much of the music. Like Australian traditional jazz in general, the Convention continues to manifest all the vital signs, but with less youthful energy than in earlier decades.

If these reservations cast something of a shadow over the music, it is nonetheless the shadow of an indisputable statistical fact: Australian traditional jazz is not being revitalised on a significant scale by young musicians. The graph is unremitting — the average age of the exponents and followers of traditional jazz is increasing, and until some new factor enters the equation, only one extrapolation is possible: that the generation carrying the standard of the music will in the foreseeable future die and not be replaced. It is only by recognising that harsh possibility that it can be averted. Unless its adherents wish to subscribe to the view that an art form kept alive by artificial means does not deserve to survive, they must develop administrative structures and youth-oriented promotional programmes similar to those which have revitalised more progressive jazz styles.

It is still too early to determine what sort of creative directions Australian jazz is likely to take as a consequence of its inroads on the consciousness of the cultural establishment of the last decade. It is imperative, however, that the music become invested with a deeper respect for and appreciation of its own local history — for without that sense of continuity, whether expressed as renewal or reaction, Australian jazz cannot develop as an authentic component of our folk culture.

INDEX

SELECT BIBLIOGRAPHY

Australian Jazz Quarterly (Melbourne) 1946–1957
Australian Music Maker and Dance Band News
    (Sydney) 1925–1972
The *Beat* (Sydney) 1949
Hughes, Dick *Daddy's Practising Again* (Richmond,
    Vic., 1977)
Jam (Sydney) 1938
Jazz Down Under (Camden, NSW) 1974 –
Jazzline (Melbourne) 1968 –
Jazz Notes (Melbourne & Hobart) 1941 –
    (intermittently) 1962
Jazz Record Review (Adelaide) 1969 –
Johnson, Bruce *The Oxford Companion to*
    Australian Jazz (1987)
Linehan, Norm *Norm Linehan's Australian Jazz*
    Picture Book (Hornsby, NSW, 1980)
Matrix (Melb.) 1954 –
Melbourne Jazz Club Newsletter 1960's
Mitchell, Jack *Australian Discography* (National Film
    and Sound Archive, A.C.T.)
Quarterly Rag (Sydney) 1955 –
Record Guide (Sydney) 1953 –
Tempo and Television (Sydney) 1937–1960

AUSTRALIAN JAZZ GREATS ON ABC RECORDS

Don Burrows at the Winery

The Rothbury Estate Society in the Hunter Valley of New South Wales was formed in 1973 and has since been a venue for dinners, wine tastings and jazz concerts.

Don Burrows played his first concert there in 1979 and this is the recording of a subsequent concert in 1983. It presents playing by seasoned musicians with the brilliant James Morrison appearing for the first time as a featured soloist. Don Burrows says: 'On a great blues track like Basin Street, James is a tough act to follow or precede.'

'Don Burrows at the Winery' features some well-loved standards and is a recording for all lovers of great jazz.

Galapagos Duck – The Voyage of the Beagle

The origin of the species known as the Galapagos Duck has little relevance to Charles Darwin but rather is related to the writings of another eminent, more contemporary Englishman, Spike Milligan. It was an evening the band spent with Spike that prompted the adoption of its curious name, which has now become a household word among jazz followers.

Apart from its name and the fact that it features very significantly in the evolution of the jazz idiom of Australia, the Galapagos Duck has little to do with the life and work of the father of Evolution. However, because of the name the band has developed a fascination with his epic voyage and this recording, which is a selection of original compositions by members of the band, attempts in musical terms to trace the Beagle's voyage.

James Morrison – A Night in Tunisia

James Morrison grew up in a musical family and is 'bursting with talent and energy'. Don Burrows is convinced that he will prove to be one of the greatest talents this country has ever produced. 'He really gets so much going,' Don says. 'He has all the energy and imagination to go with it, and he doesn't take any 'prisoners' when he plays; he just goes straight ahead.'

This recording, featuring The Morrison Brothers Big Bad Band, was recorded in front of a live audience at ABC TV's Gore Hill studios as part of the Don Burrows Collection Series.

Renee Geyer – Live at the Basement

Within twelve hours, Renee was to board a jet bound for New York. But at midnight on the night of 12 May 1986, she was holding a party of vintage musical delights to farewell her friends at Sydney's Basement Club.

The Basement has always heard the best of Renee Geyer and on this occasion the mood was especially electric. With her own blend of funk and soul, Renee and her band gave a thrilling performance. If proof were ever needed of the special place that Renee Geyer occupies in Australia's music scene, this is it.

Ricky May – Fat's Enough

In this memorable recording Ricky May, with the Julian Lee Orchestra, takes an affectionate look at the music of the great Fats Waller, one of the most widely known and loved of all the great Jazz pioneers.

Ricky May brings his own special brand of magic to some of the most memorable songs of the 'Clown Prince' of Jazz.

HOW THE GREAT JAZZ MEN REALLY SOUNDED!

ROBERT PARKER'S JAZZ CLASSICS

BIX BEIDERBECKE became a Jazz Age romantic legend in a little over half a decade, during which he played brilliant cornet and drank too much bad prohibition liquor – resulting in his premature death at 28. He was one of the first white musicians to adapt New Orleans Jazz to his own middle-class background and his genius helped to ensure the spread of hot music into the mainstream of pop culture.

DUKE ELLINGTON has been hailed as the greatest single talent to have emerged in the history of Jazz. His working life spanned half a century and this album traces his evolution from the Jazz Age to the Swing Era in new digital stereo transfers from the original 78 rpm masters, making possible a clearer insight into the subtlety and force of his unique contribution to the development of jazz.

JELLY ROLL MORTON claimed to be 'the inventor of Jazz' – a slight exaggeration – but he was certainly one of the great Jazz innovators. His work as a composer and arranger as represented in this album dispels forever the myth that early jazz was crude and undisciplined.

FATS WALLER's highly successful career was based on his ebullient personality and breathtaking techniques for playing and composition. His genius was largely devoted to inventing musical essays on the theme of 'having a good time' and he produced very little of social significance – which perhaps explains why he was (and still is) so widely loved as an entertainer.

LOUIS ARMSTRONG was undoubtedly a genius whose influence has spread throughout much of twentieth century music. His special talent lay in his ability to improvise on a musical theme. It is not possible to over-estimate his importance to the development of jazz and the superb recordings reproduced in this album captured him in the 1920s, at the height of his powers.

JOHNNY DODDS is widely regarded as the greatest jazz clarinetist to have ever lived. This album presents a selection of his finest recordings in new digital transfers from the original 78 rpm discs and gives a powerful stereo-impression of how the master may have sounded in live performance.

BESSIE SMITH was dubbed 'The Empress of the Blues' by her contemporaries and a selection of her greatest performances are heard here for the first time in digital stereo – revealing the full power, warmth and sensitivity of her consummate artistry.